MW01688586

PAINTED IN BLOOD:

REMEMBER WYOMING!

America's First Civil War

by

JAY L. GLICKMAN

6/7/00

To Dr Schulman,

Best Wishes!

Jay L. Glickman

Painted in Blood: Remember Wyoming!. Copyright 1997 by Jay L. Glickman. All rights reserved, including the right to reproduce this book or portions thereof without prior written permission from the publisher.

First Edition Trade Paperback
First Printing: 1997

ISBN: 1-879915-16-2
Library of Congress Number:

Cover Art and Design by Ken Newman

The history of no portion of our great country is more replete with curious incidents and romantic adventures than the history of Wyoming. Every foot of the soil is rendered classic by some historic fact or some curious legend. Bloody conflicts, hair-breadth escapes, starvations, heart-breaks, love adventures, prodigies of heroism, and miracles of endurance mark every page of the early history of Wyoming...."

—George Peck, D.D.
Wyoming: It's History, Stirring Incidents, and Romantic Adventures
1858

ACKNOWLEDGEMENTS

Special gratitude to Anita F. Steiner-Glickman who inspired and encouraged me.

Thanks to Ken Newman for his pictorial assistance and cover art.

DEDICATION

TO TODAY'S INHABITANTS OF THE WYOMING VALLEY, WHO ARE EVERY BIT AS RESOURCEFUL AND INTREPID AS THEIR PREDECESSORS.... AND TO THEIR HONORARY CITIZENSHIP IN THE STATE OF WYOMING

In the name and on behalf of the people of the great state of Wyoming, the people of the town of Wyoming, Pennsylvania, are offered and extended honorary citizenship in the equality state of Wyoming for 1976, the bicentennial of the independence of the American states, and for so long thereafter as human pride and trust endure.

We share one name, one past, one future, and, in welcome, pledge eternal friendship.

Ed Herschler, Governor

Attest: Thyra Thomson, Secretary of State

The Great Seal of the State of Wyoming

ABOUT THE AUTHOR

The road less traveled is the one that holds the most fascination for Jay L. Glickman, particularly in the field of original research.

The author has been writing articles throughout his lifetime on various subjects and has earned degrees in English and History from New York University. From 1971 to 1979, he was affiliated with the Famous Writers School of Westport, Connecticut and served as District Manager in that organization.

He also spent fifteen years of pioneer research on a type of antique glass, heretofore considered a mere color variation. The result of his research was the discovery that Vaseline Glass is a separate and unique type of glass, which can be verified with ultraviolet light.

He has written numerous articles dealing with the history of the glass, as well as the scientific reasons for its properties, characteristics and verification. His book on the subject entitled *Yellow-Green Vaseline—A Guide to the Magic Glass* (Antique Publications, Marietta, Ohio, 1991) was recieved by critics with excellent reviews and is today considered a landmark reference book, being the first, and so far, the only book on the subject ever written.

While researching the above book, Mr. Glickman happened to find a rare book, published in 1845, on the history of the Wyoming Valley in northeastern Pennsylvania, including eyewitness accounts of the Battle of Wyoming in 1778. With further research into original sources, this fascinating, lost piece of American history emerged, including discovery of the lost battle flag of the Battle of Wyoming.

INTRODUCTION

The Wyoming Valley of Northeastern Pennsylvania is one of the most historic sites on the North American Continent. As the reader goes forward in this book the significance of the history presented here will become self-evident.

The fact that the Wyoming Valley was the flashpoint of conflict between two overlapping land claims is central to understanding this history. This in turn led to *three* intercolonial and interstate civil wars before, just before, and after the American Revolution. These little known Pennemite-Yankee Wars marked the clash of idealogies between the new American free enterprise, freehold homestead system and the medieval remnants of European feudalism.

In parallel, the Iroquois Indian tribes of the area participated in the bloody conflict in numerous ways and for their own various reasons, causing tremendous ramifications, not only affecting them directly, but ultimately affecting all Native Americans in the future. First President George Washington's response to the actions of the Iroquois was devastating, led to the creation of the "reservation system," and set U.S. Government policy in a direction which would set the stage, tragically, for U.S. policy for plains Indians in the next (19th) century. Washington did what he did, and his full orders to General Sullivan are published herein. It will be up to the reader to decide whether Washington's acts were justified.

Using the yardstick of the American West, many historians decry the taking of Indian lands and the persecution of "Native Americans." It should be pointed out here that *all land obtained in Eastern*

Pennsylvania by white men was by purchase, not by conquest. Land was purchased in the hopes of *avoiding* conflict with the Iroquois. Also, an assumption that the West's 19th century Indian persecution was the same in the 18th century in the East should be regarded carefully, since in the latter case the Indians were often the strong majority and often the persecutors rather than the victims. It is the special circumstances of the Wyoming Valley which motivated its unique history.

Historian H.C. Bradsby wrote of the Wyoming Valley in 1893, "In historical fame, there is no spot on the Continent so well known throughout the civilized world." It was so famous that a great territory and state were named after it. Yet that fame died out on this continent to the point where the Wyoming Valley is hardly known, and few, even, of the present inhabitants of the State of Wyoming even know that their state was named after it.

To rekindle the spirit of this history, the author has relied heavily on unindexed material and previously overlooked references, as well as orally transmitted history handed down by the Iroquois throughout the generations at tribal councils. Many of the quotations and battle sequences were extracted from speeches and letters in the National Archives and at the Wyoming Valley Historical Society.

The veracity and reliability of these sources was proven, in part, by the author's rediscovery of the Tory battleflag from the Battle of Wyoming in 1778, lost and in storage at West Point since 1840!

Although this artifact discovery was the most dramatic one, there are many other new revelations contained in this book for the reader to discover.

The story of the Wyoming Valley is the saga of an eighteen-mile-long valley and its river running through it, bringing hardship, stress and glory to its inhabitants. It was the Susquehanna River flowing through the dense and fearsome forests that brought this violent history to the valley—it was the superhighway of the eighteenth century.

The use of eyewitness accounts makes this tale worth telling and allows the past to come alive. It is told through the eyes of the participants, rather than subjecting the reader to an historical checklist. Only then can the reader see its full impact on the present and the future. Only then can forgotten heroes be retrieved from a lost history.

In the case of Wyoming, Pennsylvania, there was ample political motivation to suppress or distort the history of the battles. Temperance unions attempted to erase the drinking of alcohol which took place at the time. Pennsylvania, after losing on the battlefield, found it expedient to downplay the heroic deeds of the Connecticut settlers after the land was wrested from the Yankees by court decree.

The purpose of this research and book is to set the record straight in regard to the Wyoming Valley's importance and significance on the national and international stage. Of this, there is more than ample and obvious evidence.

—Jay L. Glickman
Wyoming, Pennsylvania

PROLOGUE

The river's shades of blue and white seemed to dominate the hills of winter's faded buff grasses, bordering the ominous, dense forests. It was early spring, and the earthy smell of thawing ground increased as the bright sun in a cloudless sky warmed the river bank. A herd of white-tailed deer suddenly stopped drinking and froze, before wildly bolting into the brush.

In this land of thick, virgin forest, the deer were confined to live in river valleys. Only there was adequate undergrowth for forage, to sustain small colonies of deer. The pristine forests covering the land kept sunlight from reaching their soil, preventing the growth of small, secondary plants for grazing animals. It was a dark homeland for bears, wildcats and wolf packs. Man entered the forest at his peril; sustenance and safety were sought in the river valleys.

Warning cries of overhead birds called out an alarm, followed by an eerie silence. It was so quiet that the deer, hiding in the undergrowth, could hear the silken parting of the water from the approaching canoes.

Even before Red Hawk rounded the bend in the lead canoe, he could hear the splash of animals deserting the river for safety. It was a sound that brought him comfort. Too often in the past had he heard silence in his northern homeland or, worse yet, the howling of wolves. The supply of food there was always uncertain. Too many times had empty stomachs forced his tribe to eat the leftovers of the ever present wolves. Short growing seasons along the Genesee and Seneca limited the farming of corn, beans and squash. Game was scarce, particularly in winter. Inter-tribal warfare over hunting grounds was incessant and, together with famine and disease, the population decreased periodically.

Red Hawk remembered vividly that great meeting of five tribes, twelve years before, at Onondaga. His parents and all the other Senecas, for the first time, counseled with other Iroquois-speaking peoples, to form a confederation to stop the constant fighting over hunting grounds.

As he and his Iroquois brothers put their backs into the rhythmic paddle strokes, propelling the canoes through clear waters, he recalled the huge bonfire in the night, at Onondaga, with the deep, constant drum beats of the representative tribes. The fire sent bright-orange and red tongues of flame high into the black sky, punctuated by the hissing and crackling of pine knots, accompanied by the glorious smell of burning sap. Magically, the hundreds of drums all stopped at once and, in the silence before the fire, stood the elder chieftain Agatarho through whom the spirit Deganwiddah spoke.

Red Hawk never forgot the words of the old chief. In a powerful voice for one so aged, Agatarho gave the history of his people so it would be remembered and passed along to successive generations:

"0ur people came to a high mountain from whence they took a prospect and beheld a narrow sea. While they were consulting which way to go, and what to do, there was at length a voice spake unto them from the Great Spirit saying, 'Look over that narrow sea and behold a country for you and your children!' whereupon, they came down from the mountain and crossed the sea and came into the country. This was the first company. Afterwards, they were followed by a great many more companies who came into the same path, till they filled the country."

Agatarho and the god Deganwiddah then spoke of the need for Kanonsionni, the Longhouse. The Longhouse symbolized the League of Five Nations. The guardians of the Western Door of the Longhouse were to be the Senecas. The guardians of the Eastern Door were to be the Mohawks. The three other nations were to dwell in peace in their midst. They were the Oneidas, the Onondagas, and the Cayugas.

Deganwiddah, as channeled through Agatarho, continued: "We bond ourselves together by taking hold of each other's hands so firmly and forming a circle so strong that if a tree should fall upon us it could not shake or break it, so that our people and grandchildren shall remain in the circle in security, peace and happiness.

"You are Five Nations for you sprang each from a different handful of the seed I sowed, but you are brethren and I am your father for I made all of you; I have nursed and brought you up. Mohawks, I have made you bold and valiant, and see, I give you corn for food. Oneidas, I have made you patient of pain and of hunger, the nuts and fruits of the trees are yours. Senecas, I have made you industrious and active, beans do I give you for nourishment; Cayugas, I have made you strong, friendly, and generous, ground nuts and every root shall refresh you; Onondagas, I have made you wise, just and eloquent; squashes and grapes have I given you to eat and tobacco to smoke in Council. The beasts, birds and fishes have I given you all, so you love and take care of one another. Communicate freely to each other the good things I have given you, and learn to imitate each other's virtues. I have made you the best people in the world, and I give you the best country." (Quotes of Agatarho from Harvey, Oscar, J., *A History of Wilkes-Barre*, Vol. I W-B 1909)

Red Hawk stroked his paddle even deeper in the water rushing by, as if to shock himself back into the reality of the present. Following the course of the paddle downward, he looked at the train of bubbles he pushed into the depths and, through the sunlit, clear water, saw a large fish with chain-like markings suddenly dart out and snap at one of the bubbles. The omen puzzled him, but again he forced himself back to the real mission of his war party.

They were a mixed band of Mohawks, Senecas and Onandagas on the first leg of close to a thousand mile, southerly expedition to the lands of the Cherokees and Catawbas. The purpose of the raiding party was to take fresh captives and return to the Iroquois lands for them to be "adopted" by families who had lost members to war, famine or disease. Those families who chose not to adopt a presented captive had the right to avenge the loss of their loved one by slow torture and death of the captive.

These customs, guiding the war party's objective, restored Red Hawk's stern Iroquoian outlook on life, especially in regard to outsiders. A Seneca warrior should have no time for, or interest in, frivolities. As a child, when he was encouraged to shoot arrows at captives tied to trees, he was advised to develop a skin "seven thumbs thick." His valor and fighting skills on raids were to be measured by the the number of scalps and captives taken.

The hilly landscapes on both sides of the river suddenly eased, upon reaching the mouth of a tributary named Lackawanuck. It was here where the Iroquois stopped to rest and adorn themselves with red, yellow and black war paint. This would serve to signal their mission and hopefully strike terror into the hearts of potential adversaries. They were approaching a populated area and what was unknown could not be trusted.

In years past, Iroquois emissaries and runners had promised outlying tribes, both large and small, that aiding Iroquois raiding parties with food and shelter as they passed through their areas, would result in peaceful relations and future protection by the Five Nations.

These Five Nations were later to become Six Nations with the addition of the Tuscarora Tribe to the Iroquois Confederacy. From the stirrings in the tall grasses on shore, Red Hawk knew that news of the approaching raiding party would be dispatched to every community downstream. However, what might have been a peaceful tribe a few years ago could have changed, with the loss of some tribal members from an Iroquois skirmish, or with the removal of a peaceful tribe by a more warlike one. The Iroquois were soon to know.

After each painted warrior ate cornmeal mixed with maple sugar, a sustaining food called "yokeag," as part of his daily ration, kept in a leather bag, their southward trek resumed. Suddenly, happy cries of children resounded as the Iroquois canoes entered a large panoramic valley. Children were swimming nearby and, further down, men were casting nets into the river. Best of all was the smell of roasting venison and steamed corn. People ashore were beckoning to the Iroquois to come to the feast.

The Iroquois chief warily motioned two canoes to proceed upstream and two downstream, while directing the rest toward shore. This was standard procedure with unknown tribes to diminish the danger of ambush. The bronze, lean, Iroquois warriors looked sternly at their welcomers and were formidable in their war paint. Most of the Iroquois were over six feet tall, as opposed to the shorter and plumper natives who greeted them with food and smiling faces. Red Hawk was amazed at the outward displays of affection among family members of this tribe, who identified themselves as Susquehannocks, and their village and valley as Maughwauwama, meaning Large Plains.

What a contrast to Red Hawk's homeland! The pink and white beauty of flowering fruit trees, together with mountain laurel and dogwood, was breathtaking, even to Red Hawk's stoic gaze. Freshly planted and well-tended, light green rows of corn and beans indicated that farming, not warfare, was the main occupation of the Susquehannocks. However, scattered ancient and abandoned fortifications and parapets testified to the fact that earlier tribes had once lived here.

It seemed to Red Hawk that when he wasn't hunting far from home, he was out fighting against one tribe or another for either scalps, vengeance or captives.

He had seen other tribes of Indians enjoying life, only a few years ago on his first war party to the north and west, when the Senecas drove the Wyandottes to the shores of a great lake and then, returning southward, through grasslands, saw huge herds of large animals thundering across the prairies. The local tribes that the Iroquois encountered there wanted none of the Wyandotte captives in trade, but were only too happy to share their buffalo meat and hides with Red Hawk and his brothers. Wryly, Red Hawk reflected that the Iroquois back home had to be content with random, small herds of deer in competition with the ever-present wolf packs. These western tribes, and the Susquehannocks, now welcoming and feeding the Iroquois, seemed to have much in common.

The Susquehannocks were so open that the Iroquois soon dropped their naturally suspicious attitude and joined in the feasting and dancing of thanksgiving. Red Hawk noticed that some Mohawk brothers remained aloof and one made a threatening gesture with his tomahawk toward a Susquehannock who jumped quickly away. The Mohawk turned to Red Hawk and scornfully stated, "See, even their men are like women!"

Red Hawk ignored him for he noticed that the Susquehannocks didn't even carry weapons. Unlike the Iroquois, who were never without bow, quiver and tomahawk, these people carried only farming tools and fishing nets. Even more amazing, some were working side by side, in the fields, with their wives. Red Hawk hadn't even been home long enough to find himself a wife. Deganwiddah's exhortation to the Iroquois, to seek peace and happiness, suddenly sprang into Red Hawk's mind and he became more puzzled and distraught than ever before.

The time finally came for the Iroquois to leave. Their generous hosts wanted to fill the canoes with food and gifts. Red Hawk and his brothers politely refused some of the gifts of blankets and clothing, since space in the canoes was needed for the captives they would take in the south. As the river widened downstream, through flatter terrain, the Iroquois stayed in the center of the river, hunched low in the canoes to avoid offering a larger target.

Red Hawk's face was without emotion as the last rays of sunset illuminated his war party with a warm, orange glow. With head and shoulders low, his rhythmic paddling concealed the turmoil within him. For the first time, he was questioning his purpose in life and wondered whether he would ever find the answer.

Suddenly, a blue and orange blur above and downstream caught his attention. A greedy kingfisher had swooped into the river and taken two fish at once with his large bill. The air was filled with loud fluttering, as the bird sought altitude with the heavy fish. With an exasperated squawk, he released one of the silvery fish in midair. It dropped in a perfect arc, as the setting sun reflected a blinding golden light off the fish's body, and it landed in the canoe at Red Hawk's feet. His brothers let out an exclamation of wonder and admiration. Red Hawk knew this to be a favorable sign from Deganwiddah that his present course was correct.

Red Hawk rose in the canoe with arms outstretched in thanks and praise. Joy was his last emotion as the Lenape arrow thudded deep into his heart, and across the Great Water, a hemisphere away, the year was 1462.

For the next 250 years, the frequent Iroquois war parties racing down the Susquehanna served to intimidate all tribes in their way, including the Susquehannocks and the Lenape. The Susquehannocks fought off the Iroquois, but were wiped out by a smallpox epidemic in 1661. The Lenape, on the other hand, did their best to avoid the Iroquois, although they were intimidated by them. For the most part, the Lenape remained to the east of the Iroquois incursions.

With the arrival of the English, the Lenape saw a possible ally to help them withstand the Iroquois pressure. In order to curry favor with the British, the Lenape gave their tribe the English name, *Delaware*, not only for their tribe but for their river and valley, and worse yet, they secretly sold land claimed by the Iroquois to the Penn Estates in the southeast.

The Delaware became so bold as to change the name of Maughwauwama. To adjust this name to the Lenape dialect, they clipped short the first and last syllables of Maughwauwama so that it now sounded like *Woheahowming*, eventually sounding like *Wyoming*.

The last thing that the Delaware wished to do was to move into this neighboring river valley, for this would place their tribe in the direct contact and thus under direct domination of the Iroquois war parties. This had already occured with another tribe which had moved into the area, the Shawanese, a nomadic southern group invited into the Valley of Woheahowming by the Iroquois in an effort to keep the valley occupied and to ward off white settlement. The Shawanese, however, being a small tribe of only about 500, chose to occupy only the west bank of the Susquehanna River, which ran through the Wyoming Valley. The east side, therefore, was left uninhabited, and it was only a matter of time before the Delaware made contact with the Shawanese.

It was a beautiful day in midsummer, when the happy Delaware women and children left the braves who were hunting in the mountains, to descend into Woheahowming, to collect wild fruits and berries. Spread below them, like an oasis in the wilderness, lay the Valley with its majestic river. The blue river wound through groves of willow, sycamore and maple in their varying shades of green. Sunlight reflected off the trees and directly into the river where, every now and then, a fish would break water with a loud splash to swallow a low-flying insect.

There were signs that man had long been involved in the history of the valley. From the heights on the eastern slope, the Delaware women and children could see abandoned orchards of fruit trees, in stark contrast to the haphazard growth of wild trees. Clearings throughout the valley, now partially overgrown with berry bushes and green foliage, gave testament that villages formerly existed there. On the edge of the flood plains, other signs of forgotten tribes could also be seen—walls and fortifications built to defend the valley's inhabitants from invaders. In the distance, on the far side of the river, downstream, was a small Shawanese village.

The morning haze over the valley began to lift and laughter of the Delaware children resounded as they raced over the flowered plains. They were followed by their watchful and worried mothers, picking berries and fruits.

The laughter suddenly stopped. The Delaware had come upon a small number of Shawanese squaws and their children who had crossed the river in their canoes to also pick fruits. The Delaware children crowded around a Shawanese child who had caught a large grasshopper. A Delaware child made a grab for it and the mothers of both tribes joined in. The Delaware women contended that the Shawanese had no business being on the east bank of the river and, with knives and rocks, drove the Shawanese to their canoes and to the opposite bank. A few women and children on each side were killed.

By this time, the warriors of both sides joined their women and children and prepared for battle. The Shawanese donned their warpaint and recrossed the river, finding the Delawares ready to oppose their landing.

A ferocious battle took place, first with arrows and spears thrown at long range, then with knives and tomahawks hand-to-hand. Scores of warriors were killed on both sides and the Susquehanna River ran red. The Shawanese lost more warriors, because the Delaware were able to take more careful aim from the shore while the Shawanese paddled their canoes and fired arrows and spears only intermittently. The Shawanese were so weakened upon landing that they were not able to sustain the conflict and, after losing about half their number of braves, were forced to retreat to the western side of the river. They were never able to regain their former strength and were thus compelled to confine their settlement to the west bank.

This unplanned battle had given control of the Wyoming Valley to the Delaware tribe even though they returned immediately to the Delaware Valley where they lived.

The Delaware Valley was directly under the control of the Iroquois, and news of the battle reached Onandaga Iroquois leaders at about the same time that the Pennsylvania Governor's complaints were received concerning other lands sold earlier by the Delaware to Penn, and which were never turned over to the English. The angry Iroquois, upon hearing all this news, ordered the Delaware to return to Woheahowming and settle there, which they intended to do in the next year, 1743. Although the Delaware felt they had been spared, and their worst fears had come to pass, through the following years more Delaware continued to move into the Wyoming Valley.

The Wyoming Valley and the Susquehanna River at sunset—a scene unchanged throughout the ages.

The Descent into the Valley of Wyoming. This is an old etching by G.K. Richardson. An early 19th Century author, William L. Stone, stated in regard to this panorama, "Nearly the entire Valley can be surveyed at a single view, forming one of the richest and most beautiful landscapes upon which the eye of man ever rested!"

Lenape (Delaware) Palisaded Village. This is an old woodcut from Camponius' "New Sweden."

BRANT
N.B. The Tuscaroras are now reckon'd a
the Onondagues & Oneidos; & the Necaria
received to be the seventh Nation at Albany
80 Men of that Nation being present besides
The chief Trade with the far Indians
where they must all pass to go towar
A Scale of English Miles
The UP-PER LAKE
Oulaouaes or Necariages
Misilimakinac
LAKE of the HURONS
MICHIGAN LAKE
High Plain 70 Leagues Long
The Countrys
Conquer'd by
the FIVE NATIONS
Jagara
Oulawaes
Tusakronde
LAKE ERIE or OKSWEGO
R. St. Joseph
Car. place
Carrying place
Huakiki R.
Car. place
Car. place
The Miamis or Twightwis
Ouabache R.
Branches of the Misisipi
Ohio R.
A MAP of the Country of the FIVE NATIONS of the IRO
and of the LAKES near which the Nations
52-6

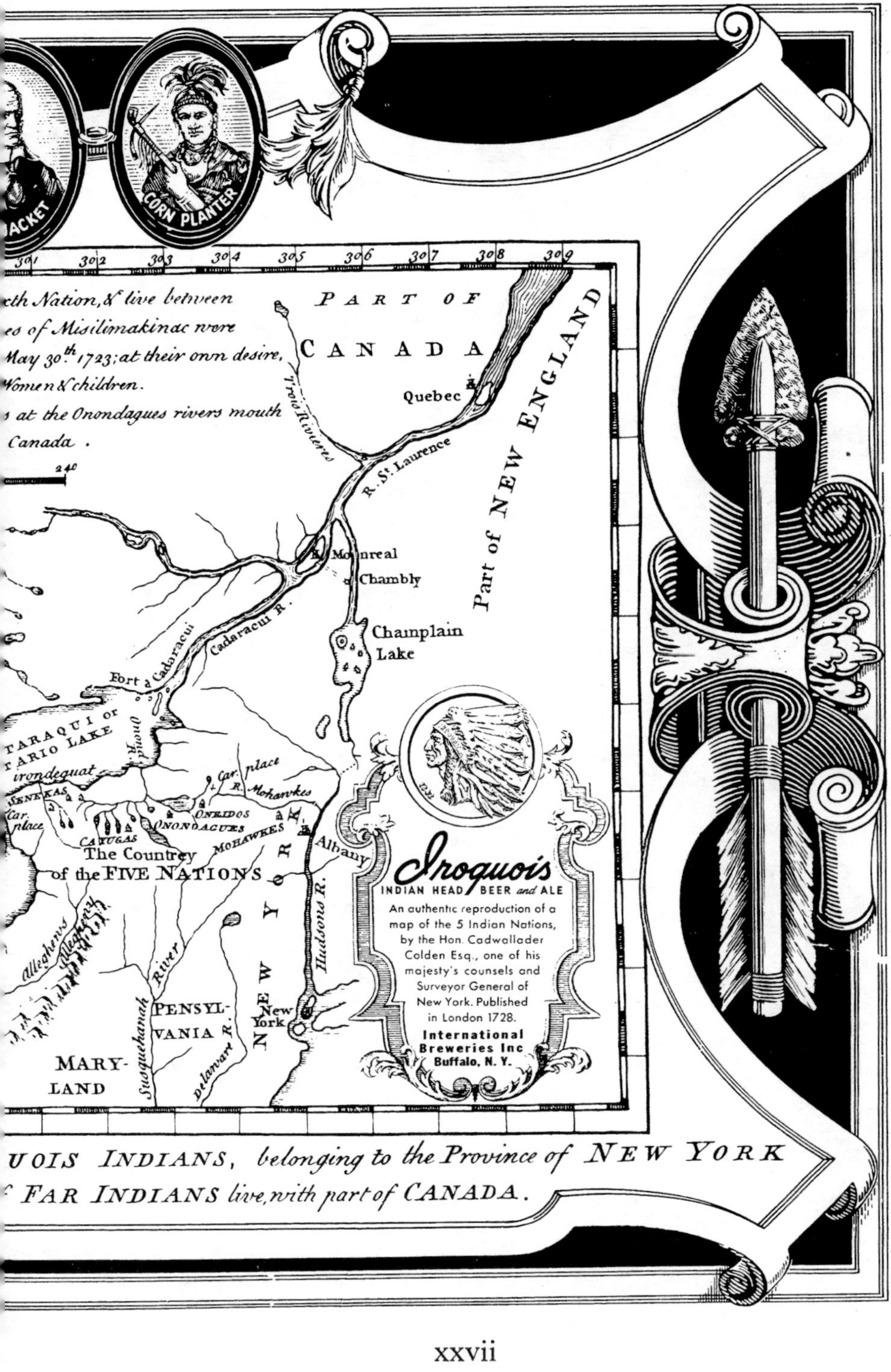

JACKET
CORN PLANTER
eth Nation, & live between
es of Misilimakinac were
May 30th 1723; at their own desire,
Women & children.
at the Onondagues rivers mouth
Canada.
PART OF
CANADA
Quebec
Part of NEW ENGLAND
R. St. Laurence
Trois Rivieres
Monreal
Chambly
Champlain Lake
Cadaracui R.
Fort a Cadaracui
TARAQUI or
ARIO LAKE
irondequat
SENEKAS
Car. place
CAYUGAS
ONONDAGUES
ONEIDOS
MOHAWKES
R. Mohawkes
Car. place
Albany
The Country of the FIVE NATIONS
NEW YORK
Hudsons R.
New York
PENSYLVANIA
MARY-LAND
Susquehanah River
Delaware R.
Alleghenys
Iroquois
INDIAN HEAD BEER and ALE
An authentic reproduction of a map of the 5 Indian Nations, by the Hon. Cadwallader Colden Esq., one of his majesty's counsels and Surveyor General of New York. Published in London 1728.
International Breweries Inc
Buffalo, N. Y.
UOIS INDIANS, belonging to the Province of NEW YORK
FAR INDIANS live, with part of CANADA.

11 TILBURY'S KNOB
PLUNKETT-BATTLE GROUND AT RAMPART ROCKS
12
SHAWNEE VILLAGE AND FLATS
13
NANTICOKE 10 VILLAGE
9 STEWART BLOCK HOUSE LOWER HANOVER FLATS
14 OLD WIOMIC TOWN
TEEDYUSCUNG'S CASTLE 7
CAREY TOWN 8
5 FORT DURKEE SOUTH ST.
15 PICKERING HOUSE
16 FELL TAVERN
SULLIVAN'S CAMP 6
FERRY 4
FORT WYOMING 3
40 KINGSTON
2 WILKES-BARRE
17
18
19
Historic Map of The Wyoming Valley in Pennsylvania
SHOWING POINTS OF INTEREST ASSOCIATED WITH ITS EARLY HISTORY
The Battle of Wyoming, July 3rd, 1778
Sullivan's Encampment, May-June-July, 1779
Fell's Discovery of the Domestic Use of Wyoming Anthracite, February 11th, 1808

29
MOUNT LOOKOUT
28
WARNING MONUMENT
26
CAMPBELL'S LEDGE
25
INDIAN VILLAGE
27
SCOVELL'S ISLAND
BRITISH
TORIES
INDIANS
30
WYOMING BATTLE
REGULARS
MILITIA
35 LAST BATTLE
24 JENKIN'S CEMETERY
37
36 STONE BRIDGE
34 WYOMING MONUMENT
TUTTLES MILL
QUEEN ESTHER'S ROCK 33
31 FORT WINTERMOOT
23 FORT JENKINS
22
FORT PITTSTON
FORTY-FORT MEETING HOUSE
38
32
MONOCANOCK ISLAND
21 ABBOT MONUMENT
39
FERRY
FORTY FORT
20 FIRST CONNECTICUT SETTLEMENT OGDEN'S BLOCK HOUSE
VILLAGE
1

CHAPTER ONE

The summer of 1742 saw a largely unoccupied, verdant Wyoming Valley, with only a small Shawanese village on the west bank. The Delawares were to arrive next year, and the Valley seemed like a magnet—attracting forces already in motion.

Surprisingly, the attracting force was not the Valley itself, but its inhabitants, the Shawanese, later known as the Shawnee. They had been ordered into the Valley by the Iroquois some thirty-five years earlier as a buffer to ward off colonization by the English and French. The Shawanese were a nomadic and warlike tribe when brought from the south. Many left the Valley after the "Grasshopper War." What remained in Wyoming was a ferocious, loosely knit and loose-living group of a few hundred renegades, the perfect target for a soul-saving, Evangelical ministry.

Such a ministry seemed destined to intersect with the Shawanese, though the movement had started thousands of miles away in August of 1727, in Dresden, Saxony, Germany. An earnest and pious twenty-seven year-old nobleman, Nicholas Ludwig Count Von Zinzendorf, threw open his estate at Herrnhut to some 300 people to start a religious organization. It became known as the "Church of the Brethren," and its members, Moravians, after their province of origin.

Although quite wealthy, Zinzendorf led a simple life, dressing plainly and, counter to the fashion of the day, never wore a wig. Although he was a high-born nobleman, he astounded everyone by treating all men as equals. Zinzendorf's message was "love of God and man." This emphasis on love had the effect of attracting hordes of people to hear the young count's preaching. Programs included Bible studies, discussions, prayers, and love-fests. Even death was treated as a joyous journey and was accompanied by the blowing of trombones and trumpets.

From this nucleus of Zinzendorf's followers, waves of Moravian Brethren migrated to the New World, to establish communities in the Pennsylvania Colony. Starting in Philadelphia, the Moravians branched into the wilderness areas of Shamokin and Bethlehem, to spread the teachings of the Brethren to the native inhabitants. In 1741, Zinzendorf himself came to the New World, to inspect the operations of the Moravian settlements and their evangelical efforts with the native inhabitants.

Zinzendorf was tireless in his activities and preachings in the wilderness. An eyewitness, James Logan, stated, "He speaks Latin and French, is aged, I suppose between forty and fifty years, wears his own hair, and is in all other respects very plain in making the propagation of the Gospel his whole purpose and business."

In his contacts with the Indians, Logan added, the preacher gave "... a practicable insight into the religion he came to teach, by simply leading a Christian life among them and, when favorable impressions had thus been made, and inquiry was excited, he preached the leading truths of the Gospel, taking care not to put more things in their heads than their hearts could lay hold of. His mode of approaching them was carefully adapted to their distinctive peculiarities."

By coincidence, on August 3, 1742, Zinzendorf, while on a visit to the Indian agent, Conrad Weiser, in the wilderness, encountered a delegation of Six Nation Chiefs. They were returning home from a conference with the Delawares and English which had been held in Philidelphia.

The key Iroquois in this group were Chief Canassatego and the Viceroy Shikellamy. Zinzendorf, after persuasive talks with them, ratified a covenant of friendship with the Iroquois.

Permission was granted to Zinzendorf to pass through and sojourn within the domain of the Iroquois Confederacy. Canassatego said, "Brother, you have journeyed a long way from beyond the sea, in order to preach to the white people and the Indians. You did not know we were here; we had no knowledge of your coming. The Great Spirit has brought us together. Come to our people; you shall be welcome. Take this fathom (string) of wampum, it is a token that our words are true."

The way was now clear for Zinzendorf to save new souls in the wilderness. In September of 1742, he wrote in his *Narrative* of his determination to journey to "Wayomink, the seat of the Nation of the Shawanese who are confederates of the Iroquois, and a people wholly ignorant of and adverse to Christians and Christianity."

Together with one of his missionary disciples, John Mack, as well as Shikellamy, Zinzendorf cut northward through the wilderness from Shamokin to a settlement called Frenchtown (now Montoursville).

Count Zinzendorf stated that he found at Frenchtown, "...a promiscuous population of French Indians, who yet are under the protection of the English." There he met the most important person in the town, Catherine Montour, also known as Madame Montour.

Madame Montour was from Quebec, the daughter of a French nobleman, Comte de Frontenae, and a Huron mother. Catherine's sister, French Margaret, was married to an Iroquois, and living in a village called French Margaret Town (now Williamsport).

When Madame Montour met Count Zinzendorf and learned of his mission to preach the Gospel she burst into tears, since she was now about fifty-five years old and hadn't practiced Christianity since she was a young woman.

Zinzendorf wrote, "I was surprised at the woman's ignorance, considering she had been brought up a Christian."

Madame Montour confided that she was tired of native life and brought two children to Count Zinzendorf and asked him to baptize them. One of the children was Madame Montour's young niece, Esther, daughter of French Margaret. Zinzendorf baptized Esther and, together with the Montours, she attended religious services officiated by Zinzendorf, before the Count set out for Wyoming.

John Mack later wrote, "... our way lay through the forest, over rocks and frightful mountains, and across streams swollen by the recent heavy rains. This was a fatiguing and dangerous journey and, on several occasions, we imperiled our lives in fording the creeks which ran with impetuous current. On the fifth day, we reached Wyoming, and pitched our tent not far from the Shawanese town (now Plymouth). The Disciple's (Zinzendorf's) reception by the savages was unfriendly, although from the first, their visits were frequent. Painted with red and black, each with a large knife in his hand, they came in crowds about the tent, again and again.

"He (Zinzendorf) lost no time, therefore, informing the Shawanese chief of the object of his mission. This the wily savage affected to regard as a mystery, and replied that such matters concerned the white man and not the Indian. Our stock of provisions was, by this time, almost exhausted and yet, the Disciple shared with the Indians what little was left. The very clothes on his own back were not spared. One shirt button after another was given away, until all were gone and, likewise his shoe buckles, so that we were obliged to fasten his underclothes and tie his shoes with strings. For ten days, we lived on boiled beans, of which we partook sparingly, three times a day, as the supply was scanty."

From his unfinished work, *History of Wyoming*, written in 1818, Isaac A. Chapman, an early Wyoming Valley native and newspaper editor, wrote, "To these unlettered children of the wilderness it appeared altogether improbable that a stranger should have braved the dangers of a boisterous ocean three thousand miles broad, for the sole purpose of instructing them in the means of obtaining happiness *after* death, and that too without requiring any compensation for his trouble and expense, and as they had observed the anxiety of the white people to purchase land of the Indians, they naturally concluded that the real object of Zinzendorf was either to procure from them the lands at Wyoming for his own use, to search for hidden treasures, or to examine the country with a view to future conquest. It was accordingly resolved to assassinate him, and to do it privately, lest the knowledge of the transaction should produce a war with the English, who were settling in the country below the mountains.

"Zinzendorf was alone in his tent, seated upon a bundle of dry weeds which composed his bed, and engaged in writing, when the assassins approached to execute their bloody commission. It was night, And the cool air of September had rendered a small fire necessary to his comfort and convenience. A curtain, formed of a blanket, and hung upon pins, was the only guard to the entrance of the tent.

"The heat of his fire had aroused a large rattlesnake which lay in the weeds, not far from it; and the reptile to enjoy it more effectually crawled slowly into the tent, and passed over one of his legs undiscovered. Without, all was still and quiet, except for the gentle murmur of the river at the rapids about a mile below. At this moment the Indians softly approached the door of his tent, and slightly removing the curtain, contemplated the venerable man, too deeply engaged in the subject of his thought to notice either their approach, or the snake which lay extended before him. At a sight like this, even the heart of the savage shrunk from the idea of committing so horrid an act, and quitting the spot, they hastily returned to the town, and informed their companions that the Great Spirit protected the white man, for they had found him with no door, but a blanket, and had seen a large rattlesnake crawl over his legs without attempting to injure him. This circumstance, together with the arrival soon of Conrad Weiser, procured Zinzendorf the friendship and confidence of the Indians and probably contributed essentially towards inducing many of them at a subsequent period, to embrace the Christian Religion."

Before Count Zinzendorf left Wyoming, to return to Germany, he composed two German hymns, both of which he titled, "*Wayomink Im November 1742*," and taught them to the native inhabitants. At the Count's final service, the voices of Zinzendorf's new converts resounded through the wilderness of the Wyoming Valley, praising the glory of God, in German!

Many Germans stayed on in the new colonies in southeastern Pennsylvania, in the areas of Lancaster and Bethelehem. But Zinzendorf returned to Germany. His mission was complete, and this marked the end of the peaceful era.

Count Zinzendorf from a contemporary German lithograph.

CHAPTER TWO

As if to mark the end of an old era and the beginning of a new age, the years of 1748 to 1753 saw an intermittent series of droughts and famines in Wyoming.

In his diary, David Mack wrote of his visit to the Wyoming Valley in 1748:

July 25—Resumed our journey and came to Wapwallopen. Found only one family at home who boiled the bark of trees for food. All the others had been driven by famine to the white settlements. At night we camped at the lower end of the flats of Wyomick.

July 26—Arose early and proceeded up the flats. People decrepit and scarcely able to move, and in danger of starvation. Lodged in one of the huts.

July 27—Crossed the river and visited the Nanticokes who moved here last Spring from Chesapeake Bay and found them clever, modest people. They too complained of the famine, and told us that their young people had been gone several weeks to the settlements to procure food. In the evening, the Nanticokes set us over the river. Visited some old people also an old man who fetched some wood to make a fire in his hut. He was so weak as to be compelled to crawl on his hands and knees. Made the fire much to the gratitude of the aged invalid.

The following autumn, a Moravian bishop, visiting Wyoming related that only sixteen people remained on the west side of the Susquehanna. Some of the Shawanese had returned from Ohio, under their Chief Paxinosa, and settled in what is now Plymouth. However, due to the droughts and famines in 1752 and 1753, they abandoned the Wyoming Valley to settle in Chenango, in New York State. Shortly afterwards, the remaining Shawanese left for Ohio, and only the Delawares remained in the Valley.

As nature abhors a vacuum, so does man and, in the rocky and infertile fields of Connecticut, the richness, beauty and comparative emptiness of the Wyoming Valley presented an irresistable attraction. By the early 1750s, what little fertile land was left in Connecticut, was being rapidly filled by a burgeoning population of land-hungry, independent inhabitants.

In 1682 and 1686, Charles II had granted a charter to Connecticut which included a strip of New York, New Jersey, and northern Pennsylvania, as well as all lands westward to the Pacific Ocean! This was the same Charles II who had granted to William Penn, a few years earlier, all lands from the source to the mouth of the Delaware River westward. Thus, what later became southern New York and northern Pennsylvania, were both deeded to Connecticut and Pennsylvania!

In June of 1763, a group of Connecticut citizens petitioned the Connecticut General Assembly with a request for a quit claim stating:

"That whereas, there is a large quantity of land lying upon a river called Susquehanna; and that there is no English inhabitant that lives on said land, nor near thereunto; and at the same time lies about seventy miles west of the Dielewey (Delaware) River, and as we suppose within the charter of the Colony of Connecticut: and that there is a number of Indians that live on or near the piece of land aforesaid, who lay claim to the same. And we, the subscribers to the number of one hundred persons, are very desirous to go and inhabit the aforesaid land, and at the place aforesaid (provided that we can obtain a quiet or quit claim of the Honorable Assembly, of attractive land lying in the place aforesaid, and to contain a quantity sixteen miles square, to lie on both sides of the Susquehanna River); and as the Indians lay claim to the same, we propose to purchase of them their right, so as to be at peace with them."

The next month, some two hundred and fifty prospective settlers met to form The Susquehanna Company and collected "Two Milled Spanish Dollars" from each to set up a "Journeying Committee," to map out the land, and to purchase it from the Indians. The Journeying Committee secretly left for Wyoming in October 1753, but the Pennemites (Pennsylvanians) soon found out.

In a letter from a Captain William Parson to Governor Hamilton of Pennsylvania, the following was stated: "Having heard that some persons under pretense of an authority from the Government of Connecticut had passed by Daniel Brodhead's (now East Stroudsburg) on their way to Wyomink upon the Susquehanna River in order to view the land in those parts ... Mr. Brodhead told me that some of his near neighbors had accompanied three gentlemen-like men to Wyomink, who produced a writing under a large seal, which they said was the public seal of the Governor of Connecticut empowering them to treat, etc."

At the same time, Conrad Weiser, the Pennsylvania agent to the Indians and interpreter wrote Governor Hamilton: "In the Fall of 1753, the Indians on the Susquehanna saw some of the New England men, that came as spies to Wayomink, and that they saw them making drafts of the lands and rivers, and are much offended about it."

Weiser added that the Indians asked him about these men, and his answer was that, "We had intelligence from New England that they came against the advice of their superiors, as a parcel of head-strong men and disturbers of the peace."

Governor Hamilton, thus warned, sent Conrad Weiser and Shikellamy to Albany, to meet with the Mohawks, to possibly prevent any sale of land to the Susquehanna Company and, on July 4th and 5th of 1754, a conference was held with "King" Hendrick (Tejanoge), Chief of the Mohawks, and about seventy of his subjects.

Hendrick was about seventy-eight years old at this time, and was described as a "venerable and noble looking old chief and a large corpulent man."

In Mohawk fashion, his head was shaved and crested with a deer's tail and eagle feathers. He was one of the five Iroquois chiefs who had journied to Queen Anne's court in London in 1710. At the age of seventy-five, he had become a Chieftain, or "King." The Mohawk's declaration by Hendrick was:

"*We will never part with the land at Shamokin and Wyomink.* Our bones are scattered there, and on this land there has always been a great Council-fire.... We have heard since we came here that our Brother Onas (Penn) and our Brother of New Engl and have had some disputes about the lands of Susquehanna; but we desire you would not differ with one another about it, for *neither shall have it....* We have appointed Shikellamy to take care of the lands. He is our representative there, and has our orders not to suffer Onas' people or the New Englanders to settle there!"

Six Days later, the very same Hendrick, together with fourteen other Six Nations Chiefs and Sachems, listed as grantors in the deed, sold the Wyoming Valley to the Susquehanna Company of Connecticut for two thousand pounds! Although Hendrick was not a signer of the deed, he was listed as a grantor and never questioned the validity of the deed, until six months later.

There were now 753 members of the Susquehanna Company—583 whole-share and 165 half-share proprietors. These comparatively large numbers did not dissuade Governor Hamilton of Pennsylvania from declaring the Susquehanna Company deed null and void.

Hamilton stated that the Indian signers had been bribed by the Susquehanna Company agent, John Lydius, with money and liquor, to sign over the deed to the Wyoming Valley to the New Englanders. Hamilton added that Lydius, a tavern owner, had been seen getting the Indian delegates drunk and then counting out bribe money on the stoop of his tavern to present to the Indian delegates. This was followed by an intimation that there were *two* Mohawk Chiefs named Hendrick, one for, and one against the deed!

Hamilton followed up his statement by inviting King Hendrick and the other Indian signers to Philadelphia. When Hendrick and his entourage arrived in January, 1755, they were lodged in the State House and treated with the greatest respect.

Now it was Hamilton's turn to wine and dine Hendrick and his followers. Hendrick, in appreciation, declared that, "The Governor and people of this province have, more than other of the Colonies, manifested on all occasions a particular tenderness and affection for the Indians!"

Governor Hamilton, with further tenderness and affection, requested Hendrick's help in breaking the Susquehanna Company's deed.

Hendrick replied, "We have considered what you have said to us about the deceitful deed which John Lydius inveigled some of us to sign. We agree with you that the deed should be destroyed. We agree with you that it is a false proceeding. We will give you our assistance, but you know that we cannot destroy the deed ourselves—that would be another mistake. ... It must be an act of the Council of the Six Nations. We will think of the proper means. We advise the Governor to send for two deputies of every Nation of the Six, either here (Philadelphia) or at Albany to kindle a council-fire with them, to consider a way to oblige Connecticut to discountenance the deed."

Governor Hamilton, through his secretary, wrote to Colonel William Johnson, Superintendant of Indian Affairs:

"We further intimated to Hendrick and now inform you that to get rid of this deed we cannot devise any other method that will be effectual, unless the Six Nations in Council, will execute a conveyance to the Proprietoraries (Pennsylvania) of all the lands lying within their grant!"

The Governor then requested Johnson to summon the Council meeting suggested by Hendrick. However, before the meeting could be called, Johnson was delegated to lead a Six Nation expedition against the French at Lake George, where King Hendrick, at the age of eighty, was killed while leading a charge in his bright-red, British uniform.

Thus, through poor luck and timing, the Pennsylvania Proprietaries lost one of the main spokesmen for their cause, among the Six Nations, a fact considered crucial to future events by Charles Miner, in his *History of Wyoming*. It should be noted here, that the former Five Nations of the Iroquois Confederacy had become Six Nations with the addition of the Tuscarora Tribe, which further strengthened the Confederacy.

King Hendrick

CHAPTER THREE

In the Wyoming Valley, Teedyuscung and his Delaware followers, who had arrived in 1754, set up their town where the city of Wilkes-Barre now stands.

Teedyuscung was originally from the Trenton, New Jersey area and was part of a clan of Delawares who moved to the Pocono Mountains. He had heard of the Moravians in 1742 and was so impressed by Christianity as to later join the congregation at Gnadenhutten, and a year later was baptized at the age of thirty-six.

In speaking of his baptism, Teedyuscung stated, "I cannot describe it—but I wept and trembled." He added that he had been a very bad man all his life, that he had no power to resist evil, and that he had never been before so desirous to be delivered from sin. He became known among the Moravians as "Honest John" and was described as a "portly, well-looking man endowed with good natural sense, quick of comprehension and very ready in answering the questions put to him ... His greatest weakness was a fondness for strong drink, the temptation he could not easily resist, and would sometimes drink to excess."

More to the point was a statement written by William Parsons, a justice of the peace and an officer in the militia: "He is a lusty, raw-boned man, haughty and very desirous of respect and command. He can drink three quarts or one gallon of rum a day without being drunk."

John Mack came to the Wyoming Valley shortly after Teedyuscung's arrival and wrote in his journal:

"Wyoming is in a critical condition. The New Englanders in right of a Royal Charter, lay claim to Wyoming. The Pennsylvanians hold it is within the Proprietary Grant and wished the Indians to sell it to them. Thus, the Indians are in a dilemma, for if they yield to the solicitations of the Pennsylvanians and oppose the New Englanders who desire to settle here, and threaten to shoot their horses and cows (and the Pennsylvanians urge them to oppose them), they know there will be a war, as the New Englanders are a people who refuse to regard the Indians as lords of the soil, and will subjugate them if they refuse to evacuate the Valley."

The Delawares in this crisis looked to Teedyuscung for leadership, and according to the Moravian Hockwelder:

"It is said by the Indians who knew him best, and who at that time had the welfare of their own nation much at heart that his great and sole object was to recover for the Lenapes that dignity which the Iroquois had treacherously wrested from them. Thence flowed the bitterness of the later against him, though he seemed to be promoting the same interest which they themselves supported."

At a conference with the Pennsylvania Governor, Teedyuscung

recalled that the Iroquois made women of the Delawares and then stated:

"The Covenant of Friendship made by our fathers and grandfathers with the English is bound so fast by a chain about our arms that, let happen what will, we will not break loose, but will be united and stand firm to each other forever. As you are at one end of the road, our uncles, the Six Nations at the other, and we ourselves are seated in the middle at Wyomink, if any mischief or disturbance should arise, whether before or behind, we shall be ready to see it and join to assist and stand by each other."

Within a year however, whether due to contacts with the French and promises of lost lands to be restored for military aid, or recognition of opportunities to be gained with British defeats, to prove the Delawares were not women, Teedyuscung had himself proclaimed "King."

John Mack during a visit to Wyoming was disturbed and horrified to find a large gathering of Delawares celebrating the pagan "Feast of the Harvest" with dancing, drinking, and carousing.

Teedyuscung had discarded his cloak of Christianity like an ill-fitting garment. He was no longer known as "Honest John," but was now known as "The War Trumpet." Upon hearing of Braddock's Defeat in Western Pennsylvania, he urged his Delawares to remember their Lenape tradition and to prove to the Six Nations and the English that they were brave warriors and not women.

With alternate drinking, revelry, and tireless ranting about his insolent Iroquois and English enemies, Teedyuscung would work himself and his braves into a frenzy and don their warpaint. From his village in the Wyoming Valley he attacked and pillaged the entire upper Delaware Valley. In one month alone, in 1755, he and his warriors killed over one hundred English settlers and burned and pillaged over fifty farms.

The following year saw a series of English victories over the French, and seeing the handwriting on the wall, Teedyuscung wiped off the war paint, and in reply to English peace overtures to the Delawares, stated:

"The Brethren, the Governor and People of Pennsylvania; We rejoice to hear from you. We desire you will look upon us with eyes of mercy. We are a very poor people—our wives and children are almost naked ... we are void of understanding and destitute of the necessaries of life. We the Delawares give you this string of wampum and desire that the bitterness that may have gathered in this dark and unhappy time may be removed. We have laid aside our hatchet and will never make use of it anymore against you or your brethren, the English."

Teedyuscung then set off for Fort Niagara to obtain the endorsement of the Six Nations for an upcoming peace council at Easton. He sought to increase his own stature as well as the Delawares' at the meeting by removing the stigma that the Iroquois had long ago inflicted upon the Delawares. The Iroquois at Fort Niagara gave Teedyuscung the following message:

"Cousins, the Delawares—You will remember that you are our women; our forefathers made you so, and put a petticoat on you and charged you to be true to us and and live with no other man. But of late you have suffered the string that tied your petticoat to be cut loose by the French, and you lay with them, and so became a common bawd, in which you did very wrong and deserve chastisement. But notwithstanding this, we will still esteem you; and as you have thrown off the cover of your modesty and became stark naked which is a shame for a woman, we now advise you not to act as a man yet, but be first instructed by us and do as we bid you, and you will become a noted man."

Armed with this less-than-ringing Iroquois endorsement of his authority, Teedyuscung delayed completion of any peace conference until the outcome of the French and Indian War was no longer in doubt.

This delaying action prompted Canyese, a Mohawk chief, to issue the following threat to the Delawares (and let the English know of it):

"Teedyuscung, on behalf of the Delawares, applied to me as Chief of the Six Nations. I told him that the Delawares were the most nearly related to the Mohawks, who had given the Delawares protection and had permitted them to sit down and enjoy peaceably the lands on which they were seated. We, Mohawks are men; we are made so from above. But the Delawares are women and under our protection and of too low a kind to be men; and we have observed you, the Delawares, have suffered your petticoats to be cut away by strangers (the French), and are running about naked, and doing things that do not become you in the condition you know you are in, subject to us. We have seen you in all your proceedings and do not approve your conduct. Since you have been so foolish to obey that stranger's voice and cut off your petticoats and have taken the tomahawk and and now appear in the character of a Man, I join and help to cut off your petticoats, and so far make a Man of you—but do not put a tomahawk in your hand. I know what is for your good and therefore, I will not allow you to carry a tomahawk."

Governor Denny, the new Governor of Pennsylvania, feeling that this above declaration weakened Teedyuscung's bargaining position, sought to take advantage of the Delaware "King," and changed the site of the proposed peace treaty from Easton to Philadelphia. Teedyuscung, who was awaiting Governor Denny at Easton, sent the following message:

"Brother, you remember very well that in time of darkness and danger I came in here at your invitation. At Easton we kindled a small council-fire... If you should put out this little fire our enemies will call it only a Jack-o-lantern, kindled on purpose to deceive those who approach it. Brother, I think it by no means advisable to put out this little fire but rather to put more sticks upon it and I desire that you will come to it as soon as possible, bringing your old and wise men along with you, and I shall be very glad to see you here."

Denny grudgingly went to Easton only to be told by Teedyuscung that he would like to meet the governor again at a future time. According to Conrad Weiser, Teedyuscung "was too often overcome with strong liquor; he spoke confused, though nothing that was wrong or false."

Three months later, in July 1757, Teedyuscung together with over three hundred Delawares and Iroquois met with Governor Denny at Easton. Even before the proceedings began, Teedyuscung shocked every one present by threatening to walk out if not provided with a clerk as befitting a King. He protested that even the Governor had his own clerk. Again Governor Denny gave in and the peace treaty was rapidly and amicably concluded with Teedyuscung making the following speech:

"We intend to settle at Wyoming, and we want to have certain boundaries fixed between you—and us; and a certain tract of land fixed which it shall not be lawful for us or our children ever to sell nor for you or any of your children ever to buy.... And as we intend to make a settlement at Wyoming, and to build different houses from what we have done heretofore—such as may last only for a little time, but for our children after us—we desire you will assist us in making our settlements, and send us persons to instruct us in building houses and in making such necessaries as shall be needful; and that persons be sent to instruct us in the Christian religion and instruct our children in reading and writing."

The Pennsylvania Governor replied, "I am pleased you have made choice of that place. It is perfectly agreeable to me, and I assure you I will heartily concur with you in using all the means in my power to have those lands settled upon you and your posterity."

Ominously, occupation of Wyoming by the Delawares, rather than ownership, was assented to by the Six Nations by Thomas King Chief of the Oneidas when he stated:

"Teedyuscung desired us to make you, the Delawares, the owners of the lands at Wyoming and other places on the Susquehanna River. In answer to which we, who are present, say that we have no power to convey lands to anyone, but we shall take your request to the Great Council fire for their sentiments, as we never sell or convey lands before it be agreed upon in the Great Council of the Six Nations. In the meantime, you may make use of those lands in conjunction with our people.

"Cousins, as you have swallowed down your throats and your own country, and your uncles, the Six Nations have made a fire for you at Wyoming, we desire you to go and sit by that fire and watch it and see that no people come there to steal our country; and *if they should come, we desire you will give us immediate notice, that we may take some measures to remove them.*"

CHAPTER FOUR

When Teedyuscung heard that thousands of New England settlers had banded together with the intention of settling in Wyoming, his first reaction was to consult the Governor of Pennsylvania, not the Iroquois.

The Governor answered, "Do not suffer them to settle. That is, collect the ancient and discreet men of your nation and go to the settlers in a peaceable manner, and endeavor to persuade them to forbear those lands."

It was August 1762 when 119 New England settlers, without their wives and children, set out on foot and horseback for Wyoming. Their route was over a rough and narrow trail which didn't allow for the use of wagons or carts. Their mission was to prepare a settlement for the arrival of their families the following year.

The New Englanders weren't in Wyoming for more than a day before close to 400 Iroquois arrived unexpectedly on their way home to Onondaga from a Lancaster conference. The settlers were ordered to leave immediately. Most did, but some twenty five brave souls stayed on until October in defiance of the Iroquois order to till the virgin soil and plant some wheat in what is now Plains on the east bank of the Susquehanna.

The following year saw more arrivals other then New Englanders. Many Iroquois suddenly appeared in the Wyoming Valley to live with the Delawares. Casks of rum accompanied these new arrivals to reward Teedyuscung and the Delawares for their hospitality.

On the night of April 19th, 1763, the revelry between the Iroquois and their Delaware hosts culminated with, the hut of Teedyuscung suddenly bursting into flames simultaneously with about twenty other surrounding Delawares huts and cabins. Teedyuscung and more than half his tribe died and the Iroquois were no where to be found.

The Moravian historian, Reichel, in his Memorials of the *Moravian Church,* wrote:

"The Iroquois, it is said, were the instigators of this cowardly act, for they hated the man who testified against their arrogant assumption and who opposed their lust of power. As long as he lived, therefore, he was a standing rebuke to their designing oppression, and although they no longer dreaded his arms, they feared his words, which left their guilty consciences no peace. Hence, it was resolved in council that he ought not to live; and when news was brought to Onondaga that the body of the Delaware King and the bodies of his men of war had disappeared in flames, the perfidious Six Nations triumphed in having destroyed an enemy whose spirit they had failed to subdue.

"A few weeks later, in May, about twelve New Englanders arrived, some with their wives, to a nearly unpopulated Wyoming Valley. Many of the native population had left the month before with the murder of Teedyuscung and many of his people. Others had left since to join the Pontiac Rebellion on the Western Frontier. The sudden Indian exodus from the Wyoming Valley thus left the area open for the incoming migration of the New Englanders, unchallenged.

"The Six Nations realized this and in May of 1763, a delegation of four deputies and a chief of the Six Nations arrived in Hartford to address the Connecticut Assembly. One of these deputies, Sayenqueraghta, a Seneca sachem rose and declared:

"We heard grevious news this Winter that you were about to come with 300 families to settle on our lands, which was very astonishing to us; and that you designed to build forts and strong places on our lands. For that reason our sachems considered upon it, and have sent us down to this place. We are come down here to acquaint you with what news we hear—that you have got a design to settle on the Susquehanna River and claim the land to the West Seas. We have heretofore given away lands to the White People, but of the sale of *this* land, the Six Nations know nothing—either that they have ever given it away, or sold it to any, and what little we have left we intend to keep for ourselves. We know not of any such sale, and if any such thing has been asked it must have been done by particular persons in a separate manner, and not of any General Meeting, or Council, of the Six Nations—as has been the usual manner of their giving or selling their lands....

"Brothers, seriously take into consideration and think how you would like to have lands taken from you in an unfair and injurious manner. *You are a praying people,* better acquainted with books and learning then we, and must need to know better what is right.... Brothers, as I have told you before, that we have been sent here by chiefs to let you know that we have heard about your design of entering upon our lands, and we deliver in this belt (of wampum) to show the minds of the Confederate Nations—that you do not encroach on these lands which we have reserved and design to keep for ourselves and our children to the latest prosperity, and will not part with them. Brothers, if you proceed to encroach on our lands we shall not be easy, but will return home to our own places and apply ourselves to the King, our father to obtain justice, and I myself will go, and on my going out of the house will return home."

The Governor of Connecticut requested that they stay over until the following week which the Iroquois deputies reluctantly agreed to. This caused a correspondent of the New York Gazette to comment: "...it is plain that this was a mere pretense—for it was with some entreaty they were prevailed upon to wait for the Governor's answer. They intended *their remonstrance should be a declaration of war!*"

Even more ominous was an extract of a letter from David Zeisberger, a Moravian minister who passed through Wyoming on June of 1763: "At Wyomick we found the Indians in motion to leave the place the same night we arrived there; they received many frightful relations concerning war being begun again ... They have planted there (at Wyoming), but leave everything behind them."

The Indians' occupancy of the Wyoming Valley had come to an end!

Von Zinzendorf's Disciple, David Zeisberger, preaching to the Indians at Wyoming in 1763 (from a black and white drawing by John Sartrain in 1864).

Massacre of the First Wyoming Settlers on October 15, 1763 (From the original drawing by F.O.C. Darley, entitled *Wyoming*. This scene is often incorrectly entitled *The Battle of Wyoming*.

CHAPTER FIVE

The Wyoming Valley rang with the metallic thud of axes in the Spring and early Summer of 1763, as the twenty some odd New Englanders cut timber to clear the land and build cabins.

The virgin soil they plowed was dark rich sediment brought by rampaging and flooding Susquehanna waters from the North over periods of centuries. The settlers were grateful to plow land so free of rocks, unlike their previous New England soils, where they constantly had to interupt plowing and planting to haul out rocks and change plow blades.

By the end of the summer they saw corn and wheat growing to such rich density and height as they had never seen before. It is no wonder that they completely ignored the three urgent demands from the Governor of Connecticut to leave the Wyoming Valley immediately.

In early July, more families came with livestock and settled on the west side of the Susquehanna River and on the east side a large blockhouse was erected.

It was just about noon on October 15th, 1763, just before the wheat harvest was to occur, that the Wyoming Valley suddenly echoed to blood curdling war whoops. From the river bank there sprang 100 Iroquois warriors in bright red and black war paint. They came in stages to overrun individual groups of settlers with flashing tomahawks and spears. Some were armed with muskets traded for or taken in previous raids in other areas.

Within minutes approximately eighteen New Englanders were killed and about seven were captured. The remaining settlers fled for their lives to the mountains in the east with the screams of their loved ones ringing in their ears as the warriors killed and scalped the victims.

Two brothers, Parshall and Nathaniel Terry, were on their way through the fields to their cabin for lunch when the warriors suddenly appeared and shot and killed Nathaniel. Parshall, who was unarmed dropped immediately into the tall grasses. The Iroquois poked around with their spears, thrusting into the dense wheat for about an hour before moving on. Parshall lay motionless scarcely daring to breathe, hearing the whistling of the spears through the grasses only inches from his body. He waited until darkness to escape.

Twin brothers, John and Emanuel Hoover, were working on a chimney while building a cabin, when they were seized and bound by the Iroquois. At almost the same time their father and another brother were killed and scalped. The Hoover brothers were marched north by some six Iroquois, together with another prisoner named Isaac Hollister, along the river where the town of Plains is now situated. There they saw an unarmed settler walking toward them carrying a small bundle—and oblivious of danger! The Iroquois immediately surrounded him and repeatedly thrust their spears through him before scalping him.

The Hoover brothers' forced march continued northward, and weeks later, they were able to escape near what is now Geneva, New York. This was in the heart of the Iroquois lands and proved that the perpetrators of the 1763 raid were Iroquois. Although John Hoover died in the forest of fatigue and hunger, Nathaniel lived to tell of his capture and escape when he returned to Wyoming many years later.

Hoover's fellow prisoner, Isaac Hollister, also captured at Wyoming, survived as well. Three years later upon his release he wrote a graphic account of his life among the Iroquois, first with the Cayuga and then the Seneca. It was titled, "A Brief Narrative of the Captivity of Isaac Hollister, Who Was Taken by the Indians, A.D. 1763":

"The Indians, after they burnt and destroyed all they could, marched off, and carried me up the Susuehanna River 150 miles to a town called by them, Weltouounque, and when we arrived there they tied me with a rope about my neck, and an Indian was ordered to lead me while others beat me with their fists. This they continued to do until I ran about a quarter of a mile. When I arrived at one of their huts, they tied me to one of the spars of the hut, where I remained at that night. The next day they let me loose, but would not let me go out of their sight. Here I tarried about three months, in which time I underwent many hardships, and like to have famished with hunger and cold—having nothing to cover with but an old coat and an old blanket which was almost worn out. My employment was to fetch wood every day, upon my back, half a mile, which made me almost weary of my life.

"At this place was brought a young Dutchman, (John Hoover), who was taken at the same time and place that I was, and when we had convenient opportunity we laid our heads together to contrive an escape. To this end we stole everything we could, without being discovered, and hid it in hollow of an old log.... we had got together about forty ears of corn and six cakes of bread, each about the bigness of a hand.... The next next day about noon we were sent after wood at the usual place, when, instead of returning back we set out with a design to reach the nearest English settlement we could. We ran all the afternoon until evening, when we made a stop and built a fire, where we remained during the night."

They traveled on through severe, bone-chilling March weather with little food, and the Dutchman died. Hollister continued:

"The evening before his death he told me that if he died first he would not have me afraid to eat of his flesh, 'for I am determined,' said he, 'to eat of yours if you should die before me....' I thought the absolute necessity I was in would excuse my pursuing the advice he gave me of eating his flesh as soon as he died. I went immediately about performing the disagreeable operation, and cut off about five or six pounds of his legs and thighs. I left the rest and made the best way I could down the creek. I had not traveled but four days before I arrived at an Indian town where I was soon discovered...."

Hollister was given parched corn and returned to his former captives. They wanted to burn him at the stake, but instead held a council, where the majority of Indians decided that because of his youth and usefulness, they would whip him instead by having him run the gauntlet. He was then completely stripped and forced to run about 600 feet between two rows of Indian men, women, and children who beat his body with whips and clubs as he ran by. One of the blows was exceptionally vicious and he fell to the ground, badly cut and bleeding, whereupon an old squaw ran to his aid and dragged him to her hut.

Hollister stated: "I tarried here about fourteen days and then they sent me to the Senecas, about 150 miles off. I lived here one year, in which time I suffered almost insurmountable hardships. For the most part of the time we had nothing but ground nuts and herbs to subsist upon in Summer, and red plums in Winter. Several of the Indians actually starved to death."

He was later freed after being held prisoner for three years.

Another settler, Noah Hopkins, also lived to tell of his escape. Noah, as a shareholder in the Susquehanna Company, was among the first settlers to come to the Wyoming Valley to build a cabin and clear the wilderness. Unlike most of the new Connecticut arrivals, he came from Dutchess County, New York, and had no family.

At the first sound of attack, Hopkins ran for the forest, hearing the war whoops of the pursuing warriors. He had run a long distance and was completely out of breath, when he saw the trunk of a large hollow tree lying on the ground. With his last burst of energy, he thrust his body feet first into the log. Trying to catch his breath without making a noise, he awaited his fate.

Before long, he heard footsteps and the voices of the Iroquois speaking in gutteral tones. Then, in horror, he heard bullets rattling in pouches and arrows moving about in quivers as two Indians sat down on the log to rest. Hopkins, paralyzed with fear, looked out through the opening of the log as if to catch his last glimpse of the world. His conscious mind told himself to be still as he noted that a light rain had begun. He thought that maybe the Indians would move on. At the same time, he subconsciously remembered his parents and his boyhood years,and that is when his focus narrowed.

At the opening of the log, a little brown spider wove a single silken thread across the entrance. With infinite patience the little spider wove one cross hair, and then another, and another, and another...

Hopkins was captivated by the sheer beauty of the dancing and dipping motion of the insect and the beautiful symmetry of the web. The spider daintily pirouetted and wove circular threads around the diagonal threads.

The drizzle had stopped and little droplets of water clung to the web as the sun came out. Hopkins marveled at the beauty of the rainbow colors emanating from the drops of water clinging to the web as the sun's rays crept into the log. The little spider, now finished, came inside the log to hide and await the capture of some careless insect in the web. Hopkins was amazed at the calming effect the sight had on him and at his strange feeling of kinship for his fellow partner in concealment.

The Indians were now fully rested and arose from the tree trunk to resume their search for victims. One of the Indians then looked at the opening of the log, and seeing a spider web completely blocking the entrance, joined the others to leave the area, convinced that the log was unoccupied.

Hopkins waited a few hours before crawling out of the log. He was famished, and cautiously went back to the settlement in hope of finding food. He had been in the wilderness for five days without anything to eat and though faint, he was shocked by what he saw: Bodies lay in the fields, scalped and mutilated. Crops had been destroyed, cattle were gone, and all the cabins and structures were burned down. The stillness and the smell of death permeated the area, yet the Valley was beautifully resplendent in Fall foliage. Hopkins couldn't dwell on this contradiction—he had to find food. He first looked along side of the river and in the river itself, with no success. Then, returning to the shore, he found the remains of a wild turkey that had been shot on the morning of the attack and left to rot in the sun. Hopkins had no choice and quickly stripped off the feathers and washed the carcass in the river before he ate it raw. Years later, he stated it was the sweetest meat he had ever eaten.

With the remains of the turkey and some herbs, roots, and grains for sustenance, Hopkins made the long, dangerous trek over mountains and rivers back to civilization. No sooner had Hopkins left the Wyoming Valley, than a detachment of soldiers from Lancaster County, Pennsylvania arrived, and in an extract of a letter dated October 23rd, the *Pennsylvania Gazette*, quoting an eyewitness soldier, printed, "Our party under Captain Clayton has returned from Wyoming where they met with no Indians, but found the New Englanders who had been killed and scalped a day or two before they got there. They buried the dead, nine men and a woman who had been most cruelly butchered; the woman was roasted and several of the men had awls thrust into their eyes, and spears, arrows, pitchforks, etc., sticking in their bodies."

The sudden attack temporarily stopped the flow of settlers into the Wyoming Valley. Neverthless, a precedent had been set and a warning message delivered. The comparatively small-scale raid was destined to be obscured by the inevitable resulting event fifteen years into the future.

BLOCKHOUSE

The block house, made of hardwood logs. These outside-the-fort defensive positions proved to be effective in the Pennemite Wars and in defense against Indian raids.

CHAPTER SIX

The raid on the first New England settlers of Wyoming Valley struck such terror and fear into the operations of the Susquehanna Company that they transacted no further business dealing with the Valley for a full four years.

The Wyoming Valley lay vacant again, this time for two more years until 1765. In that year, the Commissioners of Indian Affairs for Pennsylvania, under Superintendant Sir William Johnson, granted rights to establish and operate a trading post in the Wyoming Valley. Recipients of these rights were Captain Amos Ogden of New Jersey and his associates, Captain John Dick, and John Anderson.

The traders arrived in Wyoming in the Summer of 1765 and quickly erected a large log building near Mill Creek to house a store, warehouse, and living space. Not only did Iroquois from surrounding areas come to Wyoming to trade, but Anderson, between 1765 and 1769, went up the Susquehanna twice a year to trade with them. As it turned out, he kept himself busy between trips as well.

In 1766, an Iroquois named Jemmy Nanticoke came to Philadelphia for a conference with the Governor. He had come from Chenango, New York with a few others who had formerly lived in Wyoming. Presenting the Governor with an unusual belt of black wampum, he said:

"Brother, it is now proper for us to mention to you that there has been a great deal of wickedness of late, which hangs like a cloud in the air and hinders us from seeing each other and from transacting or settling such business as we may have with one another. By the belt therefore, we remove these clouds and we now present them to you to show our joy that the Great God of Heaven has brought us again together to see one another with the same brotherly affection we used formally to do.

"As we came down from our country, we stopped at Wyoming, where we had a *mine* in two places, and we discovered that some white people had been at work at the mine and had filled out three canoes with the ore; and we saw their tools with which they had dug it out of the ground, where they had made a hole at least forty feet long and five or six feet deep. It happened formally that some white people did now and then take only a small bit and carried it away, but these people had been working at the mine and had filled their canoes.

"You know, Brother, that by our ancient treaties we are obliged to acquaint each other when anything hurtful shall happen to either of us. According to this we now inform you of this injury done to us, which is a very bad thing, and may produce mischief between us ... We also inform you that there is one, John Anderson, a trader now living at Wyoming, and we suspect that either he or somebody employed by him has robbed our mine. This man has a store of goods there, and it may happen, when the Indians see their mine robbed, they will come and take away his goods."

The Governor replied, "We have heard what you say about the mine at Wyoming, and we assure you that we know nothing of this matter; and if Anderson has settled there, he has been guilty of a breach of our general order ... If any of our people should attempt to take away any ore from your mine you will endeavor to learn their names, and give the Governor early information."

The ore in question was called "stone coal," later known as anthracite, and its abundance in the Wyoming Valley only added to the attraction it already held for the ambitious New Englanders of the Susquehanna Company when news of the mine reached Connecticut. The Susquehanna Company, no longer able to restrain its members, finally met in January 1768 and agreed to send an emissary, Colonel Dyer, to London to have King George III legitimize their claim to Wyoming. Dyer's mission to London was a failure, as his petition fell victim to bureaucratic delay and inertia, probably due to his lack of political connections at the King's Privy Council.

The growing Iroquois unrest and boundary disputes between the Colonies themselves finally forced Sir William Johnson, Superintendant of Indian Affairs, to call a great Council to be held in October of 1768. Invited were delegates of each of the Six Nations as well as other tribes. Also invited were delegates of each of the Northeastern Colonies.

Johnson stated that his purpose in calling the Council was not only "to renew the ancient covenant chain between the Indians and the

English, but to establish a scientific frontier." The site of the Council was Fort Stanwix, where Rome, New York is now located.

Sir William Johnson was a quick-witted man from Northern Ireland who spoke with a heavy brogue. He owned Johnson Hall, a medieval type of manor in the lower Mohawk Valley in New York State, amid barbaric splendor and many scores of tenant farmers. There were also other large estates nearby, owned by allied underlords, one of whom was John Butler, who was to enter into the scene in future years.

Living as a feudal lord, unrestricted by the laws of civilization, Sir William married a Mohawk princess and had three legitimate children and unknown numbers of illegimate offspring. He always urged and encouraged intermarriage and closer ties with the Iroquois in order to maintain an alliance for the end goal of wresting Canada from the French.

Johnson himself became one of the largest land owners in America. Land acquistion was his driving force—and to this end—he was extremely crafty and cunning with the Iroquois.

He once had his heart set on acquiring an attractive, large piece of land surrounding a beautiful lake and owned by a Mohawk chief. Johnson noticed that at a conference, the chief admired a lace-trimmed coat Johnson was wearing. The chief told Johnson that he dreamed that he owned the coat and wore it to the admiring approval of his tribesmen.

Two days later, Johnson met the Mohawk chief and questioned him on his dreams, especially the one about his fine coat. Johnson then suddenly took off the coat and gave it to the Mohawk.

Johnson explained that, the night before, he had dreamed about land around a beautiful lake. The chief asked if Johnson had really had the dream. He told the chief that it was true and the chief then solemnly deeded the land to him. When the deal was completed, the chief sadly stated that he would never dream with Johnson again!

Sir William intended that the Council of Fort Stanwix was to be a major meeting of great importance and scope. In *The Old New York Frontier,* Francis W. Halsey wrote:

"In preparation for this Council, some twenty large bateaux, laden with presents best suited to propitiate the Indians, has been conveyed to Fort Stanwix. From his agent in Albany, Sir William ordered sixty barrels of flour, fifty barrels of pork, six barrels of rice, and seventy barrels of other provisions." When the Congress opened, 3,200 Indians were present, and, according to Johnson, "each of whom consumes daily more than two ordinary men amongst us," and "would be extemely dissatisfied if stinted when convened for business."

On the Colonial side, the highest echelon of the Crown's public servants were present, including Governor Penn of Pennsylvania, his associate, Benjamin Franklin, as well as Franklin's son, William, who was the Governor of New Jersey. There were Chief Justices of the various Colonies present as well as Colonel Eleazar Fitch of Connecticut, who not only represented the Colony, but the Susquehanna Company as well. Even Wyoming was represented in the person of Captain Amos Ogden.

All the polite gesturing and toasts which ensued however, appeared to have been a public display for a result taken for granted. The fact is that *eight days* before the formal Council Treaty line was established, Governor Penn returned to Philadelphia to issue warrants to survey the Wyoming Valley and to establish the "Manor of Sunbury" on the west side of the Susquehanna, and the "Manor of Stoke" on the east side.

As the Council at Fort Stanwix got under way in an atmosphere of apparent harmony, an event took place that shattered the air of smug self-satisfaction. It was at a routine dinner toast to King George III by one of the most unimportant and obscure guests, that a shocking declaration was sounded that froze, horrified, and angered every loyal Englishman present. It had the effect of a distant sound of thunder signalling an impending storm.

An almost unknown clergyman, Reverend Jacob Johnson (no relation to Sir William) stood before the distinguished Colonial delegates and offered the following toast: "...I drink the health of King George III of Great Britain and Company, comprehending New England and all the British Colonies and Provinces in North America. And I mean to drink such a Health to his British Majesty when occasion serves, so long as his Royal Majesty shall govern his British and American subjects according to the Magna Charta or the great charter of English Liberties, and hears the prayers of his American subjects, when properly laid before him.

"But in case British Majesty (which God in great mercy prevent) should supercede and proceed contrary to charter rights and privileges and govern us with a rod of iron and the mouth of cannon, and make his little finger thicker than his father's loins, and utterly refuse to hear or consider our humble prayers, then, and in that case I should think it my indispensable duty to seek a retreat elsewhere, or *join with my Countrymen in forming a new empire in America,* distinct and independent of the British Empire..."

The gathered servants of King and Crown were so offended that they demanded an apology. The Reverend Johnson was quick to oblige and the following day read a letter of apology to all present, saying that he was only a lowly clergyman unused to addressing people of such high social standards. At the end of this apology, he again repeated his inflammatory toast of the previous day!

To add insult to injury, the good Reverend referred the distinguished gathering to a "projected and predicted plan" in an anti-British essay and placed himself in agreement "with every true Son of Liberty."

Sir William Johnson was so angered and embarrassed by Reverend Johnson's outburst that he severely limited the clergyman's contacts with the Indians during the negotiations. The event confirmed Sir William's suspicions about missionary clergymen who lived and worked among the Iroquois. Most of them were New Englanders and he suspected them of being secret agents for the Susquehanna Company. He felt that the clergy were trying to obstruct any new boundaries so that the Susquehanna Company could lay claim to the Wyoming Valley, while they hid behind their religious mission.

Reverend Jacob Johnson's mission was to preach Christianity to the Oneidas. He lived among them and was respected and loved by them. His restrictions imposed by Sir William in contact with the Indians during the Council or taking part in meetings did not stop him from writing notes to torment Sir William. In one of these letters he advised Sir William to be wary of the Senecas, as they were the only tribe that came armed to the Conference, and then closed the letter with the following: "P. S. As *I am a* seer—I may be knowing to some things your Excellency possibly may not—which occasions me thus to write."

With the full support of the majority of delegates, the Council, under the guidance of Sir William Johnson, quickly drew up a boundary line for English settlement, and a deed was made and signed by the Six Nations of the Iroquois on November 5th, 1768 granting all land east of the line to the King of England. The territory included large parts of New York, Pennsylvania, West Virginia, and Kentucky for the sum of $50,600 Spanish dollars paid to the various tribes.

On the same day, the Proprietaries of Pennsylvania purchased the Wyoming Valley alone from the Six Nations for $10,000 in Spanish dollars as an outgrowth of the Fort Stanwix Treaty. Two of the signers of the deed, Tyanhasare of the Mohawks, and Senosies of the Oneidas, had also been signers of the 1754 deed which had transferred the *very same land* to the Susquehanna Company of Connecticut!

Twenty-five years later, Reverend Jacob Johnson, after moving to Wyoming, testified in an affidavit that he "... was informed by several of the Indians present that Governor Penn wanted the Indians to give him a deed for the lands on the Susquehanna, and that they replied to him that they had given the New England white people a deed of the same lands, had received their pay for the same, and could not sell the same lands again. But they had finally agreed to give Governor Penn a deed of that land, because Sir William Johnson had told them that their former conveyance to the New England white people was unlawful—that they (the New Englanders) had no right to purchase the land, which was within Penn's charter and Penn alone had the right of purchasing the same."

Having returned to Philadelphia before the deed to the Wyoming Valley was signed, Governor Penn sent an urgent communication to his agents in Wyoming. Adressed to Amos Ogden Charles Stewart and John Jennings, it stated:

"There being Occasion, as soon as may be, to settle the Proprietary manors of Wyoming, on both sides of the Susquehanna—which you have signified your inclination to undertake—you may give such settlers, as you may think proper to invite there, the strongest assurances that each shall have a lease for seven years of one hundred acres of bottom-land with wood-land sufficient to support their plantation, upon paying the acknowledgement of an ear of Indian corn per annum—if the same be demanded. And at the end of the term, if the Proprietaries incline to sell the lands, the settlers shall have the [right of] refusal—in case they incline to give as much as other people; and if the Proprietaries do not incline to sell, but to rent, the said settlers shall have the preference of others—in case they will give as good a rent as others offer.

"And the said settlers, on their part, must undertake *to defend their possessions against all persons* as shall unlawfully and without authority intrude upon the said manors or any other of the proprietary lands in their neighborhood; and shall do their utmost, and give their best assistance to magistrates and others, in a lawful manner to exclude and remove such unlawful intruders or settlers from off the lands of the Proprietaries...."

As mentioned, the Pennsylvania Proprietaries already had agents and a trading post in the Wyoming Valley, as their surveying began. This prompted the Susquehanna Company to meet hurriedly in

Hartford in December, 1768 to put into effect Connecticut's settlement of the Wyoming Valley. The stage was set for Wyoming to become the scene of the first civil war on the North American Continent.

Sir William Johnson, Superintendant of Indian Affairs

CHAPTER SEVEN

The Susquehanna Company notice of its policy and intentions towards Wyoming was immediately printed in the *New London Gazette* and the *Connecticut Courant* of Hartford on December 2nd, 1768 and omminously in the *Pennsylvania Chronicle* and *Universal Advertisers* of Philadelphia, a week later:

"Whereas, the lands formerly purchased by the New England people and others (commonly called the Susquehanna Company) from the Six Nations of Indians, and lying on the Susquehanna River, are within the grant made to the Governor and Company of the Colony of Connecticut, in the most plain and legal construction thereof; and His Majesty's prohibition as to the settling of those lands, pointing out the dissatisfaction and disturbance that such settlement might occasion to those Indians as the only reason of such prohibition; and as in consequence of His Majesty's order at the late congress at Fort Stanwix such precautions have been taken as to obviate any fresh troubles with the Indians; and the Indians being now quieted and satisfied—it appears that nothing reasonable lies in the way against the Susquehanna purchasers going on and settling those lands, purchased by them (lying within the line settled with the Indians at said congress), as soon as conveniently may be. These are therefore to give notice to the said Susquehanna Company to meet at Hartford in the Colony of Connecticut, on the 28th day of December next, then and there to consult and act as they see fit and convenient as to carrying on such settlement—and other business that may be thought proper to be done at said meeting."

The Susquehanna statement thus deftly used the sale of the Wyoming Valley to the Pennsylvania Proprietaries as a justification for settlement by the New Englanders by the simple act of just not mentioning Pennsylvania. The insertion of this notice in the Philadelphia newspaper was a deliberate challenge to Pennsylvania of Connecticut's desire to occupy and settle the Wyoming Valley.

The stage was set for more than a land grab between two colonies, it was to be a clash between the feudal system of landlord-tenant propriety of the past and the independent freehold ownership of the future.

Speed was the Susquehanna Company's main priority and an eyewitness, Joseph Trumbull, a former governor of Connecticut, described the December 28th meeting as follows:

"The Susquehanna Company, at a meeting at Hartford last week unanimously agreed to pursue the settlements. Forty men of the Company are to go and take possession of the lands by February lst, that they may get possession, if possible, before Mr. Penn. At the lst of June, 200 more heads of families are to go on... They are all in high spirits, and have no want of people to embrace the offered encouragements for settling. Their ardor will rather want restraining, than need any prompting. Mr. Penn, in their opinion, is now all their obstacle, and that point, they think, may as well be determined now as ever..."

Thus it was in January of 1769 in the midst of a terrible winter, the first forty Yankee settlers hurriedly set out on horseback from Windham, Connecticut westward to Goshen in Orange County, New York. Proceeding south to the Delaware River in Pike County, Pennsylvania, they traveled south to Monroe County, and then northwest across the Poconos to the Wyoming Valley.

The migration of the first forty Yankee settlers did not go unnoticed. A letter dated February 7th,1769 from an Easton justice of the peace, Lewis Gordon, to Governor Penn stated breathlessly:

"A few hours ago I received a letter by express from Messrs. Stewart and Jennings now at Wyoming intimating that they had intelligence from the Minisinks (northern Delaware Valley) that a large body of New England men were to set off thence for Wyoming in order to take forcible possession of those lands. This moment the Constable of the Minisinks is come down to me and informs that there are at least between forty and fifty New England men in his neighborhood, on the journey to Wyoming... I shall as soon as I can learn any of the New England people's names, and issue a warrant against them."

The first forty New England settlers arriving in the Wyoming Valley naturally proceeded to the original settlement built by the ill-fated expedition in the Mill Creek area. They found that several cabins had been built there and were occupied by Pennsylvania agents, Charles Stewart, John Jennings, now Sheriff of Northampton County, and Nathan Ogden, brother of Penn's agent Amos Ogden, plus seven or eight Pennsylvania (or, as the Yankees called them, Pennemite) settlers.

Discretion dictated a partial retreat, and the New Englanders retraced their steps northward a few miles to a place called Lackawanuck, the site of the present town of Pittston.

Here the settlers immediately went to work clearing land and building three cabins for their shelter until the Spring when two hundred more settlers were scheduled to arrive from Connecticut.

Their plans were rudely interrupted when, on March 13th, some one hundred armed Pennemites under the command of Amos Ogden, Sheriff Jennings, and Captain Alexander Patterson arrived at the Yankee cabins in Lackawanuck with an arrest warrant by Justice Gordon calling for the arrest of the settlers of those known by name:

"... and divers others, evil disposed persons to me unknown, were, in my presence, riotously, routously, and unlawfully assembled; and being so assembled did, in my presence, commit a riot to the great terror of His Majesty's liege subjects and against the peace of our Lord the King."

What took place after the appearance of the one hundred armed Pennemites has two versions. The Pennsylvania version appeared in a statement by Sheriff Jennings stating that:

"We went to Lackawanack near Wyoming. That the said intruders had built there two houses, one of which was a strong log house, built for defense. That the said intruders betook themselves to their said houses and declared they would not give up possession of the said lands, but would maintain the same as their own and put to death any persons that attempeted to dispossess expostulations, the said Justices recorded the forcible detainer, and this deponent by their orders, prepared to take the said intruders, and received two blows from some of them; but having forced into one of the said houses and taken those that were within, at length the rest surrendered, and the whole, to the number of thirty-one were taken into custody."

The Connecticut version of the incident can be found in an affidavit by two of the arrested Yankee settlers, Vine Elderkin and Thomas Dyer:

"At that place (Lackawanack) they (the "Forty") remained in a peacable manner, building huts, shelters and C. until about the middle of March when they were attacked by about 150 armed men, headed and commanded by the Sheriff of Northampton County. The subordinates of that company were mostly of low and despicable character. The whole soon made an onset, seized upon the people in one of our huts, and by their legs dragged and drew them out and off to some distance, and leveled the small building with the ground. They were about to treat the remainder of the settlers—who were then in the other hut—in the same manner, when two of their members as a committee, went out and treated with the assailants; the conclusion of which was that (as the settlers had *no orders or liberties to commit the least act of hostility*) the whole became prisoners, were disarmed and drove down to Easton under a strong guard. When arrived at Easton the court was there sitting, and the whole (were) admitted to bail in the sum of 100 pounds each...."

The great historian of Wyoming, Charles Miner, offered a third, and probably the most accurate version. Jennings had called a truce to meet with the Yankees, and instead presented them with a writ exclaiming, "Gentlemen, in the name of the Commonwealth of Pennsylvania you are my prisoners! Laugh where we must, be candid where we can."

Before the Yankees could be marched off to jail in Easton, nine escaped by merely walking off while the guards were preoccupied at a tavern en route. The remainder of the prisoners were freed almost as soon as bail was set in Easton, so quickly and efficiently was bail paid by the Susquehanna Company to get its people back.

The Susquehanna Company, as if to ignore the expulsion by the Pennemites, immediately voted to send one hundred and ten more settlers under the command of Major John Durkee, a hero of the French and Indian War. The intent was to give the expedition a military flair and thus impress the Pennsylvanians with the serious nature of their mission. Major Durkee met the original forty expelled in the upper Delaware Valley, and with expanded ranks, proudly paraded his Connecticut settlers past the Mill Creek Pennemite settlement with its twenty or so inhabitants looking on.

At the site of Teedyuscung's village, which the Iroquois had burned to the ground, the settlers set to work building a fort which they named Fort Durkee.

The inevitable panic letter from agent Charles Stewart to Governor Penn was written and sent to Philadelphia:

"This afternoon at about three o'clock 146 New England men and others chiefly on horseback, passed by our houses and are now encamped on the east side of the river. Among them is Benjamin

Shoemaker and John McDowell (Pennsylvanians from Pike County who joined the Susquehanna Company), with several of their neighbors. I spoke to McDowell, who informs me that at least as many more are on their way and will be here tomorrow, and I have other intelligence that they will in a few days be 500 strong. If this be true, we can only act defensively until reinforced. At present we are but twenty four men...

"From the view I had of these gentry, in their procession by our houses, they appear to be—at least an equal number of them—*of the lowest class*, but are almost all armed and fit for mischief. I am of the opinion that unless a party of His Majesty's forces are sent up to remove them, it will be difficult for the Sheriff to raise men enough in Northampton County to effect it; and every day will add to their strength and give them more spirits to persevere in mischief."

In the following two months, Governor Penn ordered Sheriff Jennings to deliver a proclamation to the Yankees. He also ordered militia under Colonel Turbot Francis to oust them, by force if necessary.

During this time, twenty log cabins, formed in a quadrangle, were quickly built and completed. The buildings covered half an acre and were surrounded by a palisaded stockade of upright timbers with loop holes for firearms and watch towers at the corners. The new Fort Durkee was formidable indeed.

Shortly after its completion, Sheriff Jennings arrived at the Fort to read Governor Penn's proclamation ordering the New Englanders out of Wyoming. The Sheriff stated in a later deposition:

"The next day having given notice to the people settled there of the

Sheriff's intention, the said intruders, to the number of 150 or thereabouts, assembled together and this deponent read to them with a loud voice a proclamation published by the Governor. That previous to his reading, the same Major Durkee, one of the intruders, told him they would permit him to read the proclamation, but were determined not to obey it, for that those lands were in the Colony of Connecticut and not in Pennsylvania. That after the said deponent had finished reading the said proclamation, a gun was fired over his head, and the said deponent immediately retired with the said Major Durkee. That the said intruders had built about twenty very strong log houses with loop holes to fire through, and they constantly carry their firearms on all occasions, and this deponent further doth saith that he doth believe it is impossible for him to raise a sufficient force within the said County to dispossess and arrest the said intruders—they being as 'tis said, upwards of 300 able-bodied men, and in daily expectations of being joined by 200 more."

A few weeks after the ineffectual reading of Governor Penn's proclamation to the Yankees, another scene right out of a comic opera took place. In response to Governor Penn's request for militia to remove the New Englanders, Colonel Turbot Francis marched a company of troops up from Philadelphia. On a beautiful sunny day in June, 1769, they arrived in the Wyoming Valley. The company of militia was a sight to behold. The sun reflected brilliantly off their bright crimson uniforms and blindingly off their brass buttons. Behind their streaming colors, a detachment of fifes and drums filled the air with martial music. The music abruptly stopped as the troops faced Fort Durkee. Front and forward stepped Colonel Turbot Francis who at once pompously demanded the surrender of the Fort and threatened to burn down all the buildings and kill all the people inside, and to confiscate their property and livestock. With these brave words thus having been said, the fifes and drums struck up a tune and the handsomely clad detachment resolutely marched back to their barracks at Fort Augusta, now known as Sunbury, some sixty miles away.

When Major Durkee returned to the Fort from a trip and was told of the curious demonstration by the Pennsylvania militia, Major Durkee had the defenses of'the Fort strengthened, and in thanks to two English friends of America in Parliament, Colonel John Wilkes and Colonel Isaac Barre, named the settlement and territory immediately adjacent to Fort Durkee—Wilkes-Barre.

The comedic character of the early days of the Pennemite Wars resumed two months later with continuing harassment in the Wyoming Valley. In a letter to the Governor of Connecticut by some Connecticut settlers, the following news was made known:

"In September (1769) Amos and Nathan Ogden, with twenty-six others, armed with pistols and clubs assaulted and wounded sundry of our people, whereby their lives were endangered. The same month thirteen of our people, in three canoes loaded with wheat and flour, about sixty miles below Wyoming were met and robbed of their canoes and loading by thirty armed men who came from Fort Augusta, about one half mile away. In the same month came on the trial many of our men at Easton. The charge against them was riot... In the course of the trial challenge was made by a juryman for having some time before having expressed an opinion openly against our people—but neither that nor any other exception would prevail. *The jury was treated with wine by the King's Atttorney before* verdict, which verdict was brought in against the prisoners, and they (were) condemned to pay a fine of 10 pounds each, with large costs, *in which was included the cost of the wine the jury were treated with.*"

Subsequent events became even more ludicrous! For the Connecticut counsel, Colonel Dyer, had hired a Philadelphia lawyer, Richard Peters, of whom a close friend of Peters, David H. Conyngham, wrote many years later:

"The jail at Easton then being built of logs could only hold from twenty to thirty persons, and the judges and lawyers not knowing what to do with so many demanding bread and quarters from the Sheriff, he (Peters) went among them and *advised them to go home*; and meeting Colonel Dyer, asked him to walk out with him to talk over the business they had in hand; and, returning, went to the prison when the Sheriff told them that the whole party of Yankees had gone off."

The prisoners went "home" all the way to Wyoming and none were recaptured in spite of rewards posted in all the newspapers.

The final act of comedy occured at the end of the year on a disappointing note for the New Englanders. With two hundred well armed Pennemites, Sheriff Jennings added to his entourage a small cannon called a four pounder because it was capable of delivering a four-pound cannon ball. They marched up to Wyoming where they rendezvoused with Captain Ogden and an additional fifty men. The combined force stood before Fort Durkee with the little four pounder in full display. This was the first piece of ordnance seen in Wyoming and it had its desired effect—with the surrender of Fort Durkee to the Pennemites—without a shot being fired.

Major Durkee and three other leaders were taken prisoner and shipped off to jail in Philadelphia, since the Easton jail was no longer trusted. All the remaining Yankees and their families were allowed to leave the Valley, with Captain Ogden promising to respect their private property. No sooner had the Connecticut settlers left, than Ogden seized and sold the remaining property and livestock for personal gain.

This exodus constituted the third time that the Connecticut settlers had been expelled from the Wyoming Valley. Not one life had been lost or one wound inflicted so far in this Pennemite debacle, but now there had been instilled a new ingredient—hatred—in what was to become a civil war on the eve of a Revolution!

John Wilkes on the left, and Isaac Barre on the right, two key members of Parliament who supported American independence and whose hyphenated last names were used by Yankee leader Major John Durkee to name the first town in the Wyoming Valley.

CHAPTER EIGHT

Captain Ogden was convinced he had finally put an end to Connecticut settlement of the Wyoming Valley. Leaving a garrison of ten men in possession of Fort Durkee, he retired to Philadelphia to spend the Winter of 1769-1770, basking in the public limelight of admiration.

As Charles Miner explained: "A city distinguished for hospitality would not fail to welcome to their sumptuous tables a gentleman who had served so faithfully, and accomplished so much for the public interest, and their own.... Pure wine flowed—health to the victors were quaffed—the joke passed, and Ogden, truly a most capital soldier, assured them in these moments of hilarity that the work was accomplished—the four pounder, superior to 'if' [meaning *compromise* or *negotiation*] was the true peacemaker, and he was confident that never another Yankee would dare to place his intruding foot upon the Susquehanna."

Ogden had not counted on a renegade, quick tempered and abrupt

Pennsylvanian, Captain Lazarus Stewart from Hanover, Lancaster County in Southern Pennsylvania. Leading a group of disgruntled Pennsylvania farmers, known as the Paxtang Boys, hungering for land, and having the full support of the Susquehanna Company, Stewart and his group easily recaptured Fort Durkee in the dead of Winter.

Stewart and his men were promised their own township to be named after their home town of Hanover. Their first objective after taking the Fort was to capture the four pounder and its ammunition at Mill Creek and move it to the Fort. This was so easily done that the perpetrators felt a sublime sense of security.

Ogden was beside himself with rage when he was informed that renegade Pennsylvanians, of all people, had retaken the Wyoming Valley, and this was followed by another startling piece of news: Major Durkee had somehow escaped from jail in Phildelphia and was now leading the Yankee forces. On the way to Wyoming, Ogden received the final, crushing piece of news: the new Yankee commandant of the Fort was their most able leader, Captain Zebulon Butler, and Yankee reinforcements from both Connecticut and Hanover, Pennsylvania were en route to Wyoming.

This new and more warlike phase of the Pennemite War almost immediately drew its first blood with the death of its first victim, one of the Hanover followers named Butzer Stager. This early skirmish resulted in bitter feelings towards Ogden and his Pennemites, and the Yankees and their allies, under Lazarus Stewart, did not hesitate in using their captured artillery pieces for the first time. The Yankees fired the four-pounder from the west bank where the Pennemites were garrisoned. A great deal of noise was made when one projectile after another was fired across the Susquehanna River, but with little effect. The Yankees firing the gun were farmers, not artillery men, and knew little about maintaining accuracy.

Major Durkee gave the order to move the cannon to Fort Durkee on the same shore as the Pennemite target buildings. Before long a direct hit was scored on a Pennemite storehouses, setting it on fire, and destroying most of their munitions and supplies.

Ogden sent an urgent message to Governor Penn asking for relief and aid. Penn in turn requested the aid of troops from General Gage, commander-in-chief of his Majesty's forces in North America. The message was received at Gage's headquarters in New York shortly after the Boston Massacre had taken place and there was a feeling of impending rebellion throughout the Colonies.

General Gage's answer to Penn indicated the general mood of the time in regards to the Pennemite War:

"New York, April 15, 1770—The troops in all the provinces have orders in general to assist the civil power, when it shall be legally called upon; but the affair in question seems to be a dispute concerning property, in which I cannot but think it would be highly improper for the King's troops to interfere."

When informed that no aid was at hand, Ogden surrendered the Mill Creek compound. The Pennemites were forced to leave the Valley with the Yankees left in control. This time Major Durkee gave the order to burn the Mill Creek compound to the ground to prevent the Pennemites from using it again if they decided to return.

Return they did, after a three month period of Pennemite

recruitment. This time Ogden moved back into the Valley stealthfully at night, under cover of darkness, and waited until morning when the Yankees went out into the fields, where Ogden's troops waited in groups of ten. Thusly, they took the Yankees prisoner—as they arrived to work their crops. This depletion left the Yankee garrison at Fort Durkee severely undermanned. Ogden then sent a raiding party of over 100 Pennemites under Captain Thomas Craig to take Fort Durkee. Craig was a bold and audacious leader who was later to serve with distinction alongside his present Yankee foes. On this night in September, 1770, he actually went ahead of his men and casually went up to the Yankee sentinal at the Fort's main gate. He spoke to the sentinal in low tones, as a friend. The sentinal relaxed his guard, and Craig knocked him down and waved his men on into the Fort.

The Yankees were taken by surprise and several were killed. Craig's Pennemites forced the remaining Yankees into a small room where hiding women and children were trampled. The Fort's commander, Captain Zebulon Butler, had been knocked down and wounded in the rush, and one of Craig's men was about to bayonet Butler when Craig burst into the room, drove his own men back, and thus saved Butler's life. Craig's humane instincts then prompted him to immediately tend to Butler's wounds, as well as to the other wounded.

As before, the Yankee leaders were sent off to jail, and Ogden, again feeling smugly confident in his victory, left a skeleton crew of about twenty Pennemites to garrison Fort Durkee through the winter. Lazarus Stewart, the renegade from Hanover, Pennsylvania, was the sole rebel leader not at the Fort, and thus the last one still at large.

Before leaving for Philadelphia to spend the winter among admiring Pennsylvanians, Ogden issued an arrest warrant for Lazarus Stewart.

Stewart was located in Lebanon staying with friends, and the local justice of the Peace, having been informed by Governor Penn that Stewart was "the most dangerous man in Pennsylvania," deputized three men to accompany him in arresting Stewart.

The Justice of the Peace, in his own words, as the deponent, stated in a deposition:

"Word was brought deponent that Stewart had rescued himself with the assistance of one Mathias Mause, who gave Stewart the handle of an ax, with which he had knocked down the Constable and beat him in a cruel and unmerciful manner. That thereupon this deponent went to the place where the said Stewart was, and called to sundry of the inhabitants who were there standing, and had been witnesses to the aforesaid outrageous proceeding, charging them in his Majesty's name to assist him, the deponent and the said Constable in retaking Stewart at the same time acquainting them of the crimes of which he was charged. That none of the inhabitants would obey the deponent, some of them being friends and abettors of Stewart, and the rest afraid. That the said Stewart stepped forward with a club in his hand and abused the deponent in the most opprobrious terms that about an hour after the rescue a party of armed men to the number of twenty or thereabouts, rode into the town of Lebanon and joined the said Stewart, who soon afterwards came towards the deponent, then walking before his own door, and with much scurrility and abuse with a pistol in one hand, and a club in the other, threatened him for having procured him to be arrested. The deponent, finding it necessary to defend himself, retired into his house and got his pistols. That the said Stewart attempted to follow him into the house, but one of the family fastened the door and prevented him. That the said Stewart afterwards called on the deponent to come and take him, and said there was long ago 200 pounds offered for him.

"That the said deponent was informed by Nicholas Hausaker, innkeeper in Lebanon, that the said Stewart came to Hausaker and threatened that if he ever should obey the orders of the deponent in taking, or assisting to take Stewart or any of his company, he the said Stewart would *cut him to pieces—and make a breakfast of his heart!"*

Although captured in York two weeks later, and bound with rope to a guard, Stewart escaped. In the dead of night while his captor slept and snored in a tavern, Stewart slipped his bonds and stepped out in the cold. Though handcuffed, barefoot, and coatless, he traveled all night through the woods to Paxtang, where he assumed comand of the Paxtang Boys and with them set out for Wyoming."

At three o'clock in the morning on December 18th, 1770, Stewart and about twenty-five Paxtang Boys broke into Fort Durkee shouting, "Hurrah for Hanover and King George!" They quickly seized the fort and expelled the Pennemite defenders.

A month later, Captain Ogden, with about one-hundred Pennemites, returned to the Valley and began construction on a new fort not far from Fort Durkee. This new fort was named Fort Wyoming and as its construction progressed, Captain Amos Ogden, his brother Nathan, and a delegation of Pennemites went before the front gate of Fort Durkee demanding Stewart's surrender. Shots rang out. Nathan Ogden fell dead and some of the Pennemites were wounded. That night, knowing he would be charged with murder by the Pennemites, Lazarus Stewart and some of his men slipped out of Fort Durkee and made their way up to Connecticut. This constituted the fifth time that the Yankees were evicted from the Wyoming Valley.

Governor Penn decided that by ensuring that Pennsylvanians settled in Wyoming permanently to defend their lands, he could then ensure that Connecticut settlers would be kept out. Accordingly, he ordered Fort Wyoming completed and that his agents in Wyoming sell land in one-hundred-acre lots for at least thirty pounds, while extending the leases of leaseholders. Preference was to be given to those who were actively resisting the Yankees or had suffered losses in doing so. Buyers were allowed to pay one third down and mortgage the balance. There was only one strong condition laid down for these privileges: *"Every purchaser must agree to keep one able-bodied man at least, constantly on the ground."*

Pennemite surveyors began to lay out property boundries for the first fifty-three parcels sold. Their lines were to obliterate the Connecticut property claims earlier delineated. *They* need not have bothered—the indomitable Yankees had a military expedition of seventy-four armed men en route to Wyoming under Zebulon Butler and Lazarus Stewart.

The Pennemites were warned of their coming and sought refuge in Fort Wyoming. They totaled forty-nine men and forty-eight women. Their fort was surrounded and a siege was commenced. Captain Ogden knew that aid was quickly needed and that he himself was the best man to seek aid.

It was just after midnight and all was quiet when one of the Yankee sentinels saw something suspicious floating down the Susquehanna. A shot was fired at it, then a volley, but the object kept floating down the river. It was Captain Ogden's clothes tied in a bundle with his hat on top. It was connected to a string several yards long attached to Ogden's arm as he swam downstream with the current. When out of danger, Ogden swam ashore, dressed himself in his bullet-holed clothes, and traveled 122 miles to Philadelphia for help.

When Ogden told Penn of the Yankee siege, three hundred pounds was appropriated to raise recruits. An advance party of thirty men with pack horses loaded with food and ammunition was quickly dispatched to lift the siege. Within two weeks of Ogden's underwater escape to get aid, Ogden and his aide, Captain John Dick, reached the Wyoming Valley, and Captain Butler and the Yankees knew when and where they would arrive. An ambush was set up ahead of Ogden's column, and with rifle fire from both flanks, the Yankee trap shut.

Some twenty Pennemites and their leader were able to escape to the fort, but the Yankees captured their pack horses and took their much-needed supplies.

Before another Pennemite relief column under Captain Asher Clayton could form, the Yankee seige took its toll on the Pennemite-held Fort Wyoming. Several of the garrison, including Ogden, were wounded and a few killed.

Yankee ordinance was bolstered by another seige gun. This one was home made by Yankee blackmiths in the Wyoming Valley. Obadiah Gore and his son Daniel were the primary blacksmiths of the

Valley. With great Yankee ingenuity, they were the first to use the native "stone coal" as their means of maintaining their forge at top effeciency. They conceived an idea for doubling the Yankees' artillery capacity by adding a new cannon. They hollowed out a hardwood log, hooped it from breech to muzzle with strong bands of iron, and painted the cannon black and its mouth red.

The first round fired from the new gun filled the Yankees with pride—and the Pennemites with fear. The cannon was then reloaded with a larger charge and fired. The resulting explosion split the cannon with such force and resounding reverberations throughout the Valley that one of the iron bands was later found one thousand feet away on the other side of the river.

After incessant firing of artillery and rifles for sixteen days with casualties on both sides, the Pennemites surrendered. The Yankee victory gave new confidence to the settlers which in turn brought more Connecticut people to the Wyoming Valley, and Captain Zebulon Butler was hailed as their savior. The Pennsylvania Proprietaries, in turn, faced a loss of confidence and finances as well as popular support. Connecticut was now in undisputed control of the Wyoming Valley. Thus ended the first Pennemite War. It lasted for three years and brought this first American Civil War into the same time frame as the American Revolution!

Fort Wyoming, Wilkes-Barre, 1771-1774

CHAPTER NINE

The end of the first Pennemite War brought a period of peace and consolidation to the Yankee-ruled Wyoming Valley. Increasing numbers of Connecticut settlers arrived from Connecticut in 1772 and 1773. Most of the settlers now felt safe enough to bring in their wives and children. Even though, the careful Yankees built more block houses in Hanover and Plymouth, and another block house was completed and occupied on the west side of the river—the new Forty Fort.

Seeing the need for a minister, the Susquehanna Company, upon recommendation by Zebulon Butler, offered Reverend Jacob Johnson sixty pounds a year and fifty acres to entice him to move from Connecticut to Wyoming. This was the same audacious "Son of Liberty" who had earlier defied the Crown openly, while most men stayed silent. One of his first ministerial duties was to officiate at the first marriage in the Wyoming Valley, that of Nathan Denison to Elizabeth Sill.

The first store established in the Valley was by Mathias

Hollenback, who brought goods and staples up from Lancaster. There were destined to be many customers for him, for according to the 1774 Connecticut census, Wyoming had 1,992 people.

Charles Miner, in his interviews, quoted some of the early settlers to give an idea of community life in the Valley: "Venison and shad were plenty; but salt was a treasure.... Doctor Sprague would load his horse with wheat, and go out by the bridle path, for as yet there was no road to the Delaware, have his grist ground, get a few spices, and a rimlet of Antiqua rum. The cakes baked from the flour, and the liquor, were kept as dainties for some special occasion, or when emigrants of note came in from Connecticut."

A grist mill, a saw mill, and schools were established. In keeping with Yankee practicality, a militia was establish and trained to protect the community. The latter move, above all else, antagonized Pennsylvania, still licking its wounds from the Yankee victory in the previous engagement.

In June of 1772, Governor Richard Penn of Pennsylvania issued a proclamation accusing the Connecticut settlers of disturbing the peace and giving aid and comfort to criminals. He bravely ordered them "to immediately evacuate their settlements and to depart and remove themselves off and from the said lands without delay." The Governor was now not only referring to the Wyoming Valley, but to some new Yankee settlements on the west branch of the Susquehanna near Muncy. Obviously, Pennsylvania was alarmed at the sheer numbers of Yankees arriving from Connecticut and was not about to allow the influx to continue without a fight.

A letter from a Pennemite surveyor in Sunbury to James Tilghman,

Secretary to the Pennsylvania Land office, dated April 2, 1773 states: "If Hell is justly considered as the rendezvous of Rascals, we cannot entertain a doubt of Wyoming being the Place! Burn'd Hands, cut Ears & C., are considered as the certain certifcates of superior merit; we have certain Accounts of having had several meetings lately to choose a Sovereign and settle the State & C., for it seems they have not now any Dependence on the Government of Connecticut. The time of the *Descent on the West Branch,* Fort Augusta & C. is now fixed for May next; I have no Doubt but the Desperate Tempers of these people will hurry them into some tragical affair, which will at least rouse our Government, when it may be too late to repair the mischief done by them. At the same time I am told there are some among them who would willingly become quiet subjects, and are afraid to own their sentiments."

The Connecticut defense appeared as the following newspaper advertisement:

"Susquehannah

Whereas it is reported in several Provinces on the Continent that the New England company of settlers at Wyoming on Susquehannah River, received and harbour thieves, robbers, and money-makers, that have made their escape from Justice; also servants that have run away from their masters—These are therefore to certify all to whom it may concern, that the *the above reports are false,* but on the contrary that we will give our assistance in helping to stop, secure, and return all such offenders, that they may be brought to Justice, whenever we have knowledge of them, either by advertisement or otherwise."

It was signed by the Committee of Settlers at Wyoming—Zebulon Butler, Ezekiel Pierce, Stephen Fuller and Obediah Gore, Jr.

Suddenly, outside events in Massachusetts occured which at first glance would seem to have the reverse effect of uniting the quarreling Colonies of Pennsylvania and Connecticut against a common enemy. The Battle of Lexington took place on April 19, 1775, followed by the Battle of Bunker Hill in June.

In Wyoming, that August, a town meeting "Voted that this town does now vote that they will strictly observe and follow ye rules and regulations of ye Honorable Continental Congress now sitting at Philadelphia.... Resolved by this town, that they are willing to make any accommodations with ye Pennsylvania party that Shall conduce to ye best good of ye whole, not infringing on the property of any person, and come in common cause of Liberty in ye defence of America, and that we will amicably give them ye offer of joining in ye proposals as soon as may be."

As far as Governor Penn was concerned, the presence of Connecticut people in Wyoming and new Yankee claims of sovereignty to lands to the northwest took precedence over any outside events. Penn immediately began the process of raising an army to wrest Wyoming from the Yankees.

In sharp contrast to the unrest between Pennsylvania and Connecticut, the Iroquois adopted an apparantly peaceful attitude.

At a council in August,1775, in Wyoming, three Iroquois chiefs stated, according to Jacob Johnson:

"Brothers—We must tell you we are sorry to see two Brothers are fighting one with another. Should be glad to hear the quarrel was at an end. We choose not to take part on one side or the other; but to sit down and smoke our Pipes. The quarrel to us looks unnatural. We do not understand it. We are for Peace!

"Brothers—When our young men come to hunt your way, don't dream they come to hurt you. No, they come to get things they want and trade with you.

"Brothers—We desire Wyoming may be the Place where the great men may meet, and have a Fire to sit and smoke by as a Token of Peace and Friendship and which ever hereafter may be called the Wyoming Fire."

By now, Governor Penn had raised an army of over seven-hundred men and chose as their commander a middle-aged judge named William Plunket. At the age of forty-five, Plunket held the prestigious post of President Judge of the Courts for Northampton County. He had, however, a secret past.

Charles Miner, in his *History of Wyoming*, quotes an article from the *Gentleman's Magazine* of September, 1750, which states that Plunket was an Irish highwayman who made his living in England through armed robbery. He was captured, then escaped, and emigrated to America. During the French and Indian War, he was a lieutenant and was charged with mutiny in a general court martial. Apparantly, through intervention by friends, the charges were dropped and Plunket was promoted. After the war, he became a large landowner and was appointed judge and colonel in the Pennsylvania Militia.

His first marching orders from Governor Penn took him to the small Yankee settlements on the west branch of the Susquehanna. With five hundred Pennemites against about one hundred Yankees, the victory was quick and decisive, with one Yankee killed and several wounded. The property and livestock, including horses of the settlements, were confiscated and sold. The Yankee prisoners were then dismissed, and most of them fled to Wyoming.

Governor Trumbull of Connecticut was alarmed, and petitioned the Continental Congress sitting in Philadelphia for intervention in the dispute. On November 4th, 1775, Congress issued its resolution:

"The Congress, considering that the most perfect union between all the Colonies is essentially necessary for the preservation of the just rights of North America; and being apprehensive that there is great danger of hostilities being commenced at or near Wyoming between the inhabitants of the Colony of Pennsylvania and those of Connecticut.

"Resolved, That the Assemblies of the said Colonies be requested to take the most speedy and effectual steps to prevent such hostilities."

Penn, upon being given notice of the weak Congressional response, saw his opportunity and had the Pensylvania Assembly give him authorization to strike at Wyoming. Quickly, the Governor sent William Plunket the following letter:

"I have just now received a message from the Assembly founded on a letter addressed to them from the County of Northumberland, respecting the Connecticut settlers at Wyoming, requesting me to give orders for a due execution of the laws of this province in the counties of Northumberland and Northampton. In consequence thereof I do most cheerfully order you to use your utmost Diligence and Activity, in putting the Laws of this Province in Execution throughout the county of Northumberland; and you may depend on the Faith of the House and my concurrence with them, that every proper and necessary Expense that may be incurred on the Occasion will be defrayed."

According to historian Frederic A. Godcharles, "The old Colonel was more elated than wisdom seems to have justified; proud of his easy triumph for the Proprietaries, and flattered by his admirers, he became obsessed with the belief he was the man for whom the honor had been reserved of rescuing Wyoming from the encroachments of the detested Yankees. He seems not to have appreciated the real worth of the gallant Captain Amos Ogden, or he may have overvalued his own military prowess; he became the man of the hour ... he set about to muster troops for an expedition against the Connecticut settlers at Wyoming, this in spite of the weather becoming very severe."

Yankee spies and scouts were active in keeping the Wyoming settlers informed. The following is an anonymous spy letter sent to and received by Zebulon Butler in December, 1775, from Sunbury:

"Sir—You may depend upon what I write to be facts, as I have taken great pains to inform myself, as I have ridden through the country, and I think it my duty to you. Sir; Keep this letter secret, and do not discover the author, for it would undo me in my business. You may surely depend upon their (the Pennemites) coming up to Wyoming, for they will not be stopped by the Congress, but are now mustering their men at Shamokin...

"Sir, you may depend upon their plundering you of all your effects, for they are determined to rob and plunder the country; and you will find them as inhuman as the Devil. For God's sake, put yourselves in readiness, and fight for your lives and fortunes ...

"Sir, this you may depend on to be truth. You need not depend on anything that the Congress has done, for the Governor of Pennsylvania is a Tory, I believe, and would do all that lies in his power to break the union of the Provinces, and has ordered them (the Pennemites) to go in the very face of the Congress. Your enemies are implacable. They say the Yankees won't fight; that you are all cowards and dare not fight. But in the name of God convince them of their mistake, and give these infernal dogs their deserving."

Unlike the First Pennemite War, with its civil and sometimes comic overtones, the new desperation by Pennsylvania and the background of the American Revolution dictated a completely military approach. About seven-hundred men were armed and mustered as four companies at Fort Augusta (Sunbury), and during a snowy December, the Pennemites marched on Wyoming.

The Yankees, with their efficient scout and spy network, kept track of their advancing enemies from the time they left the fort. Below Nanticoke Falls on the west side of the Susquehanna, and at the southern end of the Wyoming Valley, the Yankees—under Ensign Mason Alden together with eighteen men—set up an ambush. On the east side of the Susquehanna, below the Falls, Captain Lazuras Stewart—with twenty men—also set up an ambush to prevent any Pennemite landing from the river. Colonel Butler, with about four hundred men, retired upstream to a steep ledge of rocks which they enhanced with brush and boulders. They then waited.

The Pennemites, under Plunket, arrived in a blinding snowstorm and Alden allowed his forces to be seen before retiring. Plunket ordered a pursuit of Alden and within a half-hour of the chase, the Pennemites suddenly found their way blocked by a huge wall and rampart. Plunket was heard to cry out, "My God! what a breastwork!" before a sudden firing of muskets brought down four of his men. In panic, hundreds of Pennemites ran back to the south below the falls in headlong retreat without returning a shot.

They rested briefly and Plunket decided that their chief objective was to take the Village of Wilkes-Barre on the eastern shore of the river. Colonel Plunket then gave the order to his Pennemite Army to carry two boats by land to a site above the falls and to cross the river in detachments. It was now night, and Plunket felt that the darkness and falling snow would give his army cover and the element of surprise for an easy victory. He filled his boats with men for the crossing. Just before reaching the eastern shore, a volley of fire rang out from the dense woods. Captain Lazarus Stewart's patient waiting, after setting up his ambush, paid off, and several more casualties were suffered by the Pennemites who hurriedly backed their boats into the main channel of the river and in panic, rode headlong over the falls, downstream and through the rapids as quickly as their fear would allow them.

The next day, Christmas Day, 1775, the stubborn Plunket divided his men into two divisions and marched them up to the breastworks where his men had been ambushed the day before. He had one of his divisions frontally attack the "Rampart Rocks," and had his other division attempt to ascend a hill on the right flank to outflank the Yankees. The Yankees however, were too strongly entrenched, and after a full days' fighting, with about twenty Pennemites lost to the withering Yankee fire, Plunket withdrew downstream all the way to Fort Augusta.

Two days later, the leader of the settlers, Colonel Zebulon Butler, wrote: "By the best accounts we can get, they had fifty or sixty killed and wounded. We had two killed and three wounded, one of whom is since dead. Our enemies have all gone off, I believe for the Winter."

Unreported at the time, but recalled later in an address on July 4, 1966 by Paul A. Wallace, Humanities Fellow at Lebanon College, the following tragic fact was revealed: A few of the casualties as well as many of the survivors of the Second Pennemite War were on leave from the new Continental Army, having taken time off from fighting the British to fight each other!

Rampart Rocks (From an 1899 Photograph)

CHAPTER TEN

The new year was 1776, a year of conflict in the United Colonies, a year of exciting new ideas coming to fruition, a new nation, independence, and a common cause of liberty and equality. Sadly, this was not so in the Wyoming Valley.

The Continental Congress, early in the year, made a recommendation that persons "hostile to the cause of liberty" should be arrested. It was directed at the elimination of the danger of Loyalists, those who maintained an allegiance to the Crown, rather than to the new United Colonies. They were commonly known as Tories. One of Lazarus Stewart's Paxtang Boys offered up the following definition: "A Tory is a thing whose head is in England, its body in America, and whose neck ought to be stretched!"

The Wyoming Valley, isolated by wilderness and surrounded by Pennemites and Indians, was one of the first communities in the new nation to establish a "Committee of Inspection," a committee of vigilance in accordance with the Congressional recommendation. The Committee fed the flames of paranoia and suspicion that runs hand in hand with isolation.

The New England settlers, in a pseudo-patriotic frenzy, began to assume that all Pennemites were Tories, even though this was far from the truth. To make matters worse, Connecticut, in the spirit of national unity, prohibited further emigration to Wyoming. Suspicion and investigation were now expanded to any new arrivals from other areas, as well as to Indians.

The feeling in Wyoming was that threatening enemies were all about, and by proximity, the least threatening were the British.

The fervor of patriotism and suspicion caused the Assembly of Westmoreland (Wyoming) to look with suspicion upon a newly arrived, large family named Wintermoot, who built their own fort at the northern end of the Valley. It was thus recommended that a fort, to be named Fort Jenkins, be built a mile above Fort Wintermoot and to be under the trusted supervision of the Jenkins and Harding families. Forty Fort was to be strengthened and made larger, and other new forts were to be built in other parts of the Valley. The frugal and audacious Yankees ended their proclamation with the following statement: "That the above said committee, do recommend it to the people to proceed forthwith in building said Forts without either fee or reward from ye town."

Also established by the Assembly was the 24th Regiment of Connecticut Militia under the command of Lazarus Stewart. At the same time, federal recruiters came into the Valley to enlist men into the Continental Army, and two companies of Wyoming Valley men went off to fight with Washington. The Local militia was thus forced to go further afield to recruit new soldiers.

An ardent Pennemite, Captain Alexander Patterson made the

following statement to the Pennsylvania Legistature: "In the year 1776, there were a number of inhabitants settled near Wyalusing, under the Pennsylvania title; among them, two Pawlings, Secords, Depew, Vanderlip, and others. The Yankees at Wyoming, sixty miles distant, being more numerous, insisted that the Pennsylvania settlers should come to Wyoming and train and associate under Yankee officers of their own appointment. As may be supposed, the proposal was very obnoxious to the inhabitants of Pennsylvania, and they very properly refused, alleging they would associate by themselves, and would not be commanded by intruders & C. This gave a pretext to the Yankees for calling them Tories. They therefore went in force, tied the Pennsylvania settlers, and brought them to Wyoming, with all their movables, and confined them in a log house, until the Indians who lived in the neighborhood of Wyoming, and who loved the Pennsylvanians, came to Wyoming and requested that the Pennsylvania people should be released, declaring they would complain to Congress if they were not. They were released, and on their return without property, were ambushed and fired upon by the Yankees. The event of all this was that the Pennsylvania people were so harassed by the (New England) intruders that they were driven to seek an asylum with the Indians, and at length to retire to Fort Niagara for protection."

In addition to the Tories, the Yankees also considered the Indians a threat to the Wyoming Valley as attested to by the following muster declaration:

"Whereas the inhabitants of this town have of late been invaded by a large number of Tories, which by the blessing of God we have repulsed; but notwithstanding, are threatened with another invasion. And as we are a frontier town, and liable to be attacked by the Indians if a war should be commenced between them and us, we do think that it is out duty to be in readiness within an hour's warning, if an invasion should happen, to engage our enemies, invaders, or intruders ...

Growing friction with the Indians and possible pressure from the Tories and the British resulted in an Iroquois Council at Onandaga, which in turn authorized three chiefs to proceed to Wyoming to hold council with Colonel Zebulon Butler. Miner, in his *History of Wyoming*, stated that while the talks with the chiefs "professed peaceable intentions, the tone is one of complaint." This is in stark contrast to the friendly council held just a month before, and quoted in the previous chapter.

William Nanticoke, Indian Joseph (an Onondaga Chief), and Narondigwanok (a Seneca Chief) stated:

"Brothers—there is a great deal between us. The Devil is always putting something between us, but this is to clear your hearts that you may speak clearly and pleasantly to us.

"Well Brothers—there is a great deal of trouble around here. Your lids are all bloody, but we come to clear away all suspicion that your hearts may be pleasant.

"Well Brothers—our fire-place is almost lost and our fire almost out. We think it hard and desire it may be renewed, and the fire-place fixed here, that our mutual fire may give light from one end of this river to the other."

They then complained about the building of forts and a wrong done by a settler in the exchange of cows with an Indian. At this point, Miner makes the cogent observation that "it may be considered as creditable to the Wyoming people, that Indian jealousy could find nothing in their five years of intercourse, for their friends scattered through the Valley to complain of, except the matter of the cow exchange."

Miner continued ominously, "a report reached the valley the same month that Colonel John Butler with Indians and Canadians, was at Oswego. Notwithstanding the professions of the Six Nations, no one doubted before the close of 1776 but that they were pledged to the interest of Great Britain, and on the invasion by Burgoyne early in the following year, numbers of them were found arrayed under his standard, active, brave, and cruel as became their long established character."

Equally ominous was a fact of nature—the Susquehanna. And Miner observed, "A moderate freshet in the river, would bring their boats and canoes, in twenty four hours, from their place of rendezvous at Tioga into the heart of the Wyoming settlement."

CHAPTER ELEVEN

By the end of 1776, Washington, having suffered defeats at Long Island and White Plains, urged Congress for more troops and Congress complied: "Resolved, Thursday December 12th, that the two companies raised in the town of Westmoreland be ordered to join General Washington with *all possible expedition*."

Under the command of Zebulon Butler, the two companies quickly obeyed the order, leaving Colonel Nathan Denison now in command of the 24th Regiment in Wyoming. Denison also took over as titular head of the Committee of Inspection.

Denison, described earler as the first Connecticut settler to be married in Wyoming, was a respected and well-liked Justice of the Peace. Charles Miner, who knew him well, describes Denison:

"Judge Denison, though cheerful in the social circle, never laughed and seldom smiled. His looks were grave but pleasing—not sad but extremely sedate. Such was the character of all his deportment. His judgement was sound, as his heart was pure; but there was nothing showy about him—no attempt at effect—but all reposed in him, because his integrity was undoubted, while his good sense and intelligence inspired unlimited confidence."

Denison's first efforts as militia regimental commander was to petition Congress for aid. After much prodding of the reluctant Legislature, restating growing hostility by the Indians and the Wyoming Valley's exposed position, Congress finally gave in and resolved in April, 1777:

"That 175 firearms—either muskets and rifles—200 wt. of powder, 800 wt. of lead, and 500 flints be sent to the town of Westmoreland, on the East Branch of the Susquehanna River to the care of Col. Nathan Denison to be used by the militia there for the defence of the said town, if necessary, the armes to be returned when the service there will admit of it."

This act of Congress apparently was of great importance to the Six Nations and they quickly made a move. It has apparently been overlooked by historians that the Iroquois cunningly used overtures of peace against their enemies as much as they used the threat of war. Within a month of the Congressional aid statement, the Six Nations suddenly dropped their hostile attitude and aggressive behavior of the past few months, and sent a message of peace and reconciliation to Colonel Denison. With unabashed gaul, the Iroquois blamed the Delaware Tribe for any misunderstandings. Their message of peace was accompanied by a wampum peace belt as a symbol of good faith. This same tactic of neutralization of will and defense was to be used again in the near future with success against the American government itself.

To Denison's credit, he received and answered the Iroquois'

message amiably and his reply exuded trust, while keeping secretly alert to future events: "Brothers, we are glad you are come at this time with a message of peace to us. We cordially receive the same."

Denison, however, had the advantage of the settlers' highly efficient spy and scout network originally put into place to keep informed on the plans of the Pennemites. He had information that in the previous September, a council was held at Fort Niagara between the British and the Six Nations to have the Indians take up arms against the Americans and that scores of Tories were arriving to join the English General John Butler's Rangers.

The Fort Niagara Council was held in accordance with the following orders from Whitehall Palace, London, to the British Governor of Quebec:

"The proposal to send Parties of Indians to Virgina and Pennsylvania has been maturely weighed. It is His Majesty's resolution that the most vigorous efforts should be made, and every means employed that Providence has put into His Majesty's hands for crushing the rebellion and restoring the Constitution. It is the King's command that you should direct Lieutenant Governor Hamilton to assemble as many of the Indians of his district and placing a proper person at their head to conduct their parties and restrain them from committing violence on the well-affected, inoffensive inhabitants, *employ them in making a diversion and exciting an alarm on the frontiers of Virginia and Pennsylvania....*"

Knowing the aggressive plans of the Iroquois and the Tories, Denison probed the outer limits of his area to see how imminent the danger was. He sent John Jenkins, a fellow Committee of Inspection officer, and a Quaker named James Sutton upriver to gather information to liberate any prisoners from raids upstream. They proceeded about ninety miles through the wilderness to Queen Esther's Flats near Tioga. This is the same Esther who had earlier, as a little girl, been baptized by Count Von Zinzendorf. Now she was known as a receiver of prisoners from Indian raiding parties. The Queen, now in her fifties, treated Jenkins and Sutton with courtesy and spoke with her guests about religion and moral obligations.

According to Dr. George Peck, an early Wyoming historian, "They were invited to spend the night with the Queen, and the true spirit of hospitality seemed to characterize all her communications and arrangements. In the course of the evening, however, things took a new turn, and the travellers, for a while, were at a loss what construction to put upon the indications outside. A company of Indians came before the house, and, seating themselves upon a log, began to sing the war song. The old Queen went out to them and engaged in an earnest conversation with them for a long time. When she came in she frankly told her guests that the Indians were determined to waylay and kill them, adding with great emphasis, 'I can do nothing with them. Now you lie down until I call you.' They did so, and when all was still in the town she called them and said, 'You must go down the river. Go down the bank, take my canoe and paddle it without noise....' They slipped off ... and found their way home in safety."

A few months later, Jenkins again, with a scouting party on behalf of the Committee of Inspection, went as far as Wyalusing where they were captured by Indians and Tories.

One of the captives, an old man named Fitzgerald, was told to renounce his rebel beliefs and pledge loyalty to the King or he would die. Fitzgerald replied, "Well, I am old, and have little time to live, anyhow; and I would rather die now a friend to my country, than live ever so long and die a Tory!"

Fitzgerald was allowed to go free but Jenkins and three others were taken to Canada. Soon after, a proposal was made to exchange Jenkins for an Iroquois chief being held prisoner by the Americans at Albany. Jenkins' Iroquois guards brought him to Albany for the exchange, but upon arrival were told that the chief had died of smallpox. The Indians became enraged and demanded that Jenkins return with them to Canada, where no doubt he would have been killed in return for the death of the chief. The Indians were restrained, however, and Jenkins was freed and returned to Wyoming.

These scouting parties always consisted of young and active militia members ever on duty. Outside of them, all the able-bodied young men were away with Washington's army. The remaining men in Wyoming were old, but they formed themselves into companies called Reformados and they performed duties in the forts. They repaired or built six forts, or stockades, "without fee or reward."

The women not only cooked, but in the absence of the men, planted, cared for, and harvested the crops, and tended the sick, especially during smallpox outbreaks. In addition to these duties, the women also made gunpowder. In the Winter of 1777-1778 they would tear up their floor boards in their homes and dig out the earth. They put the soil into casks and ran water through them. They then took the water that had leached through the earth, mixed it with ashes, and boiled the mixture. When it cooled, saltpeter rose to the top. They then mixed in charcoal and sulphur to form gunpowder. The powder was then stored in the forts for use in the one pounder that Mathias Hollenback, the storekeeper, had shipped upriver.

Reports of encroaching Indians were sent to Congress with accompanying pleas for aid with little result. This suddenly gave way to an alarming event. Two Indians, who formerly lived in Wyoming and who knew the settlers, came to the Valley for a visit with their squaws. They stated that they felt a deep kinship towards the settlers but the Yankees were suspicious. In returning the feelings of friendship, the Yankees offered the Indians one drink of rum after the other. The Indians began to talk, in confidence of course, that they had been sent on a mission to report on the Valley's defenses, since an attack was soon to be launched against Wyoming.

Queen Esther soon intervened to obtain the release of the two Indians. A trade of prisoners was set up in Wyoming with Colonel Denison and Queen Esther as negotiators. At the end of the trade agreement, Denison was reported to have facetiously mocked Queen Esther by requesting her to "send more Indians."

Now the feeling of alarm turned to a frenzy, and not only was Congress again petitioned for aid, but it was requested to release the two Wyoming Companies of troops from Washington's army for home defense. Congress refused, but most of the commissioned officers resigned and headed for home, along with more than twenty-five enlisted men. In the face of these desertions, Congress finally, slowly, and grudgingly allowed the Wyoming men to go home to defend their Valley—but it was too late.

Congress' initiative to send troops and material aid to Wyoming had been sapped and delayed by distraction and indecision caused by the illusion of peace with the Six Nations. The dream of freeing the northern frontier from the threat of attack proved to be irresistible to Congress, for the Iroquois tactic of peace-seeking before attack had cast its spell on Congress, the Board of War and Washington himself, as the Iroquois and their Tory allies massed for an attack on Wyoming.

CHAPTER TWELVE

By the Spring of 1778, both Congress and the Board of War, as well as General Washington, had been beseiged by pleas from the various leaders of Wyoming for aid in both men and material. Washington's answers to the requests of Denison and Zebulon Butler always made compliance conditional upon the approval of the Board of War and Congress. in some of Washington's letters, he stated that both the Congress and the Board of War were actually considering these urgent pleas for aid.

There is no doubt that the Six Nations learned of the deliberations both by Congress and the Board of War through their highly efficient network of spies. The Senecas and their Tory allies had already made final preparations for the attack on Wyoming and an advance force had departed for Tioga.

Using the same ruse that the Iroquois had unsuccessfully attempted on Colonel Denison a few months before, the Senecas sent a secret "peace" delegation of five chiefs to Philadelphia. It is unclear whether the Board of War and the Congress sought to keep the negotiations secret as well, for there is a suspicious gap of correspondence in the Papers of the Continental Congress pertaining to Wyoming. This gap, the only one existing in an otherwise unbroken series of dates of correspondence, is from February 2, 1778 to July 6, 1778. Thusly, there is nothing in the National Archives to show that Congress was debating aid to Wyoming during this crucial period.

There is, however, a July 6th entry ironically made on the same date that Butler's Tory and Indian forces left Wyoming: "Resolved: That the Board of War be directed to send for the Seneca chiefs that have lately quitted Philadelphia and inquire whether the Seneca nation, as such, have committed hostilities against us."

This statement in and of itself shows the extent to which Congress, the Board of War, and Washington himself had been hoodwinked. Even after the Senecas had suddenly left Philadelphia, the American negotiators found difficulty in making the connection between their peace negotiations with the same tribe that had attacked Wyoming.

Both the Board of War and Congress had Pennemite members who had no love for the Wyoming settlers and who in the best of scenarios would have been reluctant to send aid. The pseudo peace negotiations with the five Seneca chiefs were enough to tip the balance and hold back aid, in the hope that a successful peace treaty would make aid unnecessary.

As Oscar Harvey stated in his *History of Wilkes-Barre:*

"It seems that when preparations were being made by the Loyalists and Indians for the descent upon Wyoming, a delegation of Seneca chiefs daringly presuming on the stolidity of Congress, repaired to Philadelphia, ostensibly to negotiate, really to amuse the members of

Congress—to put them off their guard and prevent any troops being sent to the threatened frontier. Nor did the bold and crafty chiefs leave the city until the fatal blow at Wyoming had been struck. The chiefs refused to return to Philadelphia in response to the message sent to them by the Board of War, and on July 17th, a motion was made in Congress to the effect that General Schuyler be directed to take effectual measures for detaining the Seneca chiefs at Albany; but the motion was decided in the negative."

Small wonder that the chiefs were not apprehended and brought back for trial. The scandal that a few Indians could have duped Congress, the Board of War, and Washington into inactivity and actually causing Wyoming to be abandoned to a devastating defeat, gave Congress second thoughts. Had word of this deception leaked out, reputations of the American leaders would have been irreparably damaged and the war effort compromised. That explains why Congress dropped its arrest charges and let the Seneca "delegation" escape, and why the gap in information exists in the National Archives.

Furthermore, it also explains General Washington's seething anger toward the Iroquois to be seen later in his plans for a raid of retribution and in the cruelty and brutality of his orders to the commanding officer of that raid. It was the sowing of the seeds of a future national policy of oppression, first against the Iroquois, and then against all Indian tribes.

Fort Niagara in 1759 (From an old print)

CHAPTER THIRTEEN

Throughout a snowy winter in the beginning of 1778, a polygot force of Tories, Iroquois (mostly Seneca), and various opportunists and outcasts of American society had begun to assemble at Fort Niagara. Various notices appealing to allegiance to the Crown and promises of sharing in the property and goods of the rebels had brought them there. From 1777 to 1783, Fort Niagara was to be the seat of British and Tory operations on the Northern Frontier.

Samuel DeVeaux, in *The Falls of Niagara*, published in 1839, wrote of Fort Niagara with a sublime lack of objectivity: "It was the headquarters of all that was barbarous, unrelenting, and cruel. There were congregated the leaders and chiefs of those bands of murderers and miscreants who carried death and destruction into the remote American settlements. There, civilized Europe reveled with savage America, and ladies of education and refinement mingled in the society of those whose only distinction was to wield the tomahawk and the bloody scalping knife. There were the squaws of the forest raised to eminence and the most unholy alliances between them and the officers of the highest rank smiled upon and countenanced. There, from this stronghold, like a nest of vultures, securely for seven years, they sallied forth and preyed upon the distant settlements of the Mohawk and Susquehanna. It was the depot of their plunder, there they planned their forays and there they returned to feast until the time for action should come again."

Hardly a day went by that new Tory recruits didn't report for duty. They came from all the northern Colonies, as well as Canada, to pledge their allegiance to the Crown and to train. They were outfitted in dark-green uniforms trimmed in scarlet. The caps were flat and low with a brass plate in front with the monogrammed letters "G.R." circled by the words "Butler's Rangers."

Any Indians who showed up for service were given silver medals with the likeness of King George III and a promise of returned land and a share of the plunder. Later, in 1814, in a newly ploughed field in Wyoming, historian Charles Miner actually found one of these medals and illustrated it in *The History of Wyoming*.

In early June, 1778, while the five Seneca Chiefs were negotiating a bogus peace treaty to insure Congressional inaction, the force of Rangers and Senecas moved southeast to Tioga Point. They were greeted by Queen Esther, who had earlier advised Butler of her loyalty to the Crown and of her interest in acquiring a portion of looted property. Queen Esther herself recruited most of the population in the Tioga area to the expedition.

In command of the force of over 250 Rangers, 350 Seneca Warriors, and about 100 other Indians and squaws from various tribes, was Colonel John Butler. He was in no way related to Zebulon Butler, although both men were born in Connecticut of military families. John Butler had distinguished himself as a loyal and ambitious officer in the French and Indian War. He was noticed by Sir William Johnson, a friend of John Butler's father and appointed Deputy Superintendant of Indian Affairs.

His superior, Sir Guy Carlton, described him as being modest and shy, yet coolly efficient and fiercely loyal to the Crown. His contempt for those who sought rebellion and independence from Great Britain was fully returned in kind by the rebellious Americans. As early as 1775, he left his estate and property in New York and moved to Canada where he became the rallying point for all Loyalists in the Colonies. By Royal proclamation he was empowered to raise a Tory army known as Butler's Rangers.

His basic attitude of tenacity and loyalty is best summed up by the epitaph on his tombstone in Canada which states: "Fear God and Honour the King."

The Senecas in Butler's expedition were under the command of Sayenqueraghta, also known as He Who Goes in the Smoke, or simply, Old Smoke. He was described as "a large portly man of commanding presence" by historian William L. Stone. A contemporary of his, Colonel Daniel Claus, said of Old Smoke, "He is brave, prudent, and perfectly attached to the Government (the British)— more strongly so since the alliance of the Americans with the French to whom he has an unconquerable aversion." Serving under Old Smoke was his most trusted Captain, Cornplanter, and under Cornplanter, a young, highly intelligent warrior to be heard from in the future, Handsome Lake.

In early June, the expedition arrived at Tioga Point and, with the help of Queen Esther's subjects, built a fleet of over one hundred canoes with collected provisions. Three weeks later the combined forces under Butler set off down the Susquehanna on a friendly downstream current enhanced by a "June freshet," adding an additional five miles an hour to the invaders.

Butler's party landed at the northern end of the Wyoming Valley and made their first contact with the settlers on the morning of June 30th. On a sunny day in a cornfield in what is now Exeter Borough, Benjamin, Stokley, and twelve-year-old John Harding, as well as James Hadsell, his son James Jr., Daniel Weller, John Gardiner, Daniel Carr, and a black servant named Quocko began their daily work of hoeing corn. They had come from Fort Jenkins, only three miles away and situated about a mile and a half from Fort Wintermoot.

It was in the afternoon when two men, Richard Showers and Frederick Anker, two suspected Tories from Fort Wintermoot, arrived and offered to help with the hoeing. They were allowed to hoe but soon disappeared, arousing the suspicions of the Hardings and their friends. They started back for Fort Jenkins but were ambushed.

The young settlers fought bravely, but according to Miner, James Hadsell and his son, James Jr., as well as Benjamin and Stokely Harding, were killed, and their bodies mutilated and scalped by the Indians. Weller, Gardiner, Carr, and Quocko were taken prisoner. The young boy, John Harding, jumped into the river and concealed himself amid the willows and reeds. He lay on his back with only his mouth above the surface. Although he could hear the screams and groans of his family members and friends, he kept very still. He knew the Indians were searching for him in the river. One came so close he was almost touched. At sunset they gave up the search and the boy escaped back to Fort Jenkins to warn the settlers.

Meanwhile, two prisoners, including Quocko, were marched away to where the village of Orange in Franklin Township now stands. That night they were slowly tortured by the Indians until they died.

The following morning, the gates of Fort Wintermoot were opened and the native Tories welcomed the Indian and Tory invaders with open arms. The depleted forces at nearby Fort Jenkins soon surrendered to the overwhelming army of Indians and Tories.

At daybreak, with the news of the attack having been delivered to Forty Fort, a detachment of Yankees under Lieutenant Rosewell Franklin advanced ten miles north to the sight of the ambush and found two Indians standing over the bodies of the Hardings. One of the Indians was killed immediately by one of Franklin's men, Zebulon Marcy. The other Indian tried to escape by swimming down the river, but Lieutenant Franklin and one of his men pursued the Indian in a canoe and killed him.

For many years afterward, Marcy, who survived the subsequent Battle of Wyoming, was stalked and threatened by a brother of the Indian he had killed. That slain Indian, as it turned out, was a son of Queen Esther.

The bodies of the slain Hardings were then buried in what is now West Pittston at the present intersection of Linden and Wyoming Avenues. Many years later Elisha Harding had a gravestone placed at their graves inscribed: "Sweet Be The Sleep of Those Who Prefer Death to Slavery."

Site of the Massacre of the Hardings (From a 1903 photograph)

CHAPTER FOURTEEN

The next day, July 2nd, 1778, was a day of consolidation, observation, and preparation for both sides.

In the northern end of the Valley, Major Butler and his Rangers collected all property and livestock of the captured Yankees, as well as the prisoners themselves. To ascertain the activities and location of the enemy in the lower Valley, Major Butler sent out scouts and spies.

At the lower end of the Valley, the Yankees desperately sent out scouts, not only to spy on the invading enemy, but to bring as many outlying settlers as possible into the comparative security of Forty Fort. These scouts also sought out any group of able-bodied men or militia to assist in the defense of the Valley. Towards this end, Benjamin Harvey was given a special mission.

Between Berwick and Bloomsburg there was a company of Pennsylvania Militia encamped. They numbered seventy-three enlisted men and officers under a Captain Klingman in command. Harvey carried an appeal for aid from Lieutenant Colonel George

Dorrance appealing to Klingman's national patriotism as an American as well as to humanitarian sentiments. However, feelings of hatred against the Yankees by the Pennsylvanians ran deeper than any feelings of national unity even during a war for the survival of the embryo nation. It was thus no surprise when Klingman and his Pennsylvanians ignored the desperate Yankee appeal.

Forty Fort was becoming hopelessly and quickly overcrowded for, by the next day, the 3rd of July, there were about 375 men and even more than that number comprising women and children. There were still more men en route under Captain Spaulding. This was the Westmoreland Independent Company belatedly released by Congress from Washington's Army. An advance messenger from the Company in the person of Lieutenant Phineas Pierce rode day and night to bring the message that Spaulding and his men should be arriving on July 5th.

Major John Butler, however, sought to maintain his momentum and, under a flag of truce, demanded the surrender of Forty Fort, promising humane treatment for all its inhabitants.

Zebulon Butler's answer to the demand was an outright refusal, and he immediately called a council of war among his officers. The choice was either to wait for possible relief from Spaulding's Company and possibly other militia companies, or to go out to challenge the enemy head-on in the field. The interplay of opinions became quite heated with Colonel Zebulon Butler, Colonel Denison, and Lieutenant Colonel Dorrance arguing for delay, and the firebrand Lazarus Stewart demanding an immediate confrontation and clash with the enemy.

Butler, Denison, and Dorrance stated that a small delay would possibly allow friendly forces a chance to reinforce their defenses, to which Stewart scornfully replied that these senior officers had chosen the way of cowardice. Stewart heatedly stated that the enemy had been in the Wyoming Valley for three days, murdering and pillaging, and that the Yankees could only depend on themselves, and that the time to strike was immediately, before the enemy increased its strength.

Denison uncharacteristically became incensed and angrily told Stewart to go out and die if that is what he wanted to do and ordered Stewart to be held for court martial for insubordination.

Colonel Butler was shocked to have his bravery and honor questioned, but slowly began to see the validity of Stewart's argument, particularly in the light of an overcrowded fort having inadequate supplies and provisions. He called for calmness, and gradually, all the officers were swayed to the launching of an immediate confrontation.

According to historian George Peck, who had interviewed several eyewitnesses, Butler then put aside Captain Lazarus Stewart's proposed arrest and court martial. Colonel Butler later stated, "We will march and meet the enemy, if he is to be found, and I will show the men that I dare lead where they dare follow! We go into imminent danger, but my boys, I can go as far as any of you."

Butler then gave the order to muster the troops for battle, and according to Charles Miner:

"Many old men—some of them grandfathers—took their muskets and marched to the field. For instance, the aged Mr. Searle of

Kingston was one. Having been bald he wore a wig. Taking out his silver knee-buckles, he said to his family, 'If I fall, I shall not need them. If I come back they will be safe here.' Nothing could have been more incongruous, more pitiably unfit, than the mingling of such aged men in the rough onset of battle. Dire was the necessity that compelled it. The old gentleman had a number of grandchildren. Several boys from fourteen to sixteen, are known to have been on the field ... so that there were about two hundred and thirty enrolled men, and seventy old people, boys, civil magistrates, and other volunteers."

At the Centennial of the Battle of Wyoming on July 3rd, 1878, Steuben Jenkins, grandson of Lieutenant John Jenkins, stated the following in a speech delivered on the Wyoming Battlefield before President Rutherford B. Hayes and about ten thousand people:

"They were not soldiers, trained and inured to material service, well armed and equipped for the fray. They had no great commander with an army of veterans, going forth conquering and to conquer; to sate his mad ambition or wreak his vengeance upon an innocent, unoffending people. There was no one among them who possessed an absolute command. They were principally old men and boys unfit for the active and arduous duties of the field; who from inefficiency remained at home, while the young men better fitted for those active and arduous duties, were serving in the distant ranks of our country's defenders.

"It was no war of ambition, of plunder or revenge on their part; it was to save themselves and their families from butchery, their homes from the torch of the incendiary, their flocks and herds from being slaughtered or driven off, their harvest from being destroyed, and their liberty from being overthrown.

"We cannot talk or judge of them as soldiers, for soldiers they were not. They were simply a hasty gathering of a rural settlement for defense against their invaders...."

Before the settlers set out to face the enemy on this hot July 3rd afternoon, they were offered muslin cups of water or rum by the women in the Fort. Most of the cups which were consumed contained water.

As such they marched north from the Fort with a freshly home-made Stars and Stripes at the head of the column and with drums and a fife playing "St Patrick's Day in the Morning." Only the officers and some returned continental soldiers wore the blue and buff uniforms of the American Army. The huge majority wore rustic civilian clothes.

After a march of only a mile, Colonel Butler stopped in an area affording defensible terrain, much to the disappointment of Lazarus Stewart. Stewart argued that they were over-estimating their enemy and urged less caution and more action. It was at this point that Richard Inman, one of Stewart's men, began to feel the effects of the cup of rum he had refreshed himself with upon leaving Forty Fort. - Inman laid down under a tree to rest, feeling sure that he would be awakened when the group resumed their march.

The march resumed in single file which spread out for a mile and advanced to several more miles to a point where, today, Fourth Street in Wyoming is now located. They could see smoke coming from Fort Wintermoot a few miles away. Colonel Zebulon Butler addressed his troops:

"Men, yonder is the enemy. The fate of the Hardings tells us what we have to expect if defeated. We come out to fight, not only for liberty, but for life itself, and what is dearer to preserve, our homes from conflagration, our women and children from the tomahawk. Stand firm, the first shock, and the Indians will give way. Every man to his duty."

As Colonel Denison led his men off to the right flank ending at the Susquehanna, he paraphrased the appeal of Colonel Butler to his men: "Be firm, everything depends on resisting the first shock."

At about four in the afternoon in what is now Exeter Borough, where St. Cecilia's Church now stands, Colonel Butler ordered his men to fire and advance.

The Battle of Wyoming had begun!

CHAPTER FIFTEEN

The advancing line of Yankee farmer-soldiers ran along a swamp on the left flank eastward along a lush green field some 300 yards to the Susquehanna. The line was divided along odd and even numbers—the odd-numbered men would advance, fire, kneel and reload, then the even-numbered men would do the same, filling in the void.

Every now and then some Tory skirmishers in their dark-green uniforms would jump out of the underbush in twos and threes, fire at the advancing line of variegatedly clad Yankees, and then retreat.

By now the American line had come within 100 yards of a fence and Colonel Butler ordered the entire line to fire a volley at the fence. The simultaneous fire was deafening and the gray smoke hung low in the hot, humid air.

This time over a hundred green-uniformed Tories arose from their hiding places, fired at the advancing Yankees and deliberately fell back. A cheer rose from the American ranks and Colonel Butler was heard to cry, "See the enemy retreat! Stand fast, and the day is ours!"

Enemy fire increased, especially in the center of the line, and American attention and return fire was thus directed at the center.

Suddenly, on the extreme left flank, came the blood-curdling screams of the Iroquois—the same screams that had resounded through the Wyoming Valley fifteen years before when the first Connecticut settlers were slaughtered. These Senecas, under Cornplanter, had hidden themselves in the swamp on the left and had not fired a shot until the Yankees committed themselves offensively to the center.

Out of the dense, green underbrush came about two-hundred war-painted Indians firing muskets at the long range and then resorting to spears, tomahawks, and scalping knives at close range. The war paint had been applied to faces and arms so that the red over-ran the black, with double the amount of red to indicate to their enemies that their aim was the shedding of blood.

The war whoops got closer and even drowned out the musket fire, and the Iroquois outflanked the Americans. The Iroquois then dropped their guns and tore into the left side of the American line with spears and tomahawks.

Colonel Butler gave the order to "flank off to the left" so as to present a straight line of fire to the outflanking Indians. This order in the noise and panic of the moment was misunderstood to be "fall back" and retreat. The retreat was away from the shrieking Indians on the left and to the right side, southeast toward the river.

The American officers, in vain, tried to keep their troops from giving ground. Colonel Dorrance cried out to each of his men, "Stand up to your works sir," before being wounded and captured. Also wounded and captured were Captains Ransom and Bidlack. Lazarus Stewart was killed and quickly scalped.

According to Charles Miner's eyewitness account, Lieutenant Daniel Gore was wounded in the arm by a musket ball early in the battle. He tore off a piece of his shirt to act as a crude bandage. Through his intense pain, Gore saw Captain Robert Durkee appear amid the smoke and din. Gore yelled out a warning to Durkee, "Look out—there are some of the savages under yonder heap of logs."

The warning was barely heard above the uproar of the screaming Indians and the rifle fire.

Captain Robert Durkee, younger brother of Major John Durkee who was still with Washington's army, had just arrived from fighting the British near Philadelphia. In response to Gore's warning, Captain Durkee was about to order an attack on the Indians in the area specifed by Gore, when he was struck by a musket ball in the thigh. Gore tried to help Durkee from the field of fire, but Durkee pleaded with him, "Save yourself Mr. Gore, my fate is sealed."

Gore let Durkee go, but as the Indians advanced, Ensign Mathias Hollenback, in the midst of the retreat, picked up Durkee, and without hesitation, selflessly began carrying him to the Susquehanna and possible escape.

Meanwhile, Lieutenant Gore, whose arm had been shattered, also chose to escape toward the river, and crouched down under a clump of bushes. An Indian suddenly jumped into a nearby hollow, and Gore later stated that he could see the white of the Indian's eyes, and thought that the Iroquois had seen him.

A moment later, a yell resounded on the field as a huge bullet-holed Tory Union Jack appeared, being carried through the smoke in pursuit of the Yankees. Gore saw the Indian draw up his rifle and fire at the escaping Yankees before running off in pursuit.

As the screaming waves thundered by in a cloud of smoke and dust, Lieutenant Gore lay hidden until dusk. In the growing darkness he heard nearby voices. One voice said, "It has been a hard day for the Yankees."

"Yes," replied the other, "there has been blood enough shed."

Gore later stated that he thought that one of the voices was that of Colonel John Butler, but could not be certain.

It was dark when Daniel Gore made his way across the river to Wilkes-Barre, where he was reunited with his brother Samuel. They were the only two surviving Gore brothers of five who went off to battle that morning.

Colonel Zebulon Butler rode up and down his disintegrating line yelling, "Don't leave me, my children, and the victory is ours."

There were pockets however, where men stood their ground. Private Cherrick Westover said to Private George Cooper, "Our men are all retreating, shall we go?"

Cooper replied, "I'll have one more shot first."

As a musket ball whistled by his ear, an Indian with a spear sprang toward him. Cooper whirled and fired and the Indian, caught in mid air, actually rose still further from the impact and fell face forward at Cooper's feet.

"Come," said Westover, indicating it was time to withdraw.

"I'll load first," replied Cooper.

According to Miner, "It is probable this coolness saved them, for the great body of the savages had dashed forward after the flying and were far to their rear."

At this time, with the Indians attacking south and to the right flank, one of Captain Hewitt's officers said to the Captain, "The day is lost—see the Indians are sixty rods in our rear, shall we retreat?"

Captain Hewitt replied, "I'll be damned if I do! Drummer strike up!"

He tried in vain to rally his men with every effort, but was killed in action.

Miner said it best: "Every captain that led a company into action was slain, and in every instance fell on or near the line. As was said of Bidlack, so of Hewitt, Whittlesey, and the others, 'They died at the head of their men.' They fought bravely—every man and officer did his duty, but they were overpowered by three fold their force. In point of numbers, the enemy was overwhelmingly superior."

As with Westover and Cooper, isolated squads and groups of Americans were able to keep together in their retreat. the reason for this was that a large portion of the Indians had rushed forward and to the river to cut off the retreat south to Forty Fort.

One of these surviving groups included Colonel Denison, who was mounted, and with a handful of men, managed to reach Forty Fort.

Another group included Colonel Butler, Rufus Bennett, James Stark and two or three others. They were among the last to leave the battlefield and were being hotly pursued by Indians in their flight south to Forty Fort. Colonel Butler spurred his horse to a faster gait and his group of tired soldiers was hard pressed to keep up with him.

Rufus Bennett was winded and gasping for breath but was able to keep up by grasping the horse's tail.

One of the lead Indians—with a tomahawk in one hand and a scalping knife in the other—was starting to gain on Butler's group.

The pounding of the horses' hoofs and the war whoops of the pursuing Indians, becoming ever louder, disturbed the sleep of Richard Inman under a nearby tree. He had slept all through the Battle of Wyoming, thanks to the potent rum he had consumed earlier in the afternoon.

Butler, on his horse, saw Inman stirring, and pointing to the rear with his sword, shouted, "Inman, shoot that Indian!"

Although Inman's weakness may have been a liking for rum, one of his strengths was that he was a crack shot. The lead Indian, with his tomahawk raised, was only a few yards from Rufus Bennett when Inman's shot rang out. The Indian jumped up with a scream and fell to the earth, dead. The other Indians in pursuit, hearing a shot come from an unexpected area, turned tail and disappeared. Colonel Butler and his handful of men, together with Richard Inman, reached the safety of Forty Fort without any further incident.

Years later, a further attempt to sanitize the true story of Wyoming took place. At the Wyoming Centennial on July 3, 1878, various religious and temperance groups, in their anti-alcoholic zeal, spread the story to speakers and newspapers alike that Richard Inman's sleep was caused by heat and exhaustion rather than by rum, and that rum was never offered before the Battle. This is in direct contradiction to the eyewitness accounts collected by Charles Miner after the Battle.

Daniel Washburn, a survivor of the Battle stated, "... Before we started out, our Capt. passed a pail full of rum of which I partook a small dram."

View of the Susquehanna from the Site of Forty Fort (June 1903 photograph)

Site of the Battle of Wyoming Battlefield (1878 photograph)

CHAPTER SIXTEEN

Old Smoke was not that interested in isolated groups of the enemy escaping, temporarily, from his tactic of rushing to cut off their main force at the river. His Senecas, as the protectors of the Western Door of the Longhouse, were fulfilling their responsibilities of their ancestral covenant with Deganwiddah. There would be many enemies slain and tortured to avenge the deaths of warriors killed by the French in battles he himself had survived. The pains of those tortured would ease the pain of many parents and relatives, and he would bring home scalps to show their numbers. His allies, the British, had assured him that this enemy he was fighting were friends of the hated French and were only interested in taking more Seneca lands. He knew that his brothers, the Mohawks, were not with him with their Chief Brant, because they, too, were busy at the Eastern Door in fighting the same enemy to keep their own lands from being taken.

Old Smoke had already fought the enemy, whom his friend John Butler called "rebels." At the Battle of Oriskany, they had fought bravely and seventeen Senecas including several of his captains were killed. According to Colonel Daniel Claus, Old Smoke, who was in command at Oriskany, "revenged himself by killing many Americans but was not satisfied." He now gave the order to his most trusted captain, Cornplanter, as well as to Big Tree and the other captains, to drive the enemy to the river.

The scene at the river was chaotic. Groups of Yankees—with whooping Indians in pursuit—flung themselves into the river.

At this point in the river, their goal was Monocanock Island, a low-lying piece of land separated from the west bank by shallow water.

Among the first to arrive at the river were George Cooper and Cherrick Westbrook, mentioned in the previous chapter. They easily waded to Monocanock Island where they found another early arrival, John Abbott, hiding in the tall grass. Abbott couldn't swim across the deep channel to the east bank but both Cooper and Westbrook were swimmers and helped Abbott to safety.

As more Indians and Rangers approached the river, the chances for survival of the escapees lessened. There were at least three confirmed cases of escaping Yankees being killed by Tories promising humane treatment.

Lieutenant Elijah Shoemaker was wading to Monocanock Island when he was seen and recognized by a Tory Ranger named Henry Windecker. Windecker, in a friendly tone, promised Shoemaker protection if he returned to shore. Shoemaker said, "I am afraid you will give me up to the Indians."

Windecker replied, "No, I will save you; they shan't hurt you." With that, Shoemaker returned to shore. Windecker extended his left arm to bring Shoemaker in and with his hidden right hand brandishing a tomahawk, he quickly killed Shoemaker with a blow to his skull. According to Dr. Peck, Yankees named Carpenter and Anning Owen, concealed under a fallen tree lying out in the river, were eyewitnesses. A similar incident occured involving William Hammond, who was escaping to the island when he was spotted and and hailed by a former neighbor named Secord. The two had been close friends until Secord, a Tory, joined the Rangers.

Secord called, "Is that you Bill Hammond?"

Hammond replied affirmatively, and Secord requested Hammond return, promising him protection.

Hammond answered, "No, I can swim across the river and make my escape."

"You cannot," replied Secord, "The Indians are on the opposite side, and will certainly kill you. If you will return, I will claim you as a brother and secure your life."

Thus deceived, Hammond returned to shore, grasped Secord's hand, and was tomahawked and killed. Hammond's body drifted down river to Forty Fort where it was recovered and buried.

This atrocity was witnessed by Lieutenant Lebeus Tubbs, who was lying in concealment near the shore and later escaped.

A strong Yankee Sergeant, Jeremiah Bigford, was pursued by an Indian into the river. The Indian had a spear but Bigford turned around, faced the Indian, struck the spear from his hand, seized him by the neck, and with his feet held the Indian under water to drown him. Bigford was then speared and killed by another Indian behind him. Bigford's body floated away and was found seven or eight miles away a month later. Although the body was badly decayed it was recognized by a silver brooch around the neck.

The most authenticated incident involved two brothers named Pencel who served on opposite sides.

Three escaping Yankees, Giles Slocum, Thomas Baldwin, and Henry Pencel, had reached Monocanock Island safely. They were hotly pursued by Tories, and being unarmed after dropping their weapons and fleeing, they hid behind bushes and trees. From their hiding places, Slocum and Baldwin saw that one of their pursuers was John Pencel, younger brother of their comrade, Henry Pencel. The younger brother in his Ranger-green uniform suddenly discovered Henry Pencel, exclaiming, "So it's you, is it?"

Henry Pencel fell on his knees and begged his brother for mercy, promising to serve his younger brother as long as he lived if his life was spared.

"You won't kill your brother will you?" Henry pleaded.

John replied, "I will as soon as look at you, you are a damned rebel!"

With that, John shot his brother, struck him four or five times with a tomahawk, and scalped him. All this was observed by both Slocum and Baldwin who later escaped to tell of the fratricide. They also told of a fellow Tory who went up to John Pencel after the act to say, "What have you been doing, have you killed your brother?"

"Yes," replied John, "for he was a damned rebel."

In disgust, the Tory replied, "I have a great mind to serve you in the same manner." Justice was to be reserved for a later time however, for John Pencel fled to Canada and one night while traveling home through a wooded area he was attacked and devoured by wolves.

Sometimes in the midst of tragedy an interval of comedy may suddenly appear, and the Battle of Wyoming was no exception.

Ensign Matthias Hollenback was carrying the wounded Captain Robert Durkee to the river in an effort to escape. Because of Hollenback's burden, his Indian pursuers were gaining on him and Durkee pleaded with Hollenback to leave him and to escape. Hollenback did so reluctantly, and the Indians, upon reaching Durkee, killed him with tomahawks and scalped him.

Hollenback was an active and fearless young man—a merchant with a healthy respect for money. Upon reaching the river, with the Indians in hot pursuit, he threw off his clothes as he ran. He took care to put his paper Continental money and a bill of exchange in his hat and a gold piece in his mouth, and plunged into the river with his hat on and nothing else. Retaining his hat, he swam underwater as the Indians fired at him. Out of breath, he surfaced. A musket ball grazed his skin causing him to open his mouth and his gold piece was lost in the river. He made sure he didn't lose his hat though. In his later years Hollenback declared, "I felt more the loss of my solitary guinea and was more vexed at the red rascals for the loss than I have been since by much more serious disasters."

He reached the Eastern shore wearing just his hat, and went into the woods, and there he met Solomon Bennett who had crossed over ahead of him. Since Bennet was wearing pants and shirt, Hollenback pleaded with him for clothes. Bennet with great charity gave Hollenback the shirt off his back. Hollenback then made his way to the fort at Wilkes-Barre under the protection of darkness, both to his safety and modesty.

According to Miner, who interviewed surviving eyewitnesses, "Many prisoners were lured to shore by promise of quarter, and then butchered. The accurate Indian marksmen, sure of their prey, had coolly singled out officers, and broke the thigh bone, it is supposed, as so many are found perforated, so as effectually to disable, but leaving the victim for torture. Captain Bidlack was thrown alive on the burning logs of the fort, held down with pitch forks, and there tortured till he expired. Prisoners taken under solemn promise of quarter were gathered together and placed in circles. Sixteen or eighteen were arranged round one large stone since known as the Bloody Rock."

The rock, situated at what is now Susquehanna Avenue between 7th and 8th Streets in Wyoming, is one-and-a-half feet high above ground, some six feet long, and three feet wide. The rock is a conglomerate consisting mainly of pink quartz, which partially gave it it's name of "Bloody Rock." The name was also derived from the horrible deeds performed on it.

As the sun set on that terrible day of July 3rd, 1778, Queen Esther, whose son had been killed the previous day, chose this time and place for vengeance.

Miner continues in his narrative, "Queen Esther, a fury in the form of a woman, assumed the office of executioner with death—maul, or tomahawk—or she used the one with both hands, or took up the other with one—and passing round the circle with words, as if singing, or counting with a cadence, she would dash out brains, or sink the tomahawk into the head of a prisoner. A number had fallen, her rage increased with indulgence."

Inexoribly, the time for death came around for two prisoners, Joseph Elliott and Lebbeus Hammond.

In regard to Joseph Elliott, Miner stated: "It was his fate to be dragged to the fatal ring at 'Blood Rock' where the savages, intoxicated with victory and excited by passion to wildest fury, glutted their thirst for blood. A circle was formed, two or three Indians holding or guarding each prisoner while the work went forward. Queen Esther raged like a demon. He (Elliott) saw six or seven murdered. A young man, Thomas Fuller, sprang to escape, shook off his guards, but was almost instantly overtaken and tomahawked. The confusion, the savage yells, the moans of his dying friends, the streams of blood, the scattered brains, for the moment stupefied him. With a ray of returning reason he saw death in a moment certain, and he could but die. With a might of combined courage and despair he threw off the Indians who held him, and at a spring leaped down the bank, turned off to the right a second, and at a bound, cleared a fence and fled to the river, with several of the enemy in full pursuit. He had passed Monocanock Island and entered the southern branch of the stream, when a bullet struck him in the left shoulder, inflicting a grevious wound. Being compelled to steady his wounded arm, dangling by his side, with his right hand, he does not know how he swam the portion of the river too deep to ford; but found himself on the bank and took shelter behind a tree a moment to recover breath. He at length arrived at the Wilkes-Barre fort and Dr. William Hooker afforded his prompt and skillful aid."

At the same time that Elliott chose to escape, so too did Lebbeus Hammond. Miner wrote: "Lebbeus Hammond, being a stout man, a large Indian stood behind him with his hands on his shoulders to prevent his rising. Seeing but one man on his left to receive the fatal blow before his turn should come, he concluded that, he could but die, and that he might as well make an attempt to save his life as to sit still and receive the fatal blow from the death maul of the old Queen. He gave a sudden spring, arose from the ground, knocked down the Indian that was holding him, and ran into the woods. He was pursued by two Indians, but escaped with his life. The other fourteen (prisoners) were killed, stripped, and scalped, and were left lying in the ring with their feet towards each other."

Some early historians, such as William S. Stone, found difficulty equating the kinder and gentler Queen Esther of the pre-Revolutionary Period with the evil and bloodthirsty Queen Esther of the Battle of Wyoming.

The fact which they overlooked is that during the time Queen Esther showed random acts of kindness, she was earning a living by ransoming prisoners taken by the Indians. It was well known by rampaging bands of Indians that Queen Esther's "Palace" in Tioga was a convenient way station where prisoners could be traded for food and supplies. Queen Esther would put these prisoners to work and treat them civilly while awaiting ransom.

Moreover, it must not be overlooked that Queen Esther was a Seneca with only a very thin veneer of religion and "civilized behavior" over the rough spots. When her son was killed by the Americans her character reverted to the Iroquois commitment of vengeance.

In order to bridge the supposed behavioral gap in Esther's

personality, the theory was born and nurtured that the evil Esther was really her sister Catherine. This would have been quite difficult, because according to Annette Evans in her address on July 4th, 1967, to the Wyoming Commerative Association, the Catherine described by Stone died in 1752.

There were two escapee eyewitnesses to the atrocities of Queen Esther to tell the tale and prevent historic revisionism. In addition, Esther was known to Colonel Denison, Colonel John Franklin, and Lieutenant Rosewell Franklin who all stated that it was Esther who was present and seen by them at the time of the atrocity. Finally, Dr. George Peck in his book *Wyoming*, tells of a visit by Queen Esther to Wyoming in 1777, where she was seen and talked to by Martha Bennett, later Mrs. Phillip Myers, and who saw the very same Queen Esther leading the Senecas into Forty Fort on July 4th, 1778.

The wives and mothers of the Yankee soldiers were kept informed of the calamatous events of the Battle by a series of couriers sent from the battlefield to Forty Fort. Their purpose was to inform the dependents at the Fort of the fate of their loved ones and to give them time to prepare for subsequent events or to flee.

A survivor of the Battle, Samuel Gore, many years later, told the story of his mother, together with the wives and mothers of the combatants, standing by the door of Forty Fort while the Battle raged several miles away. They were anxious to catch the first news of their sons and husbands.

A mounted courier suddenly galloped up to the Fort's gate and pantingly delivered the news that Mrs. Gore's three sons, Ralph, Silas, and George, and her two sons-in-law John Murphy and Timothy

Pierce had been killed, and that their scalped and mangled corpses lay side by side.

Heartbroken, the stricken woman screamed out, "Have I one son left?"

The humane qualities and bravery of the women of the Wyoming Valley were at this point shown to their highest advantage. Though in fear and dread of the fate of their own husbands and sons, they drew together to comfort Mrs. Gore as best they could. One can only speculate on the intense feelings of torment and forboding these women had to endure as the sun set on this dreadful day.

It was now night time in the Wyoming Valley but the horror continued. Slow torture and execution was reserved for some of the prisoners to fully exact vengeance for the taking of Iroquois lives.

Across from the Exeter side of the river, Captain Blanchard, Esquire Whittaker and Ismael Bennett, Senior and Junior, watched in horror from the fort at Pittston. They saw several naked prisoners driven around a stake through fire. As revealed later, pine knots were inserted into their bodies and body orifices and set afire. The sudden flaring of these pine knots emitted screams and the horrible smell of burning flesh.

According to Miner, the odor of the burning flesh came to the nostrils of the British Major John Butler who later declared, "It was not in my power to help it." Miner implied that cannibalism was also practiced that night by the Indians by adding, "In the morning, the battlefield was strewed with limbs and bodies torn apart, mangled and partially consumed."

Not all the eyewitnesses to these atrocities were observing them from the other side of the river. The wife of John Gardner received permission from one of the Tory Wintermoots to see her husband who was taken prisoner when the Hardings were ambushed. She was accompanied by Mrs. John Jenkins to the ruins of Fort Wintermoot. Mrs. Jenkins later related that the Indians were at that time engaged in burning their prisoners. The Indians had taken down an old pine fence and on it piled the dead, wounded, and some unwounded prisoners, and set it on fire. Mrs. Jenkins reported that the entire line of the fence was filled with the charred bones and flesh of the prisoners with some of the bodies still burning.

According to Miner, "About one hundred and sixty of the Connecticut people were killed that day and one hundred and forty escaped." But mere numbers cannot convey the horror and inhumane brutality of the aftermath of the Battle.

Historian Oscar J. Harvey stated, "To the survivors it was a night long to be remembered—never to be forgotten." How surprised and dismayed they would have been to know that with the passage of time, the denial of facts, and the revision of history, that night has not only been forgotten, but the modern argument raised is that the atrocities never even occurred!

Massacre at Wyoming. 1857 Painting by Alonzo Chappell.

The Fratricide at Wyoming. An early engraving.

Queen Esther's Rock. This old photograph taken before the turn of the 19th Century shows the rock of pink quartz before the protective cage was placed over it in 1895 (Also known as the "Bloody Rock.")

CHAPTER SEVENTEEN

Apparently sated and sobered by the previous night's excesses of vengeance, torture, and death, the following morning saw a return to reality by the invaders. Major John Butler's first order was to bury the Tory and Indian dead.

According to Solomon Bennet, one of the last Yankee survivors of the Battle, and who returned to Wyoming in 1820, the Tory Wintermoots and Secords told him of the burial. Dr. George Peck, in his book *Wyoming*, stated that Bennet "pointed out the spot where the British and Indians who were killed were buried. It was on what was called 'the island' in the marsh, under some large yellow pines which were then standing. There, sixty were consigned to their long resting place by their fellow Royalists."

The Yankee dead were left to rot in the field and their bones were not to be interred until October, three months away.

The surrender of Forty Fort was demanded by Major Butler at eight o'clock in the morning on July 4th, 1778, and Colonel Denison replied that he would give his answer in the afternoon. Denison used the intervening time to warn Zebulon Butler and his Continental detachment to flee and to empty the Fort's liquor supply into the Susquehanna.

Articles of capitulation and surrender were written providing for humane treatment of all the inhabitants of the Fort and surrounding areas. The two gates of Forty Fort were then thrown open. With colors flying and fifes and drums playing, in marched the dark-green clad Rangers headed by John Butler in his bright scarlet uniform with gold braid and buttons.

An oversized silken Union Jack, bordered in Tory buff, spanked in the morning, summer breeze. The musket ball holes in the fluttering banner gave a grim testament and reminder of the bloody battle on the previous day.

To the right of the Rangers came the Indians in files of four and led by Queen Esther. She approached Colonel Denison standing next to the stacked arms in the court yard. In a sarcastic, drawling tone, the old Queen said, "You told me to bring more Indians, Colonel Denison, see here, I have brought all these."

Colonel John Butler, upon hearing what he felt to be an insolent remark in bad form, turned to Queen Esther and retorted, "Be silent, women should be seen but not heard." Then, turning to the Indians, he turned the stacked weapons over to them with the remark, "See, a present the Yankees have made you."

Colonels Butler and Denison then signed the articles of capitulation which promised to spare the lives and property of the departed Yankees. Looking up, Butler recognized a British deserter,

Sergeant Boyd, who had formerly been at Fort Niagara but had gone over to the Yankee side.

Butler sternly said to him, "Boyd, go to that tree!"

Boyd replied, "I hope you keep your honor and will consider me a prisoner of war."

"Go to that tree, sir," repeated Butler.

Boyd walked to the tree and Butler signaled to a detachment of Indians who fired a volley, killing Boyd. That was the only life taken at Forty Fort, but it was a different situation with regard to property.

The Indians wasted no time beginning their plunder of Forty Fort in violation of the articles of capitulation. As Colonel John Franklin stated in a later deposition, "The articles of capitulation were on as good terms as we could expect, considering our situation at the time. Had the enemy held to the agreements, there should have been nothing to complain of but they were violated in every respect, except that of massacring the inhabitants. There were no personal injuries done at that time, but plundering immediately took place, even while the articles of capitulation were being committed to writing."

Colonel Nathan Denison requested a meeting with Major John Butler to protest the plundering. They met at Mrs. Myer's cabin. Mrs. Myer, then Martha Bennet, said of the Tory commander: "Butler was a large corpulent man, with fair skin. I looked at him with astonishment, wondering how such a fine looking man could come with the Indians to kill us."

Denison made his complaint regarding the Indian's plundering in violation of Butler's solemn promise to control the Indians and according to Franklin:

"Major Butler professed to have his feelings injured at such conduct, and reprimanded the Indians, saying that he had pledged his honor that the property of the inhabitants should be preserved entire; that by their plundering, his promises were violated; that if he had known that they would have conducted themselves in that manner; he would have marched them off immediately after the battle and never taken possession of the fort. Complaints were renewed, and Major Butler, turning to one of his chiefs, said, 'They are your Indians, you must stop them from plundering!' The chief withdrew, and in a few minutes returned, saying that he could not stop them—that they threatened to tomahawk him. Major Butler observed that he was sorry, but that after a successful battle, the Indians would not be commanded. They even threatened his life on some occasions, when he was endeavoring to prevent them from plundering. He requested Colonel Denison to make up a statement of all property that was taken contrary to the agreement contained in the capitulation, and send it to him at his quarters the next morning, and pledged on his honor that the full value should be paid. Colonel Denison observed that it would be difficult in so short a time to ascertain what property had been taken. Major Butler replied that he must make a statement as near as he could, and again pledged on his honor that the full value should be paid....

"After the business was finished in the fort, the enemy withdrew in a body, marching out in the same form in which they had entered. About thirty or forty Indians and Tories remained in the fort, but the main body marched to Wintermoot's Fort. The first house they came to after leaving the Kingston fort (Forty Fort) was set on fire, as was also every other house on their way. Major Butler marching at the head of the savages, all was laid in ruins before him—his pledged honor to the contrary notwithstanding."

With the departure of Butler, according to Miner:

"... the savages threw off all restraint, seized on Colonel Denison, and, taking his hat from his head, demanded also the linen frock he wore. In the pocket were a few dollars, the whole military chest of the settlement, and he made some resistance, when they, instantly lifting a tomahawk, threatened his life. Obliged to comply, he stepped backward to where sat a young woman of his family, who comprehending the maneuver, adroitly took out the purse, when he gave the coveted garment to the spoiler."

Elisha Harding described the plundering of Lieutenant Elisha Scovell's property:

"When they began to plunder, he (Scovell) took his goods and halted them in a corner of the fence and made a shed of boards over them, and sat by them all safe until everybody else was stripped; then a certain Tom Green who had married a squaw, called on him to open his chest. The reply was that Major Butler was a gentlemen of honor, and had promised him (Scovell) that nothing should be taken from him. 'Damn Butler and his orders!' and then drew his sword on Scovell's rack and with his tomahawk split the lid of the chest, and this turned the attention of the Indians to the work, and in a few minutes, poor Elisha was as poor as his neighbors."

Mrs. Sylvia Seybolt, in her eighties, told Dr. George Peck that while the plundering was in progress at Forty Fort, she saw an Indian break into her sister's trunk and take out a bottle of camphor oil. She related that the Indian opened up the bottle, sniffed it, and asked if it was poisonous. Her sister replied that it wasn't, but the Indian made her taste it. The Indian waited to see what would happen, and then drank the entire contents before going out to lay down by the river. His body was found there the next day.

The Indian women who accompanied the invading party were just as agressive as the Indian men in their looting. There was an anxious moment when Mrs. Martha Myers, who was having her clothing stripped off her body by a determined squaw, clenched her fist and hit the Indian woman with all her might. The squaw was knocked to the ground, but recovered enough to grapple with Mrs. Myers who again knocked the Indian woman down. The settlers who were present expected the Indian men to tomahawk all of them in retaliation. They were amazed when the Indians roared with laughter and one of them patted Mrs. Myers on the back saying, "Good squaw!"

Mrs. Myers commented:

"They took our feather beds and ripping open the ticks, flung out the feathers, and crammed in their plunder, consisting mostly of fine clothing, and, throwing them over their horses, went off. A squaw came riding up with ribbons stringing from her head over her horse's tail. Some of the squaws could have on two or three bonnets, generally back side before. One rode off astride of mother's side saddle, that too, wrong end foremost, and mother's scarlet cloak hanging before her, being tied at the back of her neck. We could not help laughing at the ridiculous figure she cut, in spite of the deep troubles which then but overwhelmed us."

There were many strange sights to behold. A large Indian stuffed his ample frame into John Sutton's tight grey "Quaker wedding suit" with generous amount of forearms and ankles exposed. Another was seen wearing Colonel Denison's new beaver hat with feathers sticking out like Porcupine quills.

However, by far, the most bizarre sight of all was the grand and final exit of Queen Esther from Wyoming. She had donned layer after layer of dresses and stockings to create such a rotund figure that she had to be helped on her horse and once upon the beleaguered animal, her collection of plundered bonnets was handed to her. She piled one bonnet after the other over her head and over each succeeding hat until no more would stay on, and rode out for the last time from the Wyoming Valley.

Lieutenant Colonel John Butler, Commander of the Royal American Regiment of Butler's Rangers. Like his namesake and opponent, Zebulon Butler (not related), he was born in Connecticut.

Forty Fort, 1778. From an early drawing by Edmund L. Dana

Departure of the Indians After the Battle and Massacre in July, 1778.
Original drawing by Frederick C. Yohn in 1902.

CHAPTER EIGHTEEN

The inhabitants of the Wyoming Valley, thus deprived of food and supplies, had no other option but to leave with just the clothes on their backs.

Colonel John Franklin wrote in a letter:

"After Major Butler with the main body of the enemy had left Kingston (after the surrender of Forty Fort), I set out with four others to go in search of my family, which I had left in Huntington. The Indians stopped us and said, 'Maybe some bad Indians kill you,' that we must stay in the fort two days, when they would go with us. We returned back into the fort, and at night lay down under a wagon; made several attempts to get off, but could not succeed without being discovered, until near morning (of Sunday, July 5th) when we got down to the bank of the river, rose up the bank, and crossed the road into the woods. When we reached the hill opposite to Wilkes-Barre, we looked back and saw the smoke of the buildings following us down from Kingston fort; the smoke also rising from the buildings in Wilkes-Barre. We passed down through Shawnee (Plymouth), which was deserted by all its inhabitants. We had passed through but a short distance when we discovered that the fire was following us. The whole of the settlements were laid in ruins as speedily as the enemy could spread the fire. All such property as they could not drive or carry off was burnt or otherwise destroyed. The families which lived below Kingston fort (Forty Fort) drove off some of their cattle—as many as they could find; but they were mostly in the woods and they had no time to look them up. A few families remained at Wilkes--Barre, but the great body of the inhabitants fled in every direction. Hundreds of women and children, turning their backs upon the mangled corpses of their husbands, fathers, brothers, and sons—who were left on the battle-grounds without inhumation—their dwellings enveloped in flames, and their personal property either carried off by the enemy or burnt in their dwellings. Some went down the river while others pursued the different roads to the Delaware. Numbers of women with their children in their arms, and other small children by their sides, traveled on foot through to the Delaware. A Mrs. Tubbs, an old lady upward of seventy years of age, traveled through barefoot, with a grandchild in her arms. Some families that went down the river made a stand at Catawissa. Of those who went east, many stopped at the Delaware, while several hundred continued their march on foot, with their little ones, to the States of New York, Connecticut, Massachusetts, and Rhode Island. Several died on the way. It is impossible to give an adequate idea of the fatigue and distress attending the retreat of the inhabitants of Wyoming."

Another eyewitness account, this one by William Gallup, specifically referred to the survivors at Forty Fort:

"We were not to be plundered, but they plundered us of everything. They kept us three or four days, then told us to go. One hundred and eighty women and children, accompanied by only thirteen men went together. They suffered extremely, all on foot, barefoot, bareheaded, in great want of provisions. Two women were delivered in the woods."

According to Dr. Frederick Johnson, in his address entitled "Pioneer Women of Wyoming," the following was recorded:

"The number of men, women, and children who fled from Wyoming was not far from three thousand.

"The several paths to the east were crowded with terror stricken fugitives. There were four avenues of escape open to them:

1. The Warrior's Path which left the lower part of the Valley and crossing the mountain reached the settlements by way of the Lehigh River. A party of one hundred women and children taking this route had but a single man to lead the way and otherwise protect them.
2. The route over Wilkes-Barre Mountain and through the 'Shades of Death' (also known as the Great Swamp), to the Delaware River, afterwards the Wilkes-Barre and Easton turnpike. Most of the fugitives took this route.
3. To the Delaware by way of Cobb's Gap at Lackawaxen passing where Scranton now stands.
4. Perhaps a thousand persons went by boats or rafts or on land down the Susquehanna."

It was the use of this last mentioned route that prompted a Pennemite eyewitness William Maclay to state:

"I write you this letter with reluctance, as I am certain it must give pain to any man of sensibility. I left Sunbury ... Wednesday last (July 8th, 1778). I never in my life saw such scenes of distress. The river and the roads leading down it were covered with men, women, and children flying for their lives—many without any property at all and none who had not left the greatest part behind.... Wyoming is totally abandoned —scarce a single family remained between that place and Sunbury when I came away. The panic and spirit of flight has reached even to this place—many having moved even out of this township—and almost everyone is thinking of some place of greater security.... Something in the way of charity ought to be done for the many miserable objects that crowd the banks of this river—especially those who fled from Wyoming. They are a people, you know, I did not used to love, but I now most sincerely pity their distress...."

As stated, the largest portion of the settlers fleeing Wyoming took the Lower Road, south through the Great Swamp, within which was a forbidding valley known as the Shades of Death. This swamp of fifteen miles in width was a mired tangle of brambles and treacherous bogs. It was the home of huge rattlesnakes, wolf packs, and bears. It is not surprising that this route accounted for most of the hundreds of deaths and disappearances of the fleeing people.

A former Hessian doctor, Dr. Johann David Schopf, who surrendered with the British at Yorktown, described the "Great Swamp" in his journal written in 1783 when he travelled through the area on horseback en route to Wyoming:

"Further on we got into the veritable Great Swamp, so called, which extends only fifteen miles across, but no one knows how far it lies to the north and to the south. Really, the whole of this region is not what is commonly called called swamp, several mountains and valleys being included under the name. The road cut through is nowhere more than six feet wide, which is full of everything which can make trouble for the traveller. On both sides the forest is so thick that the trees almost touch, and by their height and their matted branches making a deep shade which is cold and fearful even at noon of the clearest day. All beneath is grown up in green and impenetrable bush. Everywhere lie fallen trees or half-fallen—despite their weight, not reaching the ground. Thousands of rotten and rotting trunks cover the ground and make every step uncertain, while between lies a fat bed of the richest mould, that sucks up, like a sponge, all the moisture, and so becomes swampy almost everywhere.

"One cannot with difficulty, penetrate this growth, even a little way and not be in danger of coming too near this or that sort of snake, being hidden from the sharpest eye in the waste of stones, leaves, and roots.... A particularly deep and narrow valley in this great swamp is the 'Shades of Death.' Its steep mountain sides are distinguished by a great number of the tallest and slimmest pines with white spruce and hemlock ... our fellow travelers were of the opinion that all these hills and valley would never be used for anything because they thought cultivation would be impossible or certainly too troublesome...."

A third eyewitness recount, by Mercy Ross, who took this dangerous route, states that it took ten days to get through the Shades of Death and the woods. She stated:

"Hannah (Ford), wife of Josiah Rogers died on the route, and was buried under the root of a fallen tree, and Mrs. Ross was so worn down from the excitement and fatigue of the journey and starved for want of food, that when the burial was over and the party about to move on, Mrs. Ross said that she could go no farther, and would like to be buried along side of the other woman. She was however, appealed to on behalf of her children, and was urged to get up and go on with the party, which she was finally induced to do.

"They first met the abode of civilization before they were taken up by the Government and furnished with provisions. She had five children with her, all of whom were about naked, so badly were their clothes torn and worn in the journey. About the first of October, three months after the Battle, her last child was born in Connecticut. In March 1782, she remarried and moved to Wyoming, to the place of her former husband."

The bravery of the fleeing women of Wyoming was exceeded only by their strength of character as exemplified by Mrs. Jabez Fish. She had assumed her husband to be dead, and though overcome with grief, hunger, and fatigue, she cared for her children as best she could in her flight. Despite this, her infant child died and there was no way to dig a grave. Rather than leave the tiny body to be eaten by wolves she carried it twenty miles through the wilderness until she came to a German settlement near Easton where the people, though poor, fed and cared for her and gave the infant a decent burial.

It was during this flight that the wife of Captain Stephen Gardner had a vision which could easily have been ascribed to fatigue and hunger. In her vision, Mrs. Gardner's daughter, who was living in Connecticut, appeared to her with a baby in her arms. She told her mother that she herself was dead and she wanted Mrs. Gardner to have her grandchild. To show the reality of the vision, the daughter touched her mother's wrist leaving a permanent mark. When Mrs. Gardner reached civilization, after regaining her strength, she found the mark on her wrist to be a compelling force to return to Connecticut. Everything in her vision proved true; her daughter had died, and had asked that Mrs. Gardner raise and care for the child. Mrs. Gardner devoted the rest of her life to this task in accordance with her dead daughter's wishes.

These refugees from Wyoming became the most common source of news from the scene of the Battle. Although Zebulon Butler had reported the facts of the Battle to Washington and the Board of War in Philadelphia, the newspapers were far more interested in detailed narrative. The first stories published, as a result, were wildly exaggerated versions of what really happened at Wyoming. As Charles Miner stated, "The false account was immeasurably worse."

Historian Oscar J. Harvey wrote:

"There is no doubt that the Wyoming refugees—particularly the women, and the youth of both sexes—when they arrived at the inhabited parts of the country in the course of their flight, were not only physically exhausted, but had naturally, become worked up to a high degree of excitement, and a consequent condition of excessive exasperation against the author of their ills. It followed, therefore, as a matter of course, that when they told their tales of the enemy's doings in Wyoming, they told them with hyperbolical amplification.... Many of their hearers in repeating these stories, added to them certain details of their own fabrication, and thus it came to pass that many accounts of the Wyoming battle and massacre were put in circulation."

The first false reports were published in a Poughkeepsie, New York newspaper. The account, allegedly quoting some Connecticut-bound escapees from Wyoming, stated that when Colonel Nathan Denison asked what terms of surrender Major John Butler would grant, he was told, "The hatchet." It was added that in compliance with this dreaded promise, surviving Wyoming settlers, including women and children, were locked in their houses which were then burned down.

Other falsehoods which were disseminated by other publications, were that the Tories and Indians burned down Forty Fort, that Zebulon Butler and John Butler were cousins, and that seventy Continental soldiers were methodically killed and tortured. It was also fallaciously stated that Zebulon Butler was drawn into battle by promises of a peace parley, when in reality, the Yankees went into battle with every intention of defeating their enemies.

Despite disclaimers and letters to various editors by Butler of what really occurred at Wyoming, the false information prevailed. Such reliable eyewitnesses as Colonel Butler's son, Lord Butler, Elisha Blackman, Rufus Bennet, John Franklin, and Mathias Hollenback all refuted these exaggerations and endorsed the facts as related in this book.

However, one false account after another was published, many by people who should have known better. Dr. James Thatcher, Surgeon General of the American Army published these false reports in his book, *Military Journal*, as did the great Chief Justice John Marshall in his *Life of Washington*. In a later revision, however, Marshall corrected his errors, admitting he had used erroneous sources.

Dr. George Peck Wrote in 1858:

"The grave errors of historians in relation to the early history of this famous locality seem to be imperishable. They have been corrected and refuted, over and over, and yet they continue to be propagated and palmed up to the public."

All this did not stop the exaggerated and false news of Wyoming from going overseas. In England it strengthened opposition to the Revolutionary War in Parliament and calls for England to quit the Colonies were heard for the first time.

In France, the news reinforced sympathy for America with requests for more aid to the new American nation, and in Italy the news later prompted an Italian historian named Charles Botta to even further wild exaggerations in his *History of the War for the Independence of the United States of America.*

However, nowhere were the accounts made so bizarre as in Germany. There, where the story of Von Zinzendorf in Wyoming was taught in the schools, Wyoming was thought of as a German Colony in America. The narrative of Wyoming was used to spur a rising tide of German nationalism.

The following account is an English translation of a piece entitled *The German Thermopylae*, which appeared in a German publication and was later republished in the *Pittsburgh Post* in 1850.

"There are, we presume, but a few of our readers who have not heard of the beautiful Wyoming Valley, that rich and fertile tract of land situated in the State of Pennsylvania, and which has often been celebrated by poets and writers. This Valley was first and chiefly settled by Germans. It contains rich farms, fields, and meadows, together with valuable timber, and was visited with fire and sword by a party of American Tories, British, and Indians in the year 1778, at a time when the male population of the settlement (which number amounted to about 350 souls) had joined the army of the great and immortal Washington, at a distance of several days journey, where they expected to encounter the main army of the enemy.

"The Colonel of the Wyoming Germans was Hollenback, a Justice of the Peace. He was an intimate friend of Washington, who knew how to appreciate his distinguished qualities, as well as his rare intelligence; although as regarding religion, their views and opinions differed greatly from each other, as it is well known that Washington was a strict believer in the Bible, whereas Hollenback did adhere to the doctrines of Thomas Paine, who was a philospher and freethinker.

"The heart rending call in distress of their parents, wives, and children, whom they had left at home, soon reached the ears of the Wyoming Volunteers, and in an instant Hollenback found himself surrounded by his men, who urged him to meet the enemy, whose force consisted of more than 2,000 men. In vain were the representations of Washington, who being aware of the superior numerical strength of these barbarous and plundering hordes, had prognosticated to all a sure death. Terror and agony moved the heart of everyone at the thought of the dear ones whom they had left behind unprotected, and they clenched their fists in eagerness for combat and vengeance at the gloomy prospects of their ruined happiness; and it was now no longer possible for them to remain with the army.

"At the sound of the trumpet, and headed by their Colonel, they began to return homeward in great haste, marching day and night until they arrived at their settlement, where, they beheld the smoking ruins of destroyed dwellings, near to which the enemies had comfortably erected their tents, their morning fires blazing triumphantly in the air, intermingled with their huzzas ...

"With doleful looks Hollenback regarded his little band, who, gnashing their teeth for rage and venegeance stood near the place of destruction, and the looks of his men announced to him the innermost thoughts of their hearts. There was none who would have trembled at an assault on the hordes of murderers. 'Brothers,' exclaimed Hollenback, 'against such cowards, who watch for our absence, and who now rejoice in victory over women and children only, everyone of us can stand the ground against eight of them. Let us send these brutes to hell in such a manner that even the Devil himself must have respect for the Germans of Wyoming Valley!' And raising himself from the saddle, he waved his sword in the air, and spurred his horse onward. Thundering hurrahs followed his words and his men rushed forward eager for the ensuing combat.

"At the first volley more than 100 of these redskins (who formed the advance guard of the enemy) were weltering in their blood. The enemy were quietly reposing in their camp, but in an instant the whole army of the enemy was apprised of the assault, and from all sides they rushed upon the gallant little corps. The sun rose, spreading its animating beams upon the exhausted Germans, who made arrangements to make their stand behind a row of ruins, and to wait for the approach of their enemies. The first assault of the enemy was repulsed, and many kissed the earth in death, caused by the dense drift of bullets sent forth from behind the entrenchments.... The enemy soon engaged its whole army in a furious combat, but they were not able to stand their ground against the discharges of the pieces of the little band, which rattling, cleared their ranks. Repulsed repeatedly, and again hurrying into the fight, the enemy could not gain a foot of ground, although their guns began to clear the ranks of their powerful antagonists.

"During twelve long hours, these German Spartans manfully resisted the superior force of the enemy. Finally, and with the last glowing of the setting sun, the fate of the day was decided; 300 Germans had fallen in defense of their adopted country, and fifty more lay badly wounded, who would not seek for quarter, and still strove to make a last effort against the enemy—who seeing their determination, had almost been driven to madness on account of their bravery.

"What a noble military achievement! What persevering heroism! Had these men been Americans they would up to this day, have been remembered by the nation as 'The Immortal Wyoming Boys.' But they were only Germans, and their memory—which is as worthy of immortality as that of the Hellenes of Thermopylae—remains silently recorded in the book of history of two Pennsylvania counties!"

Partly as a reaction to the claims of exaggerated cruelty and atrocities by the Tories and Indians, and partly due to self interests of certain groups of people, the truth was again ignored in favor of the other extreme.

This opposite attitude of apparent indifference to Wyoming may have started with the first news item published in the *Pennsylvania Packet* of Philadelphia on July 14th, 1778:

"Mr. Butler, formerly an Indian Agent under Sir William Johnson, with a considerable force consisting of regular troops and Indians, have made an attack on the settlement at Wyoming, and have done some mischief. The particulars are not yet come to hand."

When the particulars did "come to hand," the following account was published by Captain Alexander Patterson, an avid Pennemite in 1804:

"It is well known at that time (1776) on the frontiers of Northampton and Northumberland Counties that the conduct of those (Wyoming) Yankees occasioned the session of the Five Nations from the United States. As was natural to imagine, those Pennsylvania settlers who had been so cruelly robbed of their property would endeavor to regain it. Their address and moving complaints induced Joseph Brant, a well known Indian chief and a Colonel Butler, Superintendant of Indian Affairs, to come with them to Wyoming, with a number of Indians, for the recovery of their goods and chattels. The party had arrived at Abraham's Plains; the Yankees were apprized of their being at that place and must needs to go fight them, led on by that old murderer, Lazarus Stewart—first having drunk two barrels of whiskey to stimulate their spirits. They marched in riot, with drums beating and colors flying. The result was that a number of them were killed; those who asked quarter were humanely treated, nor was a woman or child molested, only enjoined to quit the country and leave it for the righful owners. Surely there was no propriety in calling that transaction a massacre or murder! The wretches brought it upon themselves—and so be it!

"Your petitioner had at that time been assigned a district in the

Quartermaster General's Department, north of the mountains in Jersey and Pennsylvania. Notwithstanding the former enmity all the vagrants that left Wyoming at that time, came to him for succor. His charity superceded prejudice, and for their support he ordered them rations out of the public stores. If there were any widows among them, they were very merry ones, and their conduct induced no respect; nor could it be expected, as most of their women, like their men, were of the lowest order of beings."

These early violations of the truth eventually provided the fuel for modern "political correctness" which holds that, at best, the conflict and atrocities at Wyoming never happened, and at worst, if so, were merely a political ploy to deprive innocent Indians of their land.

As if in answer to these past and present distortions of truth and history, Lord Butler, the son of Zebulon Butler, wrote in 1820:

"To perpetuate truth is, or ought to be, the object of history; at all events, history should never be made the vehicle of falsehood."

Flight of the Inhabitants from Wyoming. Original drawing by Denman Fink in 1902.

CHAPTER NINETEEN

Although the main body of Tories and Indians left the Wyoming Valley for New York State a few days after the Battle of Wyoming, the threat of sporadic raids on the Valley remained.

These raids after the fact were not haphazard expeditions of random forces as previously thought. They were planned incursions designed to keep American troops pinned down on the Northern frontier and away from Washington's main forces. This is borne out by a statement made by Major John Butler in a letter from Niagara in the winter of 1778-1779. He wrote:

"Mr. Secord is sent to Chemung for the purpose of keeping a constant watch upon the rebels toward Wyoming, from whence I daily expect intelligence, as parties have been out that way for some time."

Further confirmation of Indian activity appears in official records made at Fort Niagara in January 1779 which stated that 1581 warriors were present at the Fort while 1,042 were "absent on the war-path."

In spite of these ongoing raids, the first Yankee settlers began to return to the Wyoming Valley to secure whatever crops had not been destroyed. As early as mid-July, 1778, they returned to the Valley to rebuild and salvage what they could.

The return of the Connecticut settlers to Wyoming to reclaim their lands, prompted this mean spirited communication from the Pennemite members of the Pennsylvania Supreme Executive Council to the Pennsylvania Legislature dated August 7, 1778:

"The final catastrophe, which has befallen the Connecticut settlers on the river Susquehanna, deplorable as it is, recollects the disputed footing on which these sufferers stood. Compassion for them as well as justice to this State, require that they be reminded of the precarious nature of their tenure before they establish themselves."

The first American troops cautiously returned to the Valley. Colonel Thomas Hartley's regiment entered Wyoming on August lst followed by Captain Spaulding's Westmoreland Independent Company.

Colonel Hartley, in his report of August 1, 1778, to the Supreme Executive Council of Pennsylvania wrote:

"... Four-fifths of the inhabitants fled with such effects as they could carry from this country. Many of the men are returning ... A most extraordinary panic seems to have struck the people. The Wyoming settlement is almost totally destroyed. The most of the surviving inhabitants have fled to Connecticut, or are now removing as paupers to that State. There is no prospect of their returning or reestablishing themselves at Wyoming this fall."

A few days later, Colonel Zebulon Butler, with some sixty Continental troops and forty militia returned to the Wyoming Valley. Writing to Colonel Hartley, he stated, that upon his arrival:

"... We discovered two small parties of Indians yesterday, and fired at them, and discovered two other parties this day. What number there is about is uncertain. If your Honor should think it consistent to have some part of the troops under your command advance as far up the river (from Sunbury) as this place, or as far as you should think proper, I think it will be a means of keeping the savages from murdering and robbing the inhabitants of these frontiers.

"Our present situation appears rather dangerous and alarming, and as our whole interest and the little remaining prospect of our crops depends on our maintaining this Post and keeping possession of the country, therefore every person will consider himself under the strongest tie and obligation to do his utmost in the defence of the place against our common enemy. And it is impossible that we can make ourselves formidable in any degree without submitting ourselves to good order and discipline, therefore the martial law is to be strictly adhered to and obeyed as well by the militia as well as (by the) Continental troops and all who join the detachment under the command of Colonel Butler."

A week later Colonel Butler sent a dispatch to the Board of War in Philadelphia restating his idea for a limited expedition to relieve Indian pressure on Wyoming and the Northern Frontier:

"I think it would serve ... for three or four hundred men to go up the river. There are a number of Tories and some Indians, supposed to be about a hundred on the River. The lowest down is about twenty miles above us, and so extend up the River fifty or sixty miles. Some part of them have come out of the States of York and Jersey and there are a large number of horses and cattle with them since our defeat at this place."

Colonel Hartley in Sunbury, replied to Colonel Butler at Wilkes-Barre in a letter dated August 22nd, 1778:

"My firm intention is to act offensively against the enemy adjoining these frontiers. I go to Muncy tomorrow, and am collecting a clever body of men there. The detachment of my regiment which was in Northampton County is now ordered to Wyoming. This will strengthen us with upwards of a hundred good men. I order Captain George Bush of my regiment to join them....

"My plan is this: That on the 31st of August, I march with all the force I can collect to Wyalusing where we will arrive on the 2nd or 3rd of September. That to provide against any misfortune, you remain in Wyoming in garrison with between eighty and a hundred men of these who are worst prepared for an expedition in the woods; and that Captain Bush should command all the remainder of the forces at Wyoming—regulars and others—and march on the same 31st of August to Wyalusing to affect a junction with me on the 2nd or 3rd of September—taking care to send on spies to inform me of their approach and situation. The troops that move from Wyoming must draw forty rounds of cartridges per man, carry four days provisions on their backs, and twelve days more of flour with them on pack horses ... The expedition from the north and the expedition to the westward into the Indian country will appear about the beginning of September, and our movement may have a happy effect. I trust these frontiers will soon be cleared of the savages."

As if in defiance of this hope of ridding Wyoming of Indians, two young militia men, Luke Swetland and James Blanchard, were taken prisoner by a Seneca raiding party and marched northward and were presumed to have been killed. Another young man named Isaac Tripp also was taken prisoner with his grandfather a few days later on their way to oversee some land the old man owned in Providence, a tiny settlement now within the Scranton city limits. The grandfather, Isaac Sr., who was seventy-eight years old, was released because of his age and Isaac Jr. was given up for dead. As will be seen, both Swetland and Tripp were to live to give richness and meaning to the saga of Wyoming.

In compliance with Colonel Hartley's marching orders, one hundred thirty men under Captains George Bush, Simon Spalding, and John Franklin marched from Wyoming on September 14, 1778, to Muncy, on the West Branch of the Susquehanna. The force joined Colonel Hartley and two hundred more men, and the combined group of over three hundred troops set out for Tioga.

Although the element of suprise was lost when a deserter from Hartley's expedition warned the Indians, the Indians nevertheless fled from the American forces. After a few successful skirmishes, Hartley and his troops took Tioga Point. A Tory prisoner informed Hartley that a force of three hundred green-uniformed Tory Rangers under John Butler had deserted Tioga only a few hours earlier to consolidate at Chemung, twelve miles away, and prepare for battle. Hartley saw this as a trap and a potential ambush situation. He felt his lines of supply to be dangerously extended and ordered a withdrawal to Wyalusing and then Wyoming. First, however, he ordered Tioga as well as Queen Esther's "Palace" burned to the ground.

Queen Esther's "Palace" was a modified, low-lying Iroquois long house with both living quarters and warehouse space. Queen Esther used her "Palace" and adjoining buildings to house guests, prisoners, and plunder. Together with Chemung and Fort Niagara, it was looked upon as a source of all enemy incursions and attacks on Wyoming.

According to historian W.E. Griffis, an officer present at the burning of Queen Esther's "Palace" saw a huge iron cauldron inside the building that he thought too valuable for destruction. He buried the large pot in the ground nearby before burning the "Palace" to the ground. He never forgot his buried treasure and ten years later he returned with some other veterans. They dug up the pot and used it to make a batch of corn liquor which they then happily consumed with many relevant toasts all around. Year after year thereafter, the veterans returned to repeat the ritual.

Hartley ordered a withdrawal from Tioga to Wyalusing, assuming correctly that John Butler had set up an ambush at Chemung. At Wyalusing, Hartley's forces rested, allowing the enemy's advance forces to catch up and attack Hartley's rear guard as the expedition prepared to return to Wyoming. Colonel Hartley later commented:

"About two o'clock a very heavy attack was made upon our rear, which obliged the most of our rear guard to give way whilst several Indians appeared on our left flank. By the weight of firing we were soon convinced we had to oppose a large body. Captain Stoddert commanded in front, I was in the center ... whilst Captain Spaulding was dispatched to support the rear guard. We gained the heights almost unnoticed by the barbarians. At the critical moment, Captains Hawkins Boone and John Brady and Lieutenant Robert King and a few brave fellows landed from the canoes ... The war-whoop was given by our people below, and communicated round. We advanced on the enemy on all sides, with great shouting and noise. The Indians after a brave resistance of some minutes, considered themselves nearly surrounded, and fled with the utmost haste by the only passes that remained, and left ten dead on the ground ... From every account these were a select body of warriors sent after us, consisting of near 200 men. Their confidence and impetuosity probably gave the victory to us. They would have murdered us all had they succeeded, but the great God of Battles protected us on the day of danger. We had four killed and ten wounded. They received such a beating as prevented them from giving us any further trouble during our march to Wyoming."

Colonel Hartley added, "It is hellish work to be fighting those devils—we gain neither honors or laurels on these frontiers, but we have the satisfaction to think we save our country."

No sooner had Hartley and his expedition returned to Wyoming than a surprise Indian attack killed three men who were working in a potato field on the Kingston flats on October 3rd.

Hartley and his command then returned to their barracks in Sunbury and sent the following message to the Supreme Executive Council:

"From our observations we imagine that the same party that fought us, after taking care of their dead and wounded, had come on to Wyoming, and are now in that neighborhood. I would respectfully propose that Congress would be pleased to send a Connecticut regiment to garrison Wyoming as soon as possible. The Indians are numerous, as well as Tories ... It is too late for an expedition against Chemung this Fall. We must only secure our posts for the Winter, and early in the Spring a body must march against their towns on this river."

Colonel Hartley's comment concerning the Indians whom he had just fought following his expedition back to Wyoming was unfortunately correct. Following their raid in Kingston, on October 3rd, Indian raids increased in scope and intensity throughout the Fall and Winter of 1778.

The now-decimated garrison of some 169 men had been put to work by Colonel Butler building a new fort named Fort Wyoming in Wilkes-Barre. To construct this fort, two rows of logs were laid down horizontally, four feet apart and the space between the rows was filled with tamped down earth forming walls six feet deep and seven feet high. Inside the square enclosure covering a half acre, a platform was attached to the inside wall allowing the defenders to fire over the top. All around the outside wall Butler's men dug a deep trench in which were placed the sharpened tops of pine trees pointing outwards and ready to impale any unfortunate invaders who stumbled into the moat.

It was in this atmosphere of fear and the dread of impending and intermittent Iroquois raids, that Colonel Butler issued the following on October 21, 1778:

"Orders. That there be a party consisting of a subaltern, two sergeants, two corporals and twenty five privates to parade tomorrow morning with their arms and C. to go as a guard to those that will go to bury the remains of the men killed at the late battle at and near the place called Wintermute Fort; and it is expected that the main inhabitants of this place will universally turn out and assist in burying their late friends, that lost their lives in said battle."

It had been a dry, hot summer and fall ever since that ill-fated July 3rd and the bodies were dried up and unrecognizable. Being mostly bones and inoffensive, the task of gathering them up with spades and wooden pitchforks went fairly easy.

The burial party, under the command of Lieutenant John Jenkins Jr., used two ox carts to haul the bodies, and they had no problem in quickly filling both carts. They then dug a large hole near the highway, put the bodies in the common grave, and went back to the battlefield for more skeletons.

Fearing an attack by marauding Indians, the burial party quickly loaded the ox carts again, deposited them in the grave, hurriedly shoveled earth over the bones, and made a mound for identification at a future date. It didn't take long for the mound to wear down. It was plowed over and its exact location forgotten by the men involved. Fifty four years elapsed before the grave was rediscovered.

Many more bones had to be left on the battlefield that would have been buried had the circumstances been without danger for the burial party. In July 1779, Lieutenant Samuel Shute wrote:

"Went to the field where the two Butlers fought last Summer. There are a great many men's skulls to be picked up on the field—some with part of their hair on, the other part taken off with the scalps; others with bullet holes in, or with the skull split with the tomahawk, which was a very affecting scene."

There was no time to mourn the dead in that ill-fated period of the fall and winter of 1778-79 for it was the living who had to contend with the constant infiltration and depradation of the Iroquois. The ever-present danger of murder and capture brought many a sleepless night to the people of the Wyoming Valley.

Colonel Thomas Hartley. He commanded the first punitive expedition against the Iroquois after Wyoming.

CHAPTER TWENTY

Like angry bees whose hives had been invaded, the Iroquois whose northern country had been invaded now took to the offensive against Wyoming. They came in fast-moving bands of six to about twenty, large enough to cause damage and yet too small to create an effective defense against.

Besides the Swetland and Tripp attacks, and abductions referred to earlier, more settlers yet were to die and disappear at the hands of the Iroquois.

A militiaman, William Jameson, who had survived the Battle of Wyoming, was shot by the Iroquois near Hanover, south of Wilkes-Barre. He was wounded and fell off his horse. He tried to reach the woods to hide but the Iroquois overtook him and he was tomahawked and scalped. He lived for two more days even though part of his brain had been dashed out.

In November, at a mill near Nanticoke Falls, settlers William

Jackson, Edward Lester, his wife and four children, and an old man, Hageman, and his wife and daughter were captured by the Iroquois and marched up river. They then halted and Jackson, Lester, and Lester's oldest son were killed and scalped. Amazingly, the old man, Hageman, "escaped with Six wounds, and survived, although the food he took oozed from a spear wound in his side," as Miner tells it. The rest of the party was marched up to New York State by their captors.

The raids on the Wyoming Valley continued unabated. John Perkins was killed five days later in Plymouth and two days later Captain Robert Carr and Phillip Goss were ambushed near Wapwallopen, and were killed as they tried to escape by canoe. Almost at the same time, Robert Alexander and Amos Parker were also killed in the southern end of the Wyoming Valley.

A few days later, Isaac Inman in Hanover heard the calls of a wild turkey in the woods and went off in the afternoon to hunt for his supper. Although a shot was heard, the hunter never returned and a heavy snow began to fall. It wasn't until the following spring that his body was found, shot and scalped, with a war club left by his side to indicate the tribe and clan that had done the killing.

The Iroquois raids now became even bolder and more merciless. The entire four-member Utley family were killed and scalped near Nescopeck. The marauding Iroquois, after killing the mother, placed her mutilated body in a rocking chair for sport. Charles Miner was told, by an eyewitness to the grisly discovery, that the appearance of the scene of the slaughter was "enough to awaken horror and pity in a breast of marble."

Many of these attacks resulted not only in murder, but kidnapping as well. Most of these people taken were young and were given out to be adopted or used as manual laborers, farm help and servants. Some were later released, some escaped, others were never heard from again. The most famous case involved a little five year old girl often referred to as the "Lost Sister of Wyoming."

Jonathan Slocum was a Quaker who lived close to Fort Wyoming in Wilkes-Barre. He felt that his status as a religious non-combatant and his proximity to the Fort would keep his family safe from attack. It was a false sense of security, however, which brought him and his older sons to finish harvesting a corn field while his wife and two young children, Ebenezer and Frances, stayed home.

Mrs. Slocum heard the sudden rifle shot that morning, flung open the door, and saw before her the body of a neighbor boy, fifteen year old Nathan Kingsley Jr., and an Iroquois about to scalp him. The Kingsley family was living with the Slocums, since the father, Nathan Sr., had been taken by the Iroquois. Mrs. Slocum in panic grabbed her infant son and ran out the back door. Three Iroquois ransacked the house finding thirteen year old Ebenezer Slocum, who was lame, his sister Frances and the slain Kingsley boy's younger brother. When Mrs. Slocum saw them leading two of her children from the house, she ran back, pleading with the Iroquois not to take her children, pointing to the feet of Ebenezer, saying, "The child is lame; he can do thee no good!"

The Iroquois released Ebenezer, but ran off with little Frances and the young Kingsley boy despite the pleading of the mother. Although soldiers from the Fort came quickly to search for them in the adjoining woods, they were nowhere to be found. Grief stricken, Mrs.

Slocum returned to a thicket where she had hidden her infant son, and a soldier searching the area saw a movement in the bushes and raised his rifle to fire, but recognized Mrs. Slocum just in time.

The tragedy for Mrs. Slocum didn't end with the abduction of her daughter Frances. About a month later, her husband, Jonathan, her father, Isaac Tripp Sr., William Slocum, one of his sons, and Mrs. Slocum's brother were feeding cattle in a meadow near Fort Wyoming. Suddenly her husband was shot dead and her father speared and tomahawked. Both bodies were found scalped. Her brother William, who was wounded in the heel, escaped to sound the alarm. The Iroquois, however, escaped into the hills. Within a month Mrs. Slocum had lost a daughter, a husband, and a father to Indian depredations, all of which occured within the town plot in the center of which the fort was located!

It is no wonder that a frustrated Colonel Hartley wrote the following to the Supreme Executive Council of Pennsylvania: "Had one or two regiments been sent to Wyoming as I requested, these calamities would now not have happened."

Even the winter did not stop the raids. On February 18th, 1779, Lieutenant Asabel Buck, Stephen Pettebone, Elihu Williams Sr., and Frederick Follett were returning to Fort Wyoming from Kingston when they were ambushed by twenty Iroquois. Buck, Pettebone, and Williams were killed instantly and Follett was seriously wounded with seven spear wounds. Follett pretended to be dead and the Iroquois quickly scalped him and the three bodies of his comrades and fled. All this was done on the Kingston flats in broad daylight and within sight of the troops in the Kingston block house and Fort Wyoming. Follett was lying in a large pool of blood when the troops reached him. The Fort doctor, Dr. William Hooker Smith, held out no hope for his survival. Despite the fact that Follett's stomach was laid open, he made a miraculous recovery.

On the same day, apparently the same band of Iroquois killed and scalped Abel Dewey, Robert Alexander, and Amos Parker and took Michael Kelley and his daughter prisoners. These consecutive actions apparently appeared in a report by Major John Butler concerning a band of Delawares that "had a skirmish with the enemy at Wyoming in which they took three prisoners and seven scalps."

Early spring saw an increase in the number of Iroquois and a higher degree of audacity and confidence shown by them. On March 21st, two elderly men, Captain James Bidlack and Josiah Robins, were proceeding on horse back from Kingston to Plymouth. An Iroquois suddenly jumped from cover to seize the bridles of the horses. Both Rogers and Bidlack wheeled their horses and broke away, but Bidlack's saddle strap broke hurling him to the ground. He tried to escape but was overtaken by the Indians and made a prisoner. Rogers, meanwhile, raced his horse to the Kingston block house and safely reached his goal even though his clothing was pierced by several bullets narrowly missing his body. The garrison of the block house emerged to do battle with the pursuing Iroquois and Colonel Butler dispatched twenty-five men from Fort Wyoming to aid the block house garrison. Butler also fired the four pounder cannon at the charging Iroquois. They suddenly retreated, hoping to draw the troops into an ambush. The troops however saw a large number of Iroquois on the edge of the woods and prudently withdrew while a small skirmish ensued. During this period, the Iroquois drove off all the horses and cattle they could find.

Two days later, a force of between two hundred and fifty and three hundred Iroquois suddenly burst from the woods screaming their blood curdling war whoops. They swept across the Kingston flats and, in a semi-circle, charged across the shallow Susquehanna directly towards Fort Wyoming. The troops at the Fort were prepared and opened up with defensive deadly fire. The four pounder cannon was brought to bear and the chief leading the charge was cut in two by one of the cannon balls.

Adjacent to the Fort was the log house of Thaddeus Williams who that day was sick and confined to his bed. Caring for him was his elder son, Sergeant Thomas Williams, as well as Thomas' younger brother, who was also caring for his aged mother in the house.

Part of the Iroquois force attacking the Fort branched out to assault the house. The Iroquois rushed to the door twice trying to break it down and other attackers fired through openings in the logs seriously wounding the sick father. The Iroquois constantly let out their screams and whoops to terrify the occupants. Sergeant Williams maintained his coolness as did his younger brother. There were three rifles and plenty of ammunition in the house and the boy loaded one rifle as his older brother fired the other. The brothers were thus able to maintain a rapid and accurate field of fire power which took its toll on the Iroquois. Their whoops and yells decreased as more and more fell. When an Iroquois hit the ground, Sergeant Williams cooly waited for another to pull away the body and he would shoot him as well.

Suddenly, the screaming started again, and more Iroquois returned, this time with flaming arrows. As William's younger brother snuffed out the fire brands before they set the house on fire, Sergeant Williams took careful aim and brought down the Iroquois leader who was carrying a flaming torch. The Iroquois had enough and they dragged away their dead and wounded to join their brothers who had attacked the Fort and were now also retreating back across the river. All the Iroquois then carried away their casualties under withering fire and drove the settlers' livestock before them.

In his report to the Board of War, and to General Washington, Colonel Zebulon Butler wrote that although none of his men were killed, the Iroquois drove off fifty-one head of cattle and ten horses, and burned three barns filled with grain and hay. He stressed that the enemy was still in the area and their losses in the attack were unknown.

Butler sent the report by messenger to the Board of War in Philadelphia and upon its receipt one of the members of the Board, in the presence of the messenger, said, "It is impossible, it can't be so!" When Butler heard of this hasty reaction after all the pleas for aid, he became enraged that the Board had deluded itself into thinking that Wyoming did not need more men and material. Butler angrily wrote to Washington, "...that no officer who properly regarded his own honor, would, without the slightest evidence call in question the honor of a brother soldier."

On the evening following the Iroquois attack, one of the few Iroquois left on the battlefield near the Fort was found to be wounded in the thigh. The Iroquois was recognized as Anthony Turkey, who formerly lived in the Wyoming Valley but who had been seen on several raids against the settlers. The troops called out to him, "Surrender, Turkey, we won't hurt you!" Turkey turned on the soldiers and was killed.

The vengeful bitterness of the soldiers and settlers prompted them to put the body in an old canoe. They put a bow and arrow in his hand in a shooting position and lashed the seated body to the canoe. Pinned to the body was a written "pass," informing the reader to "let the bearer go to his master—King George or the Devil."

Lastly, a dead rooster was tied to the bow of the canoe and it was sent downstream. The canoe reached a point near Catawissa, and a man, seeing a drifting canoe rowed out to claim an easy prize. When he got close enough to see an Iroquois aiming an arrow at him, he quickly rowed back to shore to get his rifle and once more went out to do battle with the canoe's occupant. Upon finding the true situation, he towed the boat to shore, to the amusement of the town people, who then sent the canoe on its way.

Most American field officers, including Colonel Butler, who were stationed along the frontier, felt their forces had been neglected by the Board of War in accomodating Washington's need for men and supplies in the more populated areas. Had they known of Washington's consumate and covert interest in an overwhelming blow against the Six Nations in their own territory, these officers' anxieties would have been lessened.

As early as September, 1778, Washington in a letter to Governor Trumbull of Connecticut, wrote:

"I feel with you for the unfortunate frontiers exposed to all the inroads of an enemy, whose natural barbarity in war has been increased by the arts and influence of a civilized nation. I had early ordered for the defense of the inhabitants, Colonel Hartley's Regiment, Colonel (William) Butler's, Colonel Alden's, with the remains of Morgan's Rifle Corps. These, I believe, have been of considerable service, but I am unhappy in not having it in my power to afford them at present a more complete and sufficient security from this army to the purpose of carrying the war into the enemy's country."

Washington's practical purpose for this desire to strike into Indian country was to destroy their crops and livestock, which they raised to supply food for themselves and a large portion of the British Army. Another purpose was to relieve pressure on the Northern Frontier to free up needed troops and supplies for attacks on the main forces of the enemy.

Though Washington's dignity and coolness of purpose hid his true feelings from the outside world, his writings indicate that he never forgot the defeat he suffered at the hands of the Indians in the French and Indian War when he was a young aide to General Braddock. He was also obviously stung by the bogus Seneca peace overture—just before the attack on Wyoming on July 3rd, 1778. His unedited orders to Sullivan, which will be explored later, indicate that Washington learned from his mistakes. Washington was too level-headed to let passions consume him. Rather, by cool and secret planning, he chose the right time to strike, without mercy, at his long time adversaries, the Six Nations of the Iroquois.

An interesting letter sheds light upon Washington's private and covert efforts to obtain intelligence relating to the activities and location of the Iroquois. In such a letter from Colonel Patterson, dated March, 1779. to Colonel Butler, he wrote:

"Mr. Lemmon goes to your post to wait the return, and take into his care, Gershon Hicks; who is not to be examined or searched until he goes before his Excellency General Washington. I enclose to you his Excellency's letter. Be careful that your people, who are out on duty, or fatigue, receive Hicks, who may appear painted, and in a canoe...."

At about the same time, General Hand, on direct orders from Washington, sent a series of inquiries to Colonel Butler. Washington wanted to know the distances and routes to the Iroquois settlements as wall as their location and size. Butler was also questioned on availability of food in the Iroquois areas as well as means of transportion and condition of roads and terrain.

Colonel Butler replied with his answers to these inquiries which he made with the assistance of Lieutenant John Jenkins, who had earlier been a prisoner of the Iroquois and Tories in the Iroquois area and at Fort Niagara. Washington actually had Jenkins come to his headquarters for a personal briefing.

In a letter to Governor DeWitt Clinton of New York, dated March 3rd, 1779, Washington indicated that he had learned much about the Iroquois both from his own mistakes and from his gathered intelligence in the field:

"I am therefore to inform your Excellency that offensive operations against the hostile tribes of Indians have been meditated and determined upon some time since, and that preparations have been making for that purpose, and will be carried into execution....

But the profoundest secrecy was judged necessary to the success of such an enterprise.... With respect to the force to be employed on this occasion, it is scarcely necessary to observe that the detaching of a considerable number of Continental troops on such a remote expedition, would too much expose the country adjacent to the body of the enemy's army.... They should be a corps of active rangers, who are at the same time expert marksmen and accustomed to the irregular kind of wood fighting practiced by the Indians. Men of this description, embodied under proper officers, would be infinitely preferable to a superior number of militia, unacquainted with this species of war, and who would exhaust the magazines of ammunition and provision without rendering any effectual service."

Washington's first task was to find the right leadership for such an important expedition. He offered the command to one general after another, but was turned down repeatedly. They would each give different excuses for declining, but the real reason was obviously the lack of glory and honor to be obtained in combat against Iroquois rather than professional British soldiers.

Washington ruefully wrote a letter to the President of Congress:

"The plan of operations for the campaign being determined, a commanding officer was to be appointed for the Indian expedition. This command, according to all present appearances, will be probably of the second, if not the first, importance of the campaign. The officer conducting it has a flattering prospect of acquiring more credit than can be expected by any other this year; and he has the best reason to hope for success. General Lee, from his situation, was out of the question; General Schuyler (who by the way would have been most agreeable to me) was so uncertain of continuing in the army that I could not appoint him; General Putnam I need not mention. I therefore made the offer of it—for the appointment could no longer be delayed—to General Gates who was next in seniority."

By this time Washington could almost anticipate that Gates would turn down the command, and took the unusual step of enclosing the offer to General Gates in an envelope addressed to a young general named Major General John Sullivan. The letter, dated March 6, 1779, stated:

"Congress having determined upon an expedition of an extensive nature against the hostile tribes of the Indians of the Six Nations, the command is offered to Major General Gates as senior officer; but should he decline, it is my wish it should devolve upon you. That no time may be lost by General Gates' non-acceptance, I have put this letter under cover to him, and have desired him to forward it to you, should that be his determination. Should it, therefore, be sent to you, I must request you to set out as speedily as possible after the receipt of it; to headquarters, as the season is already far advanced. Upon your arrival, the whole plan of the expedition shall be communicated to you, and measures concerted for carrying it into execution. Nothing will contribute more to our success in the quarter where we really intend to strike, than alarming the enemy in a contrary one, and drawing their attention that way. To do this you may drop hints of an expedition to Canada.... I would wish you to keep this motive of your journey to headquarters a secret, because if it is known that an officer of your rank is to take command to the westward, it would be immediately concluded that the object must be considerable."

General Gates almost immediately declined the offer to lead the expedition in the following letter to Washington:

"Last night I had the honor of your Excellency's letter. The man who undertakes the Indian service should enjoy youth and strength—requisits I do not possess. It herefore grieved me that your Excellency should offer me the only command to which I am entirely unequal. In obedience to your command I have forwarded your letter to General Sullivan."

Washington was actually miffed by Gates' quick refusal as attested by a comment in a letter to Congress in which he stated:

"My letter to him (Gates) ... was conceived in very candid and polite terms, and it merited a different answer from the one given it."

Thus, by default, Major General John Sullivan was given command of the expedition against the Six Nations of the Iroquois. He was Washington's fifth choice!

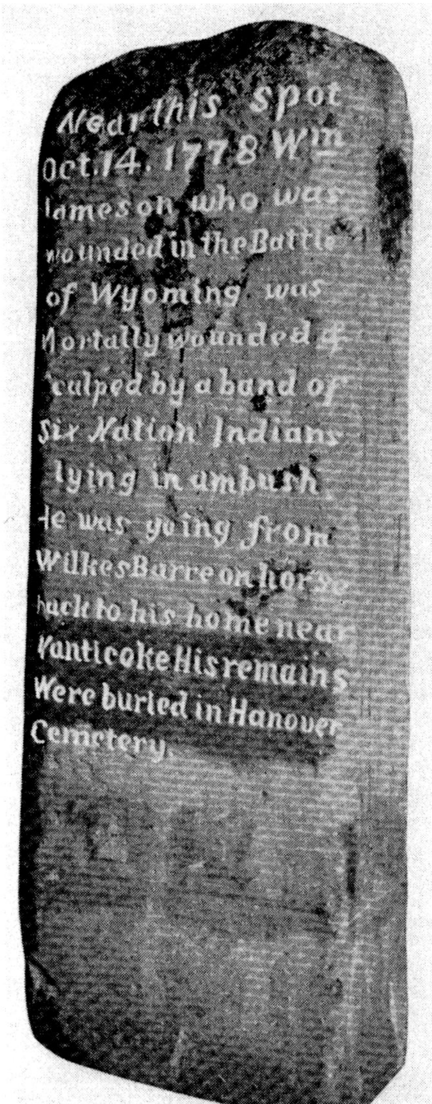

William Jameson Monument. Ambushed and killed by Indians on October 14, 1778, he was the last Wyoming Valley casualty of Indian Raids. (Courtesy of the Wyoming Valley Historical and Geographical Society)

CHAPTER TWENTY-ONE

Major General John Sullivan was thirty-nine years old when Washington gave him his first completely independent command. He was five feet eight inches in height, and walked very erect, which together with his broad shoulders made every effort of giving a commanding presence. His manner was dignified and sometimes arrogant, and when he couldn't have his way, his complaining and whining created a complete reversal of character. Another contradiction was that, though he was blessed with intelligence and ambition, he was also impulsive and argumentative, giving rise to cautious behavior and unpredictability. In spite of these contradictions, he was a born leader, accentuated by his personal appearance. He had piercing dark eyes and black curly hair and his barrel-chested, chunky body was usually displayed in expensive and perfectly fitting dress uniforms. He was a disciplinarian and was intensely loyal to his troops, especially when they performed and displayed well on the parade ground.

Sullivan was a New Hampshire lawyer from a poor background. He had quickly acquired a reputation as an efficient and ruthless collector of unpaid bills. Often he would take property and goods in compensation, and became rich, although he was an unpopular figure with many people in his town of Durham. To enhance his social image and contacts, he joined the New Hampshire militia and took part in the first military offensive measure against the Crown. In December 1774, he and other members of the militia broke into Fort William and Mary to obtain gunpowder, cannon, and munitions which were later used at Bunker Hill. He was made a brigadier when the Revolution broke out.

Except for a brief success at Trenton and Princeton, honor and glory evaded him. He was captured at the Battle of Long Island and then exchanged. When another officer was given a command he wanted, he wrote a complaint letter to Washington, who replied:

"No other officer of rank in the whole army has so often conceived himself neglected, slighted, and ill treated as you have done, and none I am sure, with less cause than yourself to entertain such ideas. If distant armies are to be formed there are several Gentleman before you, in point of rank, who have a right to claim a preference."

After unsuccessful campaigns at Brandywine and Germantown, he was given a command in Rhode Island and ordered to capture Newport with the aid of a French fleet. However, he constantly argued with his French allies in demanding that only his military plans be executed. He also complained that his troops were not being adequately supplied and pursued a campaign against the Commissary Department and other suppliers. After all this internal conflict,

Sullivan won a limited victory over the British, but never captured Newport.

It was after the Rhode Island campaign that the command of the expedition against the Iroquois was offered to Sullivan. Upon meeting with Washington at Middlebrook, New Jersey, the intelligence reports from Wyoming, the briefing accounts of Washington's spies, and Lieutenant John Jenkins' reports were turned over to Sullivan.

Washington issued the following orders, the portions in parenthesis being the parts edited out of Washington's writings either by himself or by contemporary biographers. The original text of the complete orders to Sullivan is quoted here:

"SIR,— The expedition you are appointed to command is to be directed against the hostile tribes of the Six Nations of Indians, with their associates and adherents. The immediate object is their *total destruction* and devastation, and the capture of as many persons of every age and sex as possible. (It will be essential to ruin their crops now in the ground, and prevent their planting more.)

"The troops to be employed are Clinton, Maxwell, Poor, and Hand's brigades, and the independent companies raised in the State of Pennsylvania. In Hand's brigade, I comprehend all the detached corps of Continental troops now on the Susquehanna, and Spencer's regiment. Cortland's I consider as belonging to Clinton's brigade. Alden's may go to Poor's, and Butler's and the rifle corps to Maxwell's or Hand's according to circumstances. Clinton's brigade, you are informed, has been ordered to rendezvous at Canojoharie, subject to your orders, either to form a junction with the main body on the Susquehanna by the way of Otsego, or to proceed up the Mohawk

River and co-operate in the best manner circumstances will permit, as you judge most advisable.

"As soon as your preparations are in sufficient forwardness, you will assemble your main body at Wyoming, and proceed to Tioga, taking from that place the most direct and practicable route into the heart of the Indian settlements. You will establish such intermediate posts as you think necessary for the security of your communications and convoys; nor need I caution you, while you leave a sufficiency of men for their defence, to take care to diminish your operating forces as little as possible. A fort at Tioga will be particularly necessary, either a stockade fort or an entrenched camp. If the latter, a block-house should be erected in the interior. I would recommend that some fort in the centre of the Indian country should be occupied with all expedition, with a sufficient quantity of provisions; whence parties should be detached to lay waste all the settlements around, with instructions to do it in the most effectual manner, that the country may not be *merely overrun, but* DESTROYED. I beg leave to suggest, as general rules that to govern your operations, rather than receive, attack, attended with as such impetuosity, shouting, and noise as possible; and to make the troops act in as loose and dispersed a way as is consistent with a proper degree of government, concert, and mutual support. It should be previously impressed upon the minds of the men, wherever they have an opportunity, to rush on with the war whoop and fixed bayonet. Nothing will disconcert and terrify the Indians more than this.

"(I need not urge the necessity of using every method in your power to gain intelligence of the enemy's strength, motions, and designs; nor need I suggest the extraordinary degree of vigilance and caution which will be necessary to guard against surprises from an adversary so secret, desultory, and rapid as the Indians. If a detachment operates on the Mohawk River, the commanding officer should be instructed to be very watchful that no troops come from Oswegatchie and Niagara to Oswego without his knowledge; and for this purpose he should keep trusty spies at those three places, to advertise him instantly of the movement of any party, and its force. This detachment should also endeavor to keep a constant intercourse with the main body. More than common care will be necessary of your arms and ammunition, from the nature of the service: they should be particularly inspected after a rain, or the passage of any deep water.) After you have very thoroughly completed the destruction of their settlements, if the Indians should show a disposition for peace, I would have you encourage it, on condition that they will give some decisive evidence of their sincerity, by delivering up some of the principal instigators of their past hostilities into our hands—Butler, Brant, the most mischievous of the Tories that have joined them, or any others they may have in their power, that we are interested to get into ours. They may possibly be engaged, by address, secrecy, and stratagem, to surprise the garrison of Niagara and the shipping on the lakes, and put them into our possession. This may be demanded as a condition of our friendship, and would be a most important point gained. If they render a service of this kind, you may stipulate to assist them in their distress with supplies of provision, and other articles of which they will stand in need, having regard, in the expectations you give them, to our real abilities to perform.

"I have no power at present to authorize you to conclude any treaty of peace with them; but you may agree upon the terms of one, letting them know that it must be finally ratified by Congress, and giving every assurance that it will. (I shall write to Congress on the subject, and endeavor to obtain more ample and definite authority. But you will not by any means listen to overtures of peace before the total *destruction* of their settlements is affected. It is likely enough that fear, if they are unable to oppose us, will compel them to make offers of peace; or policy may lead them to endeavor to amuse us in this way, to gain time and succor for more effectual opposition. Our future security will be in their inability to injure, in the distance to which they are driven, and in the terror with which the severity of the chastisement they will receive will impress them. Peace without this would be fallacious and temporary. New presents, and an addition of force from the enemy, would engage them to break on the first opportunity, and all the expense of our extensive preparations would be lost.) When we have effectually chastised them, we may then listen to peace, and endeavor to draw further advantages from their fear. But, even in that case, great caution will be necessary to guard against the snares which their treachery will hold out. They must be explicit in their promises, give substantial pledges for their performance, and execute their engagements with decision and despatch. Hostages are the only kind of security to be depended on.

"(Should Niagara fall into your hands in the way I have mentioned, you will do every thing in your power towards preserving and maintaining it, by establishing a chain of posts in such manner as shall appear to you most safe and effectual, and tending as little to reduce our general force as possible. This however, we shall be better able to decide as the future events of the campaign unfold themselves. I shall be more explicit on the subject hereafter.) When you have completed the objects of your expedition, unless otherwise directed in the mean time, you will return to form a junction with the main army, by the most convenient, expeditious, and secure route, according to circumstances. The Mohawk River, if it can be done without too great risk, will perhaps be most eligible on several accounts. Much should depend on the relative position of the main army at the time, (and it is impossible to foresee what may be the exigencies of the service in that quarter. This, united with other important reasons, makes it essential that your operations should be as rapid, and that the expedition should be performed in as little time, as will be consistent with its success and efficacy.

"And here I cannot forbear repeating to you my former caution, that your troops should move as light and as little encumbered as possible, even from their first outset. The state of our magazines demands it, as well as other considerations. If much time should be lost in transporting the troops and stores up the river, the provisions for the expedition will be consumed, and the general scarceness of our supplies will not permit their being replaced; consequently, the whole enterprise may be defeated. I would recommend it to you the purpose, that the general officers should make an actual inspection of the baggage of their several brigades; and absolutely reject, to be left behind at proper places, every article that can be dispensed with on the expedition. This is an extraordinary case, and requires extraordinary attention.) Relying perfectly upon your judgment, prudence, and activity, I have the highest expectation of success equal to our wishes; and I beg leave to assure you, that I anticipate with great pleasure the honor which will rebound to yourself, and the advantage to the common cause, from a happy termination of this important enterprise."

After examining the documents and orders, Sullivan decided he needed 3,000 men and a commensurate quantity of supplies and flat-bottomed barges for their transport, and almost immediately confronted the bureaucratic slowness of pace exhibited by the Board of War, prompting Alexander Hamilton, Secretary of the Treasury to write: "General Sullivan appears to be very anxious to have his supplies of every kind forwarded to him that he may begin his career—He is in his usual pother; but dispatch is certainly very desirable."

When Sullivan got to Easton, he found that the building of the road from Easton to Wyoming had hardly progressed from May 7th to June 18th. Sullivan used his excellent leadership abilities and efficiency to have the road, leading through sixty-five miles of wilderness and swamp land, completed to Wyoming. He immediately moved his men up the road and upon their arrival, his men marveled at the beauty of the Wyoming Valley.

One of his men stated in his diary that Wyoming was a beautiful place "through which runs the Susquehanna in a swift, delightful course." He added that the land was fertile and that the river teemed with shad, trout, and pickerel. General Maxwell remarked that the area would have been flourishing had it not been for the enemy depredations.

General Sullivan, however, was too busy complaining to notice his surroundings. He wrote to Washington that the salted meat provided was inedible, the bread was moldy, the quality of the troops was inadequate, and objected to the absence of Pennsylvania soldiers in Wyoming to reinforce the expedition.

General Greene, on the other hand, wrote sarcastically, "I think his army was liberally supplied and I hope his success will be equal to the preparation for the expedition." Greene added that he hoped Sullivan would avoid his army becoming too unwieldy for a wilderness campaign and wryly observed that Sullivan liked to do things in abundance. Green also wrote, "He is a friend of the Soldier, although it may be a bane upon the Citizen."

Washington was infuriated by Sullivan's delay in moving out. He had ordered Sullivan to travel light and Sullivan's delay for more supplies prompted him to write, "If you do not lighten yourself to the greatest possible degree, you will not only imminently hazard a defeat, but you will never be able to penetrate any distance into the Indian country."

Nevertheless, troops and supplies continued to arrive in Wyoming making the secrecy which Washington hoped for impossible. Finally on July 31st, the expedition of some 3,400 men departed up river on 214 boats, as well as by land. With banners flying and fife and drum bands playing, the boats, loaded with soldiers, artillery and ammunition, came upon Monocanock Island and the site of most of the carnage from the previous year's battle. At that point there was a moment of silence and the bands suddenly struck up a solemn dirge. To the soldiers in the barges there was no doubt that at least part of their mission was vengeance.

Without resistance, Sullivan's Expedition advanced to Wyalusing and then to Tioga, which was taken on August 11th. The scene was described by an army chaplain as follows:

"... Such an army crossing a river with so much regularity at a place so rapid and in width 330 yards, afforded the spectator a pleasing sight, and must have struck our enemies with awe. I must doubt whether the army of Alexander the Great encumbered as many difficulties with as much good humor as ours has evinced.

"The river being forded, we entered upon what is properly called Indian country.... The army being formed as usual we proceeded, sometimes in single files, and then in double, through a thicket, till we entered those beautiful plains where the Tioga Branch unites itself with the main river. On this level spot stood Queen Esther's Palace, burned by Colonel Hartley last fall. Over these plains our army marched towards the mouth of the Tioga in order of battle, the light troops being joined by two three-pounders from the regiment of artillery. The view of this was grand beyond description, as the ground for a great circuit was level, and the grass high and green. Drums were beating, fifes playing, colors flying ..."

Sullivan launched what he hoped to be a surprise attack on Chemung by advancing at night, but the village was deserted. A probing column pushed on a mile past Chemung and was ambushed. This constituted the first enemy resistance and a loss of four killed and eight wounded. The column returned to Chemung bringing back its killed and wounded.

Sullivan ordered the village destroyed including the main building of the town which Sullivan called the "Chapel and Council House."

Inside this house, Major James Norris found an idol "which might well enough be worshipped without a breach of the 2nd Commandment on account of its likeness to anything either in Heaven or earth." In addition to burning down the houses of the village, Sullivan also ordered all cornfields and gardens burned as well.

On August 22nd, General Clinton arrived in Tioga from eastern New York State bringing the combined forces to 4,400 men. The Tory spy network informed Major John Butler of this enlarged, approaching American force, and Butler warned the commander of Fort Niagara that this army consisted of "some of the best Continental Troops commanded by the most active of Rebel Generals."

Sullivan's next objective was Newtown, an Indian village south of what is now Elmira, New York. Expedition advance forces received information of an enemy breastwork on high ground ahead constituting a potential ambush. Sullivan decided to surround the enemy but his artillery opened up too soon, causing the Indians to retreat, and leaving their Tory allies exposed so that they, too, retreated. This was the last full-scale resistance the Indians would offer, and the rest of the campaign was spent razing settlements and destroying crops.

Catherine's Town was destroyed and then the army approached the Indian town of Kendaia on Seneca Lake. The advance party spotted a white man coming toward them and thinking him a Tory, they began to beat him with their rifle butts. Luckily one of the soldiers was from Wyoming and recognized the young man as Luke Swetland who had been captured by the Indians a year before. Swetland told the soldiers that he had been adopted by a Seneca family to replace their dead son and had been well treated. He stated that the Tories and Indians were fleeing in terror and living on nothing but green corn.

Advancing on Genesee Castle, Sullivan sent out an advance party of scouts under a Lieutenant Boyd. They were ambushed, but a few escaped to warn Sullivan of the ambush. Meanwhile, Boyd and Sergeant Michael Parker (who had been the only prisoners taken in the premature ambush) were horribly tortured by the Iroquois. Sullivan reported:

"They had whipped them in the most cruel manner, pulled out Boyd's nails, cut off his nose, plucked out one of his eyes, cut out his tongue, stabbed him with spears in sundry places and inflicted other tortures which decency will not permit me to mention; lastly cut off his head and left his body on the ground with that of his unfortunate companion, who appeared to have experienced nearly the same savage barbarity."

Sullivan's execution of a portion of Washington's orders that had been edited out of his official writings—that part about preventing future crops—was carried out by salting the land and cutting down all fruit trees. In regards to the part of the orders calling for total destruction of the Six Nations, clothing from small pox victims was left in deserted Indian villages for the returnees to pick up and use with the hope that an epidemic would sweep through the tribes.

After Sullivan destroyed Genesee castle and its outlying farm lands and orchards, he ordered a return to Tioga and Wyoming, destroying any and all Indian villages and farmland on the return trip.

Thousands of angry, beaten, and demoralized Indians fled to Fort Niagara. The two weakest tribes, the Cayuga and Onandaga sent new peace offers to Washington but he ignored them, possibly in reminder of the bogus peace offering by the Seneca which seduced him (as well as Congress) into inaction.

By November 1779, 2,628 Indians had fled to Fort Niagara, and that winter over 380 men, women and children had died of small pox and influenza.

Dr. Russel F. Weigley, Chairman of the History Department at Temple University, summed up the results of Sullivan's Raid:

"Sullivan had achieved the total destruction and devastation of the Iroquois territory that Washington had ordered. Forty towns and 160,000 bushels of corn were destroyed. The brutality of Sullivan's expedition set the style of warfare that would characterize the army's Indian campaigns."

Even more graphic is a paragraph written by J. Watts de Peyster, a descendant of a British Loyalist of the Revolutionary period:

"In 1779 occurred the famous invasion of the territory of the Six Nations by Sullivan. In one sense it was triumphant. It did the devil's work thoroughly. It converted a series of blooming gardens, teeming orchards and productive fields into wastes and ashes. It was a disgrace to developing civilization.... When white men scalp and flay Indians, and convert the skins of the latter's thighs into boot-tops, the question suggests itself—which were the savages, the Continental troops or the Indians? It is scarcely an exaggeration to say that, for every Indian slain and hut consumed in this campaign, 1,000 white men, women and children paid the penalty; and it almost unexceptionally admitted that the inextinguishable hatred of the redskins to the United States dates from this raid of Sullivan...."

The victorious army in blue paused in their return home under a late September sunset. Their jovial spirits were uplifted even further when it was announced that each of the five brigades, totaling over 4,000 men, would receive five gallons of rum to be watered down to grog.

Lieutenant Colonel Adam Hubley, who served under Sullivan in the Expedition, made the following entry in a journal that he kept, recording the growing drunkenness that night as the celebration progressed:

Saturday, Sept 25th 1779. After dinner the following toasts were drunk, the drums and fifes playing at intervals.

lst The thirteen states and their sponsors.

2nd The honorable, the American Congress.

3rd General Washington and the American Army.

4th The commander-in-chief of the Western Expedition.

5th The American Navy.

6th Our faithful allies, the united houses of Bourbon.

7th May the American Congress, and all her legislative representatives be endowed with virtue and wisdom, and may her independence be as firmly established as the pillars of time.

8th May the citizens of America, and her soldiers, be ever unanimous in the reciprocal support of each other.

9th May altercations, discord, and every degree of fraud, be totally banished form the peaceful shores of America.

10th May the memory of the brave Lieutenant Boyd, and the soldiers under his command, who were horribly massacred by the inhuman savages, or by their more barbarous and detestable allies, the British and Tories on the 13th inst., be ever dear to his country.

11th An honourable peace with America, or perpetual war with her enemies.

12th May the kingdom of Ireland merit a stripe on the American standard.

13th May the enemies of America be metamorphosed into pack horses, and sent on a western expedition against the Indians.

This encampment took place not far from the town of Newtown, where only the wall of a burned-out house remained. On this wall an American soldier had painted in blood, *REMEMBER WYOMING!*

Major General John Sullivan, Commander of the U.S. Government's punitive expedition against the Iroquois.

CHAPTER TWENTY-TWO

On June 2nd, 1780, James Madison wrote the following in a letter to Thomas Jefferson:

"The expedition of General Sullivan against the Six Nations seems by its effects rather to have exasperated than to have have terrified or disabled them."

After Sullivan and his expedition returned to Wyoming in early October, 1779, they quickly returned to their former posts and units, and Sullivan retired from the army. Wyoming was left as it was before the expedition took place: a small frontier post with barely over a hundred troops to defend it. It was hoped that Sullivan's campaign had chastised and quieted the Indians, and a calm winter seemed to bear out this hope.

The unusual period of peace in the Wyoming Valley was suddenly shattered on March 27th, 1780, when the alarm cannon's roar reverberated through the Valley. It warned the settlers and the troops that the Iroquois had returned to exact their revenge.

Lebbeus Hammond, who had earlier escaped Queen Esther's captivity and killings, was captured by a pair of Iroquois. A few hours later, four Iroquois captured Thomas Bennett and his sixteen-year-old son Andrew while plowing their fields above Forty Fort. The Iroquois hurried their captives twelve miles north to Kingston Mountain where they overtook two other Iroquois and their captive, Lebbeus Hammond. The six Indians and three captives camped for the night, and the next day were force-marched further north towards Meshoppen.

En route, they encountered a raiding party of thirty Indians led by a Tory named Moses Mount, who was known by Bennet and Hammond. Mount questioned the two captlves about the strength and defenses of Wyoming. The captives told Mount enough of an exaggeration to discourage the raiders. They said that Wyoming had over 300 well-armed and provisioned troops as well as a cannon. Mount said they would bypass Wyoming and strike to the south, but 500 Iroquois were on their way and another 500 would leave Fort Niagara shortly, to revenge Sullivan's Raid. When the tall stories were done, the little band of Indians and captives continued north.

That night Thomas Bennet was given the task of building a fire. Due to his age he was the least feared and was allowed to go unbound. Bennet asked the Iroquois leader for an awl to fasten a button, to which the Iroquois replied knowingly, "No want button for one night." Bennet's request was refused, but it had warned him of impending death.

The Iroquois then left to hunt and get water from a stream nearby. Bennet whispered to Hammond that they had to escape or be killed, and Hammond agreed. The Iroquois became tired after a heavy meal of venison and due to their long march. They lay down next to the fire and tied young Andrew Bennet between them. Except for an old one who stood guard, the Iroquois all fell asleep. The old one sat by the fire, sleepily picking the meat from a cooked deer head with his knife. By his side was his spear, and as Bennet sat by the Iroquois' side, Bennet casually took the spear and absently rolled onto his thigh. At the moment that the old Iroquois was least attentive, Bennet struck, thrusting the spear into the his side and he fell onto the burning logs.

With the agility of a young man, he cut his son and Hammond loose and three of the Iroquois were tomahawked and killed while they slept. Another was wounded, but escaped and later died. The remaining Iroquois escaped unhurt. The former captives made their way back to Fort Wyoming returning with their booty captured from the Indians: five rifles, spears, tomahawks and the most poignant of all, the silver-mounted sword inscribed with the name of Lieutenant Thomas Boyd which the Indians had taken from him before they tortured and killed him.

Major John Butler made a terse comment about the escape when he wrote from Fort Niagara in a report dated April 29th, 1780:

"Scouts have been out during the Winter. One party returning with prisoners, through carelessness, let them untie themselves at night, so that after killing five Indians they escaped."

On the same day that Bennet and Hammond were taken prisoners a band of ten Iroquois raided Hanover and shot Asa Upson as he was making maple sugar. They then tomahawked and scalped him, taking with them a fourteen-year-old boy named Jonah Rogers who was helping Upson. Slipping down river to Fishing Creek, they then surprised and attacked the Van Campen family, capturing twenty-year-old Moses Van Campen, a lieutenant in the Pennsylvania Militia. Van Campen's father, brother, and uncle were killed and scalped but the Iroquois spared the life of Peter Pence, a young man from Sunbury whose real name was probably Bentz and became a frontiersman after the Revolution.

The raiding party and their captives were suddenly intercepted by Captain John Franklin and four men on a scouting mission, but the Iroquois wounded two of them and broke off the engagement to push on to the north. Before long they came across another family making maple sugar. Abraham Pike, his wife and daughter were all captured. The wife and child were releaed but the Iroquois set out again with Pike as a prisoner.

Pike was an Irishman and a deserter from the British Army. He knew what fate awaited him if he was forced to complete the journey to Fort Niagara.

That night, fifteen miles below Tioga Point along the Susquehanna, Pike told the others of a plan he had to escape. All the captives were bound except young Jonah Rogers, who had "procured" a knife and an ax from one of the less alert captors. When all the Iroquois were asleep, Rogers cut Pike loose and then freed the other men also. One of the Iroquois awoke and Peter Pence fired at him, wounding him. The rest ran off, and Moses Van Campen and Pence fired at the fleeing Iroquois. Three were killed and the rest escaped. Pike scalped the dead ones and recovered the scalps of the people the Iroquois had killed. These scalps, together with twelve rifles and thirty blankets, comprised the booty taken. The newly liberated men and boys quickly built a raft, and with their spoils of battle descended the Susquehanna to Wyoming and safety.

Fifty-three years later, Jonah Rogers at the age of sixty-seven wrote an account of this event in the *Wyoming Republican* which he concluded with the sentence, "On the 6th of April, while the 'go-to-bed drum' (as it was called) was beating at Wilkes-Barre Fort, we reached the block house in Kingston, having suffered much with hunger during our travel."

Zebulon Butler reported the series of attacks and dramatic escapes to the Board of War and to General Washington. At the end of his reports, he mentioned the difficulty of maintaining an adequate defense without the proper amount of men and money, and of having to use volunteer militia.

The Board of War replied with a lecture on pinching pennies:

"With respect to your having engaged some of the Militia to do duty, the Board approves of your conduct. While in actual service they should receive Continental pay and rations. But the Board relies on your discretion, that you will keep them no longer in service than the safety of your Garrison absolutely requires; and the Public Finances are now so much exhausted that, unless it is maintained on the most economic principles, it must be given up from necessity.

"From circumstances it is presumed that you will not have occasion to employ more than 30 militia, and these must not be kept a moment longer than requisite ..."

George Washington replied with sympathy and hope:

"... I am extremely sorry to find that parties of the Enemy have appeared and committed hostilities in the neighborhood of Wyoming. It is not in my power to afford any troops from the army and I should hope those already there and the inhabitants will be able to repel at least any incursions by light parties. It was my intention, as I informed you that you should join your regiment immediately after your return; however, I am induced from the face of things to let you continue where you are for the present and you will remain till further orders. Should further depredations and mischiefs be committed by the enemy—you will take occasion to inform me of them. I am, sir, Yr most Obe't Servant, G. Washington."

In true Yankee spirit, the settlers organized their own committee for self-protection to send out scouts on a strictly volunteer basis. The members included Lieutenant Rosewell Franklin and Ensign John Comstock under the leadership of Captain John Franklin. Twenty-nine men volunteered.

Captain Franklin was a born leader and at the same time, a soldier, a Justice of the Peace, a farmer, a hunter who seemed always successful in supplying the community with meat, and a committee leader or member in every phase of government in the Wyoming Valley.

When John Franklin was a boy of seventeen, his parents were made aware that he was gifted with a remarkable memory and a strong intellect. He had accompanied his parents to church one Sunday in his home town of Canaan, Connecticut. It was a plain meeting house without a ceiling so that the beams and rafters were exposed to view. John had noticed that his austere father had sat through the sermon with a great deal of uneasiness, but couldn't understand why.

When the family returned home, his father said, "John, it is my duty to give you a severe thrashing and you shall have it presently, so prepare yourself."

John asked, "But you won't whip me, father, without telling me what for?"

"No, certainly not—your conduct at church is the cause, instead of attending to the sermon, you were all the while gaping about as if you were counting the beams and rafters of the meeting house."

John replied, "Well, father, can you repeat the sermon?"

"Sermon, no!" answered his father, "I had as much as I could do to watch your inattention."

John said, "If I'll tell you all the minister said, you won't whip me?"

"No, John, no," answered his father, "but that is impossible."

Young John Franklin then proceeded to recite the sermon verbatim, complete with inflections and points of emphasis.

"And now father," added John, "I can tell you exactly how many beams and rafters there are in the meeting house!"

In her book *Early Times on the Susquehanna,* Mrs. George A. Perkins described Franklin in his later years as "... a tall patriarchal looking man, bent with years and the cares and labors of early life; of a depressed though expressive countenance; his face pitted with small pox; rather negligent of his personal appearance, though always the gentleman—and always commanding the respect and attention of those who knew him. He frequently wore a long blue cloak, and on public occasions a three cornered hat, and small clothes, and always carried a little cane, used particularly on funeral occasions to preserve order in the procession, of which, he was marshal in those days. Sometimes he visited the schools, giving a word of advice, and always presiding at town meetings.

"As a young man of thirty-one in 1780, he was a whirlwind of energy and on June 6th, he led a scouting expedition of five men sixty-five miles up the Susquehanna. Near Wysox they captured three Tories—Adam and Jacob Bowman and Henry Hoover. They were all members of Butler's Rangers and had come down from Fort Niagara. Captured with the Tories was "a fine lot of plunder valued at forty-six pounds, eighteen shillings and eleven pence. Captain Franklin and Sergeant Baldwin each shared a silver watch, several pocket compasses, silver buttons, and sleeve buttons. A scarlet broadcloth coat, several gold pieces, and a beautiful spy glass attest the consequence of the prisoners. The canoes sold for four pounds, ten shillings. Colonel Z. Butler purchased the spy glass from the victors, estimated at three guineas, hard money."

The Tory prisoners were sent under guard to Continental Army headquarters at Morristown, New Jersey. There they were tried and convicted and returned to Fort Wyoming as prisoners of war.

Iroquois raids now bypassed Wyoming and struck at areas to the south. Whether this was because of the resistance and escapes of previous raids or because of the scouting of Captain Franklin and his men is not known, but the Iroquois turned their attention to more vulnerable areas.

Mahoning was attacked in May and several people were killed and scalped, and Benjamin Gilbert, a Quaker, and Abigail Dodson, a girl of twelve or thirteen, were taken prisoner and sent to Niagara.

In September, a band of thirty Iroquois struck at Scotch Valley, now known as Conyngham, and Sugarloaf, northwest of Hazleton. The Tory inhabitants of the area had heard that a detachment of Pennsylvania militia were on their way to Fort Allen to disperse and arrest them. They made contact with the Iroquois on the north side of the Susquehanna and told them of the approaching militia. The Iroquois quickly dispersed to Sugarloaf Valley and set up an ambush to await the militiamen.

On Sunday, September 10th, Captain Daniel Klader in command, with Lieutenant John Meyer second in command, arrived with forty-one Pennsylvania militia. In an open field, now occupied by the Hazleton Country Club, the tired soldiers threw off their knapsacks and rifles to rest. Suddenly, musket fire rang out and with shrill war whoops the Iroquois were upon them. Captain Klader and thirteen men were killed, stripped, and scalped. Lieutenant Meyer and two soldiers were taken prisoner and the remainder of the detachment fled and escaped. One Iroquois was killed and their chief, Roland Montour, Queen Esther's nephew, was wounded in the arm and died the following week.

The raiders and their three captives headed for the Susquehanna which they followed to Harvey's Creek, burning Benjamin Harvey's sawmill and the Shickshinny grain mills enroute. That night, Lieutenant Mayer escaped to Fort Wyoming and told the story of the Sugarloaf Massacre. Some of Captain John Franklin's scouts actually intercepted some of these Iroquois upriver, recovering some booty taken south of Wyoming.

At this point there occurred a distasteful echo of the past that seemed a portent of the future. Food and provisions for Wyoming were not arriving from Sunbury and some foods became scarce in the Valley. Colonel Butler wrote on October 8th, 1780, "... we are entirely out of bread and meat. We live on eels and corn, and the eels seem to be most done."

On October 24th, Wyoming was startled by the news that Colonel Hunter, of the Pennsylvania militia at Fort Augusta (Sunbury), had stopped the boats bound for Wyoming with provisions for the garrison. This was done in spite of the fact that the war against their common enemies, the Iroquois, Tories and British, was still in progress. Charles Miner stated in regard to this situation, "This was the first incident which had occurred for three years, exhibiting the smothered, but, by no means extinguished jealousy, that existed on the part of Pennsylvania, towards the Connecticut garrison and settlement."

Luckily, this period of food scarcity took place during a time that Wyoming seemed to benefit from an apparent immunity to Iroquois raids. Soon the harvest was in, and food was once more abundant in Wyoming though the blockade on the Susquehanna still persisted.

The Fall passed without incident and then on December 6th, the peace was suddenly shattered in the midst of a snowstorm. That evening, Benjamin Harvey, his daughter Lucy, his son Elisha, and George P. Ransom, a Continental soldier, together with four militiamen and a woman named Lucy Bullock, were drinking hard cider around the fireplace in Harvey's home in Plymouth. A heavy snow that had fallen all day blanketed the area and kept the group indoors. Soft knocks on the door were heard followed by sharper knocks. Benjamin Harvey unbolted the door and five Iroquois in full war paint rushed in and tied up the occupants. These five Iroquois, under the command of Lieutenant John Turney, comprised the entire raiding party. They had left Fort Niagara for the purpose of resuming raids on Wyoming.

The raiders marched their nine captives out into the cold night and through the snow to the top of Shawanese Mountain. There, the Indian leader painted the faces of the two women in Iroquois style and said to them after untying them, "Go, tell Colonel Butler I put on this paint."

Lucy Harvey and Lucy Bullock said their farewells to the captives, never expecting to see them again. They hurried through the snow, down to the valley and through the dark forest to the Wilkes-Barre ferry, where they awakened the ferryman, who took them across to Fort Wyoming. When the women told their story to the fort commander, he ordered the alarm cannon to be fired. By this time however, the captors and the captives were far beyond the sound of the signal. When morning came the raiding party, which had traveled all through the night, were far from their pursuers under Captain Franklin and all that was found was their canoes.

The captives were bound but still forced to carry their own plundered goods on their backs. None complained more than Benjamin Harvey, who was fifty-nine years old and six-foot-three and in the best of condition. Harvey berated and cursed his captors calling them "British red coats and red devils." With that, Turney turned Harvey over to the Iroquois who decided to kill him. They tied Harvey to a tree. Then the old chief measured off fifty feet, selected three young braves, and gave each of them a tomahawk. The chief pointed to Harvey's head as their target. The first brave threw the tomahawk which traveled end over end to sink into the tree five or six inches above Harvey's head. The second and third braves also missed. The young braves became angry over their embarrassment and apparent lack of skill and wanted to try again. However the old chief saw the misses as intervention by the Great Spirit and called off the execution.

After much suffering from cold and hunger in the wilderness in the midst of winter, and pushed to the point where they had to eat one of their horses to survive, they finally arrived at Fort Niagara. When spring came, Harvey and the rest of the prisoners were sent to a farm to grow crops for the Iroquois and Tories at Fort Niagara, but Benjamin Harvey, because of his age, was released and allowed to go home with just the clothes on his back. He followed the Chemung and Susquehanna Rivers homeward, but on the last leg of his return he saw signs of Iroquois activity, and he detoured through the wilderness and got lost in a heavy rainstorm. Harvey had no food. After the rain, he climbed a ridge and saw water shimmering in the sunlight through the trees. Thinking the water to be the Susquehanna, he descended the ridge and found the body of water to be an unknown large lake, which was subsequently named after him. Following the lake's outlet, now known as Harvey's Creek, he came to Nanticoke and was soon reunited with his loved ones.

The winter of 1780-1781 now set in, aggravated by a return to food shortages caused by a persistent blockade of foodstuffs down the Susquehanna. Colonel Butler complained to the Board of War which in turn notified Congress and a Congressional committee reported the following to Congress in November: "That in their opinion the causes of the distress under which the garrison of Wyoming now labors, and has labored for some time past, originate from a jealousy subsisting between the States of Pennsylvania and Connecticut on account of a territorial claim. They find however, that the Post of Wyoming was originally established by Congress as a necessary means for the defense of a frontier and for the purpose of protecting the inhabitants of that quarter from the encroachments of the savages. That ever since its establishment, it has been under the direction of Congress, the Board of War, or the Commander-in-chief; has been garrisoned by Continental officers and soldiers and supplied with provisions from the Continental stores.

"They do not, therefore, think it advisable that this post should be discontinued by Congress until they are informed by the Commander-in-chief that it is unnecessary for the general defense. But your committee is of the opinion that it is becoming the wisdom of Congress, at the same time, that they carefully guard the citizens of these states against the attacks of the common enemy, to remove as far as in their power, every cause of jealousy or discontent between states which might endanger the harmony of the general Union."

The very same day, Congress adopted the following resolutions:

"Resolved, That the Commander-in-chief be directed, if he shall judge the post at Wyoming necessary to relieve the garrison as soon as may be by troops from the Continental army not belonging to the lines of Pennsylvania or Connecticut, or citizens of either of the said states; and that the present and future garrison continue to be supplied by the Commissary General from the magazines of the Continent, by purchase, or out of the quota of provisions raised by any state for the use of the Continent.

"Resolved, That the State of Pennsylvania be informed of the steps Congress has taken to remove every subject of jealousy or discontent, and that they be requested to order the supplies which were stopped by Lieutenant Hunter, on their progress to Wyoming, to be immediately forwarded to that garrison, to relieve its present urgent distresses."

On December 29, 1780, Washington at New Windsor, New York, wrote the following to Colonel Butler in Wilkes-Barre:

"Congress having in order to remove all cause of jealousy and discontent between the States of Pennsylvania and Connecticut, directed me to withdraw the present garrison of Wyoming and to replace them with troops from the Continental army not belonging to the Line of Pennsylvania or Connecticut, or citizens of either of the said states, I have for that purpose ordered Captain Mitchell of the Jersey Line to relieve you. You will, therefore, upon his arrival deliver up the post to him, and march with all the men at present under your command, and join the army in the neighborhood of this place."

In a very private and revealing letter from Joseph Reed, President of the Supreme Executive Council of Pennsylvania, to Colonel Hunter at Sunbury, the admission was made that there was pressure exerted by Pennsylvania to replace Connecticut soldiers at Wyoming:

"The Congress having lately, *on our representations*, passed a Resolve directing General Washington with troops of a state indifferent to the dispute subsisting between this state and Connecticut; and his Excellency having, agreeable thereto, ordered a detachment of the Jersey Line under Captain Mitchell to occupy that post, we now think it is our duty to revoke the order formerly given to you to stay the passing of provisions and supplies from this state, and request you give to Captain Mitchell—who is a gentleman of fair character and a good officer all the assistance and civility in your power.

"As we are informed that there are quantities of provisions in that country, we request you to consult Captain Mitchell on the appointment of some person to act as Purchaser at Wyoming and its vicinity on behalf of the state. As he is to act under the state, it is needless to add that he must be a *person well affected to its interests*, as well as trustworthy in other respects."

In February 1782, Colonel Butler and his troops were replaced and they proceeded to their new post on the Hudson, from which Butler then wrote to a Connecticut representative in Congress urging that Connecticut judges be appointed to Wyoming stating:

"My reason for urging this is our settlers have been very much distressed with fears from the Pennsylvania enemies since our men were called away, but finally concluded the Civil Law was sufficient to keep out Pennsylvania settlers. But now, to have no Court, it will shock them and the opposite party to take advantage of it."

Dr. William Hooker of Wyoming also suspected a Pennemite conspiracy when he wrote the following to Butler:

"Congress was wearied out with complaints against you and Captain Spaulding's company and at length you were removed from the post—I think by the suggestion and influence of the Pennemite claimers. The second step was, troops sent from the Jersies to this post—and in that state a great part of the claimers live. These troops are commanded by Captain Mitchell, who to my satisfaction, is a party man.... If we are betrayed the Lord only knows what will become of us ..."

An old wound, covered by a facade of national unity against a common enemy, was now reopened, and the infection therein was one of greed and avarice for land.

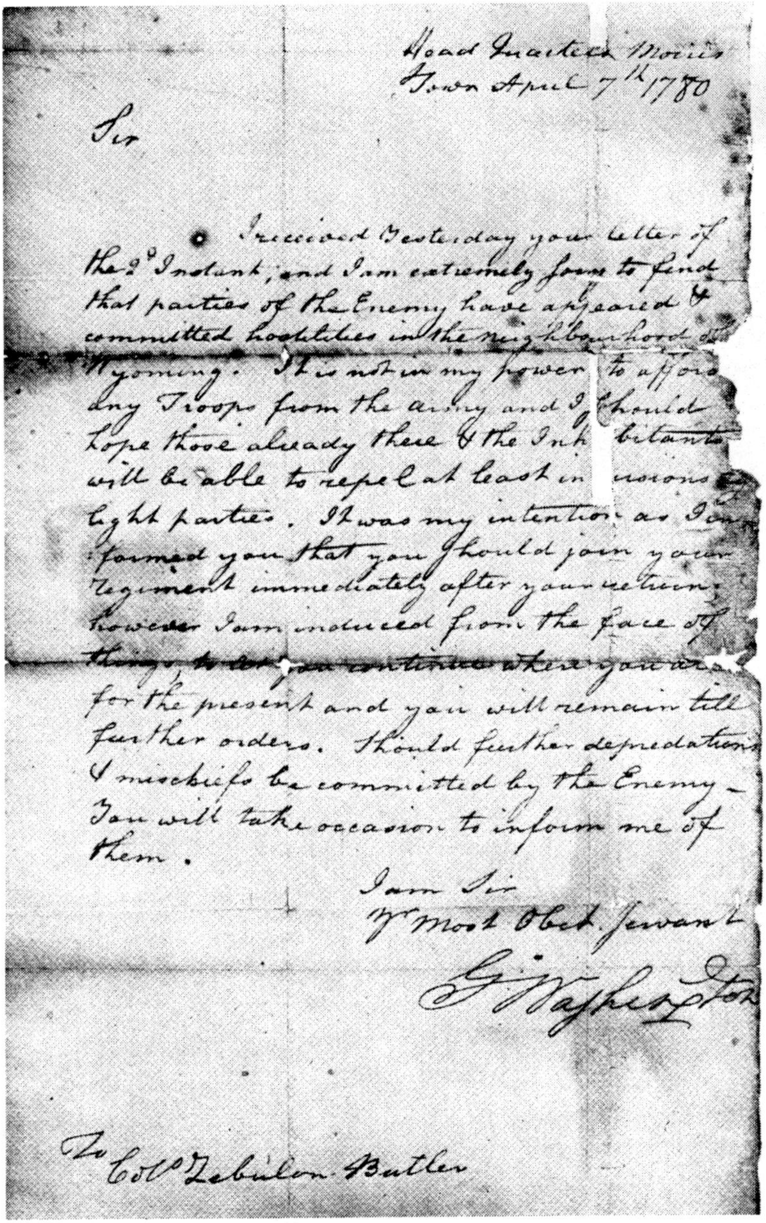

Head Quarters Morris
Town April 7th 1780

Sir

I received Yesterday your letter of the 2d Instant; and I am extremely sorry to find that parties of the Enemy have appeared & committed hostilities in the neighbourhood of Wyoming. It is not in my power to afford any Troops from the army and I should hope those already there & the Inhabitants will be able to repel at least incursions of light parties. It was my intention as I informed you that you should join your Regiment immediately after your return; however I am induced from the face of things, to let you continue where you are for the present and you will remain till further orders. Should further depredations & mischiefs be committed by the Enemy — You will take occasion to inform me of them.

I am Sir
Yr Most Obet. Servant
G: Washington

To
Colo Zebulon Butler

Copy of the letter of reply from General George Washington to Zebulon Butler, April 7, 1780, offering sympathy to Wyoming.

CHAPTER TWENTY-THREE

As if to test the new garrison of New Jersey troops in Wyoming, the Iroquois raiding parties returned to Wyoming in June, 1781.

A group of twelve Iroquois suddenly appeared before a block house in Buttonwood in the Hanover Area three miles south of Wilkes-Barre. They made an uncharacteristic frontal attack on a prepared defensive position and took the consequences. There were women within the block house to load rifles for the men who laid down a field of effective fire power. When the alarm cannon brought a party of soldiers hurrying to the block house they found pools of blood but the Iroquois had carried off their casualties, and Lieutenant Rosewell Franklin had killed at least one of them.

Eight days later, Iroquois appeared in Shohola, north of Wyoming, killed an old man, and took three prisoners. The raiding party was overtaken along the Delaware and the prisoners were liberated. A mortally wounded Iroquois, before dying, said his group had been out for a long time and was the same party that had attacked the block house in Hanover.

In the midst of all these renewed Iroquois attacks, the Reverend Jacob Johnson returned from exile in Connecticut with his family. He was full of spirit, fire and brimstone, preaching the righteousness of religion, liberty, and the Connecticut claim. He was warmly and lovingly welcomed by the settlers of Wyoming Valley. As Miner relates:

"... in season and out of season he went from place to place, awakening sinners to repentance, arousing the people to new efforts and sacrifices against the tyranny of England, and exhorting them by all means to adhere to and support their righteous claim to their lands."

In the midst of years of attack by the Iroquois, and eviction by the Pennemites, he quickly raised the spirits of the people throughout the Wyoming area, but his own spirits were suddenly dashed when his daughter, who was also the wife of Colonel Zebulon Butler, suddenly died of typhoid fever while her husband was on duty in New York. Typhus was to claim several more lives that summer before it ran its course.

Before the summer was out, yet another Iroquois attack would take its toll. On July 3rd, on the road from Wyoming to the Delaware, George Larned and his aged father were shot and scalped near their home. George's brother John shot and killed one of the attacking raiders, but the rest broke into the Larned home and carried off George Larned's wife and four-month-old infant. Other settlers pursued the Iroquois who abandoned their horses, scalps, and plunder, and finding the infant too great a burden, dashed out its brains.

Apparently the Iroquois never forgot their defeat at the hands of Lieutenant Rosewell Franklin and his men at the Hanover block house in the previous June. Again they attacked Hanover and carried off Franklin's son of sixteen and his foster son of thirteen. A detachment from the Fort pursued the Iroquois, who nevertheless escaped with their young captives and stolen horses.

This raid obviously was not enought to slake the vengeance of the Iroquois against Lieutenant Franklin. The following April, Franklin was outside the Hanover block house searching in the woods for some missing hogs. His wife and four children were in the house when eight Iroquois broke in, seized the mother and the children as well as plundered goods, and set fire to the house. The Iroquois ran off into the woods.

Lieutenant Rosewell Franklin saw his house on fire, and finding his family gone, hurried to Fort Wyoming to fire the alarm cannon. A rescue party of seven men under Sergeant Thomas Baldwin set out immediately, taking a route to hopefully cut off the marauders. Baldwin and his men arrived at Wyalusing Creek sixty miles from Wyoming and lay in wait and hiding. Although the ambush was well-hidden, the approaching Iroquois detoured the area chosen by Baldwin. Though Baldwin and his men fired at the fleeing Iroquois, they had to be careful not to hit the captives. In the midst of the firing three of the Franklin children, two little girls and a boy, ran from their captives to safety. Enraged, the Iroquois shot Mrs. Franklin. The Iroquois leader then raised infant Ichabod to his shoulder as a warning to the pursuers not to fire, and he fled with the remaining Iroquois. Franklin's infant son was never seen again. Mrs, Franklin's body was given a decent burial and the remaining three Franklin children were returned to Wyoming by the rescue party.

The postscript to the story is equally tragic. Although Lieutenant Franklin's son and foster son were returned from captivity after the war, the sad memories sustained caused Franklin to seek a new life with his children in New York State. He settled on untitled lands in controversy between New York and Massachusetts. He had two successful years of farming but then his house and crops were burned by others seeking title. This last event proved too much for Rosewell Franklin and, courageous and perservering as he was, he put an end to his life.

Toward the end of 1781, news of Cornwallis's surrender at Yorktown brought joy and hope to the people of the Wyoming Valley. Equally welcome was the return of Benjamin Harvey, described earlier, and the release and return of Captain James Bidlack. Both men had been released due to their advanced age and their lack of usefulness to the Tories.

On July 8, 1782, the last death at the hands of the Iroquois occurred in the Wyoming Valley. John Jameson, brother of William, as related earlier, killed and scalped by Iroquois in Hanover after Hartley's Raid in October of 1778, was himself set upon by Iroquois four years later.

John and his youngest brother Benjamin, not quite fourteen years old, were traveling on horseback with their neighbor, Asa Chapman, on their way to Wilkes-Barre from Hanover. Three miles below

Wilkes-Barre, Jameson, seeing some movement in the woods exclaimed, "There are Indians!" He was shot three times before he could wheel his horse around and he fell dead.

Chapman was behind him and had time to turn his horse, but he was wounded. He clung to his horse, however, and got to Wilkes-Barre where Captain John Franklin removed the rifle balls. But it was too late. Asa Chapman died after his farewell to his wife. The only survivor was the boy, Benjamin, who later returned to find the scalped body of his older brother. This was the last scalp taken by the Iroquois in the Valley and a painting depicting the final attack and titled "The Last Scalp" was later presented to the Wyoming Historical and Geological Society.

In 1879, John Jameson's grandson erected a marble pillar in Hanover with the following inscription:

"Near this Spot, 8 July, 1782, Lieut. John Jameson, Benjamin Jameson, and Asa Chapman, going to Wilkes-Barre, were attacked by a band of Six Nation Indians lying in ambush. Lieut. Jameson was killed and scalped. Chapman was mortally wounded and Benjamin escaped. They were the last men killed by Indians in the Wyoming Valley."

There were a series of British defeats after the surrender of Cornwallis and, in February 1782, in London, it was resolved by the House of Commons "...that it is the opinion of this House that a further prosecution of offensive war against America would, under present circumstances, be the means of weakening the efforts of this Country against her European enemies and tend to increase the mutual enmity so fatal to the interests both of Great Britain and America."

Peace negotiations were held in Paris and a peace treaty was signed in November, 1782, and took effect in the following January, 1783. This cessation of hostilities however, did not signal the end of Wyoming's troubles. These problems in turn were small in comparison with the turn of events that were to plague The Six Nations of the Iroquois.

What the Treaty of Paris did, to the amazement and consternation of the Iroquois, was to cede their ancestral lands to their sworn enemy, the United States of America. The Six Nations were led to believe that they were winning the war against America and from their standpoint, it could be argued that they actually were. Perhaps the Iroquois didn't feel conquered, but the young American government certainly felt that they had been.

Sidney F. Wise, Directorate of History for the Department of National Defense in Ottawa stated:

"When hostilities ceased in 1782, pending the outcome of peace negotiations in Paris, the Six Nations and their Loyalist allies were in effective military control of most of the tribal lands of the confederacy, and had succeeded in pushing the frontier of settlement back at many points. The rage of the Indians, when they discovered that the treaty of peace had ceded their lands to the new nation was intense. Colonel Maclean, the commandant at Niagara wrote to Haldiman (the Governor) in May 1783 paraphrasing their protests to him: 'They told me they never could believe that our King could pretend to cede to America what was not his to give, or that the Americans would accept from him what he had no right to grant ... the Indians were a free people subject to no power on earth ... They were but a handful of small people, but they would die like men, which they thought preferable to misery and distress if deprived of their hunting grounds ... If it was really true that the English had basely betrayed them by pretending to give up their country to the Americans without their consent, or consulting them, it was an act of cruelty and injustice that Christians *only* were capable of doing.'

"In the end, like the Loyalists, the Six Nations had to accept that the war was lost, and with it the prospect that their way of life might continue as they had known it. Some elected to remain in northern New York, but a great part of the Six Nations joined the Loyalists in settling what became the province of Ontario....

"So while for Iroquois and Loyalists both, Wyoming may have been a victory, and while their capacity to fight was not seriously affected by the Sullivan Expedition, they were losers in the end, and by the fortunes of war were compelled to work out their destinies in another land far removed from their original homes."

From the American point of view, the United States of America needed public i.e. Iroquois land to supply the needs of returning soldiers and their new families. Many veterans of Sullivan's Expedition saw these lands during their trek through Iroquois country and made it a point to try to obtain some of these tracts after the war.

Faced with poor credit and heavy debts, the new nation could only use land to stabilize a weak currency and to pay government debts and expenses. At first, both the states and the federal government claimed sovereignty over the Iroquois lands, but it was finally agreed that lands in western New York and Pennsylvania had state sovereignty and that all lands south of the Great Lakes and west of New York and Pennsylvania were subject to federal sovereignty.

The states and federal government also agreed that land was to be acquired from the Iroquois by "diplomacy" which unilaterally gave the Iroquois certain lands to live on, while declaring sovereignty over the remainder. There was implicit within this "humanitarian" gesture, the threat of force if not accepted by the Iroquois.

Neither the United States nor the separate states of New York and Pennsylvania recognized the Iroquois Confederacy as a state, but instead practiced a policy of "divide and conquer" by dealing with individual tribes or tribal segments so as to maintain a position of strength over a weaker contractual opponent.

The Fort Stanwix Treaty Council of 1784 entailed negotiations filled with coercions and insulting demands of the type inflicted upon conquered enemies. The result of the Council was the yielding of all Iroquois lands west of New York and Pennsylvania and the receipt by the Iroquois of a reservation in New York.

Two years later the Six Nations publicly repudiated the treaties drawn up at Fort Stanwix and threatened to go to war. However, in the intervening two years, it finally dawned upon the Iroquois that they really were a conquered people and they let the treaty stand by not resuming hostilities.

The various Iroquois tribes began to sell their lands in Pennsylvania and New York, and by 1789 all lands in eastern and central New York and Pennsylvania had been sold to the respective states except for small reservations. A third of all Seneca lands was bought by a land company for $5,000 plus an annuity of $500 per year. Many Iroquois, especially Mohawks, moved to Canada, as farmers and frontiersmen moved in.

The Iroquois who moved onto the reservations saw a complete change in their lifestyles. Deprived of their hunting grounds, they were forced to live on the public dole and off charity. They were expected to conform to their conqueror's mold and their children were sent to reservation schools where their culture and traditions were ignored in favor of white-society values.

The result was a breakdown of Iroquois moral values and the rise of family break ups, alcoholism, and suicide. It was this disintegration and decline, especially among the Seneca, that prompted three chiefs, Big Tree, Cornplanter, and Half Town, all veterans of the Battle of Wyoming, to present the following letter to George Washington:

"Father: The Voice of the Seneca nations speaks to you; the great counsellor in whose heart the wise men of all the *thirteen fires* (13 states) have placed their wisdom. It may be very small in your ears, and we, therefore, entreat you to hearken with attention; for we are able to speak of things which are to us very great.

"When your army entered the country of the Six Nations, we called you the *town destroyer*; to this day when your name is heard, our women look behind them and turn pale, and our childred cling close to the necks of their mothers.

"When our chiefs returned from Fort Stanwix, and laid before our council what had been done there, our nation was surprised to hear how great a country you had compelled them to give up to you, without your paying to us anything for it. Everyone said that your hearts were yet swelled with resentment against us for what had happened during the war, but that one day you would consider it with more kindness. We asked each other, *'What have we done to deserve such severe chastisement?'*

"Father: When you kindled your 13 fires separately, the wise men assembled at them told us that you were all brothers, the children of one great father, who regarded the red people as his children. They called us brothers, and invited us to his protection. They told us that he resided beyond the great water where the sun first rises; and that he was a king whose power no people could resist, and that his goodness was as bright as the sun. What they said went to our hearts. We accepted the invitation, and promised to obey him. What the Seneca nation promises, they faithfully perform. When you refused obedience to that king, he commanded us to assist his beloved men in making you sober. In obeying him, we did no more than yourselves had led us to promise. We were deceived; but your people teaching us to confide in that king, had helped to deceive us; and we now appeal to your breast. *Is all the blame ours?*

"Father: When we saw that we had been deceived, and heard the invitation which you gave us to draw near to the fire you had kindled, and talk with you concerning peace, we made haste towards it. You told us you could crush us to nothing; and you demanded from us a great country, as the price of that peace which you had offered us: *as if our want of strength had destroyed our rights.* Our chief had felt your power, and were unable to contend against you, and they therefore gave up that country. What they had agreed to has bound our nation, but your anger against us must by this time be cooled, and although our strength is not increased, nor your power become less, we ask you to consider calmly—*Were the terms dictated to us by your commissioners reasonable and just? ...*

"Father: You have said that we were in your hand, and that by closing it you could crush us to nothing. Are you determined to crush us? If you are, tell us so; that those of our nation who have become your children, and have determined to die so, we may know what to do. In this case, one chief has said he would ask you to put him out of his pain. Another, who will not think of dying by the hand of his father, or his brother, has said he will retire to the Chataughque, eat of the fatal root, and sleep with his fathers in peace.

"All the land we have been speaking of belonged to the Six Nations. No part of it ever belonged to the King of England, and he could not give it to you.

"Hear us once more. At Fort Stanwix we agreed to deliver up those of our people who should do you any wrong, and that you might try them and punish them according to your law. We delivered up two men accordingly. But instead of trying them according to your law, the lowest of your people took them to your magistrate, and put them immediately to death. It is just to punish the murder with death; but the Senecas do not deliver up their people to men who disregard the treaties of their own nation."

The Last Scalp. Artist unknown. Courtesy Wyoming Valley Historical and Geographical Society.

CHAPTER TWENTY-FOUR

The end of the Revolutionary War brought peace to Wyoming in the form of an end to Indian raids, but was immediately replaced by the war that had existed before the Revolution—the war of land claims between the Pennemites and Yankees. Two of these struggles had been fought in the arena of the Wyoming Valley and both had been won by the Connecticut settlers. Now that the unifying forces of the Revolution were gone, the Third Pennemite War was apparently imminent.

Soon after the surrender of Cornwallis, in November of 1781, Pennsylvania presented a petition to Congress requesting a hearing on the claim of Pennsylvania to the Wyoming Valley, citing the State of Connecticut as its opposition, and the following year both sides agreed to an independent Court of Commissioners to make the decision. The court met in Trenton and, after sitting for forty-one judicial days, gave its opinion on December 30,1782: "We are unanimously of opinion that Connecticut has no right to the lands in controversy."

As Miner stated, "Clear, comprehensive, and explicit, Pennsylvania was satisfied, and Connecticut submitted without breathing a sign for the loss of so noble a domain, the right to which she had so strenuously maintained, or a murmur at a decision which seemed to the surrounding world so extraordinary."

At first the transition went smoothly. The garrison of New Jersey troops was replaced by Pennsylvania soldiers. Many Wyoming citizens signed a proclamation transfering their loyalty to the jurisdiction of Pennsyvlania in hopes of an amicable settlement of conflicting land claims. However, their hopes were dashed in April of 1783 when the Pennsylvania Commissioners arrived in Wilkes-Barre, accompanied by a committee representing Pennsylvania land claimers whose chairman was Captain Alexander Patterson.

This was the same Alexander Patterson mentioned earlier as one of the original agents appointed by John Penn to take an active part against the Connecticut settlers. He had helped to arrest the first forty settlers and brought them to the jail in Easton.

He was also a major land claimant, in that many large tracts of land in the Wyoming Valley were leased to him by the Pennsyvania Proprietaries. He thus had a major vested interest in the eviction of all Connecticut settlers and could never be accused of hiding his true feelings.

In his calmer moments, he referred to "abandoned desperadoes, excluded from society in every part of the Union, and whose practice had been to bully the State and pillage its citizens."

In one of his angrier moods he labeled the Connecticut settlers as "fair weather, chimney corner, defamatory, gin shop Jacks, intrusive vagrants, and the most infamous set of wretches ever collected in any part of the terraqueous globe!"

To many of the older Wyoming inhabitants, who remembered Patterson and the earlier armed conflicts with the Pennemites over land claims, it was, as Miner stated, "a moment of intense painful anxiety."

The Pennsylvania Commissioners let their intention be known in a letter to the opposing Committee of Settlers: "It cannot be supposed that Pennsylvania will, nor can she consistent with her constitution, by any ex post facto law deprive her citizens of any part of their property legally obtained."

The statement could not help but conjure up visions in the minds of the Wyoming settlers of expulsion from their homes and lands and abandonment of all they had worked and many had died for.

It was more precisely spelled out when Patterson informed the commissioners of the proposal of the Committee of land claimers. Calling it "just and charitable," Patterson proposed that the settlers were to be given one year before they would have to move out, widows would be given a year more, and the Reverend Jacob Johnson would have a full two years in which to move out!

On behalf of the Committee of Settlers, John Jenkins' response was one of blunt rejection:

"... As we conceive that the proposals of the committee, which they offer as a compromise, will not lead to peace, as they are so far from what we deem reasonable, we cannot comply with them without doing the greatest injustice to ourselves and our associates, to widows and fatherless children. And although we mean to pay due obedience to the constitutional laws of Pennyslvania, we do not mean to become abject slaves as the Committee of Landholders suggest in their address to your honors."

With this defiant reply by the Connecticut settlers the Pennsylvania Commissioners beat a hasty departure from Wyoming after sending them this notice:

"Gentlemen—We are now possessed of your answer to the proposals of the Committee of Landholders of Pennsylvania.

"We are sorry that there does not appear any prospect of accommodation between you. Therefore we must beg the favor of you to notify your people to meet with us tomorrow morning at 8 o'clock when we shall take the liberty to lay the whole proceeding before them...."

At this meeting the settlers were told that the Wyoming Valley would be divided into three townships, and judges were elected *two hours after the notice for the election was posted.*

With that, the Pennsylvania Commissioners left Wyoming, leaving the settlers to the tender mercies of the Pennsylvania land claimers and their leader, Alexander Patterson.

The Pennemites made appropriate preparations for their promotion of peace and justice as seen in a letter from Secretary Armstrong of the Supreme Executive Council to Captain Robinson of the Pennsylvania garrison at Fort Wyoming dated May 5, 1783:

"... Among other steps which have been thought necessary for the defense of the Wyoming settlement, a further supply of ammunition is now forwarded. It consists of two boxes of muskets, cartridges, and 300 flints. As one expedient to quiet that restless, discontented spirit which seems still to exist among the Connecticut claimants, Council have thought it proper to send you a few additional copies of the late proclamation upon that subject. You will find some means to spread them abroad among the people, and, as far as your influence will go to second their operation by securing peace and promoting justice."

As attested by the return self-serving letter, Captain Robinson took it upon himself to be a self-appointed judge until a Justice of the Peace arrived on the scene:

"With respect to the inhabitants,there are a great many wrangling disputes chiefly owing to a pelfering[sic] as well as letigious[sic] spirit which seems very natural to some of them.

"In all cases, they have immediate recourse to us as there is no civil officer in the place and many of them thought to avail themselves of the opportunity, imagining no law was to take hold of them, they proceeded to take and make use of their neighbor's property at pleasure and even to dispossess others.

"Upon which I immediately interposed, choosing such as I thought freeist of the letigious[sic] disposition and who best knew the affairs of the place for information and have so far prevailed in that respect as to preserve (by their own accounts) a better regulation than has ever been among them before.

"But notwithstanding their seeming compliance, there is still a refractory spirit among them, though they wish to keep up a good appearance—of these affairs I am well aware and am very careful to keep them at a proper distance.

"And your excellency may be assured that no endeavor shall be wasting on my part to keep good order among them till civil authority takes place ..."

In September, 1783, the newly "elected" Justice of the Peace arrived in Wyoming along with a large number of Pennsylvanians who claimed land in Wyoming. It was none other than Alexander Patterson. He was acting as agent for the land claimants and at the same time was expected to be an impartial Justice of the Peace! Patterson's first act was to change the name of Wilkes-Barre to Londonderry. His second act was to remove Captain Robinson and his company of troops from Wyoming and to replace them with Captain Philip Shrawder, a close friend of Patterson's, together with his own company of militia intensely loyal to the Pennsylvania land claimants. They were garrisoned at Fort Dickinson, formerly Fort Wyoming, and named after the president of the Supreme Council of Pennsylvania.

Colonel Zebulon Butler had returned from the army with his new wife in August of 1783 to find Pennsylvania soldiers treating the inhabitants of the Wyoming Valley rudely and, from time to time, stealing property. Butler protested and bluntly swore "to set fire to 'em." With that, a writ was issued and Colonel Butler was arrested for high treason, a capital offense. Soldiers marched him off to the fort where he was treated with indignity and the next day Judge Patterson had Butler sent to Sunbury under military guard. The sheriff there released Butler since there were no documents available charging Butler with any crime, and the Colonel returned to Wyoming.

The Pennemites then went after Captain John Franklin. He was arrested for trespassing for farming his own land! Franklin was brought before Judge Patterson where he pled good title to his land and requested trial by jury. Judge Patterson immediately dismissed the charge, but then came up with some new ways to add misery to the lives of the settlers.

Two new companies of soldiers arrived in Wyoming in late October and Patterson assigned them to be quartered without recompense with the various families of Wyoming. Those people who drew the ire of Patterson were assigned eight to ten soldiers to be billeted under their roofs. Colonel Butler was given special treatment and was assigned no less than twenty soldiers.

Sheldon Reynolds in his *Frontier Forts of Pennsylvania* stated, "The soldiery having no enemy to engage, either Indian, Tory, or British became rude, licentious, and insolent, and were used almost exclusively for the oppression of the Connecticut settlers, in hope of driving them to acts of violence which could be construed into resistance to the State Government."

Emboldened by his apparent power, Justice Patterson, himself, at the head of a military guard, descended upon the settlement of Shawnee (now Plymouth). He had eleven people arrested without charges, including a sickly man of sixty-five named Prince Alden, as well as three other elderly men: Captain James Bidlack, Benjamin Harvey, and Samuel Ransom. They were held for various lengths of time ranging from a few hours to ten days. During this time the detainees were forced to lie on the muddy, earthen floor of the fort, and treated as criminals, and threatened with summary execution. In the meantime their families were thrown out of their homes and Pennsylvania land claimants moved in.

Another method used by the Pennemites to confiscate homes and property was to declare any given group of settlers as tenants and then have them evicted for non-payment of rent.

In protest to their treatment, the settlers, under the leadership of

Colonel Butler, John Jenkins, and Captain John Franklin, secretly met at a house where they blackened the windows and drew up petitions of grievances to Pennsylvania and Connecticut. The Pennsylvania petition, as expected, was immediately dismissed but the Connecticut petition was referred to Congress. The Congressional Committee assigned to the petition consisted of Thomas Jefferson and Arthur Lee, of Virginia, and Hugh Williamson of North Carolina.

As if things weren't oppressive enough in the Valley, nature now intervened to make matters worse. The huge snowfalls of the winter of 1783-1784 were suddenly followed by extended thaws. The resultant flood, according to Reverend Jacob Johnson, destroyed over one hundred and fifty homes in the Wyoming Valley. Johnson added:

"The distressed of the war obliged us to build on our lowlands, yet few or none were ever exposed to danger before this time—the water and ice have risen 12 or 15 feet higher than ever was known in our days, and in some turns of the river, 25 feet higher than what is usually raised in former floods, and was so sudden that after the banks were overflowed, and the water had begun to be in the houses, it raised 10 feet perpendicular in 15 minutes, and almost from mountain to mountain!

"This is the distressed and unhappy situation of the unfortunate inhabitants of Wyoming, who have suffered every danger this side of death during the distresses of the war, many of their most near and tender connections having bled and fallen, and their whole country laid waste by the relentless fury of the savages."

All food and livestock were gone and over 1,000 people were destitute. Dickinson, the President of the Executive Council, requested state aid from the Assembly, but under pressure from the land speculators no aid was sent. The only thing that saved Wyoming from starvation was the seasonal shad run up the Susquehanna.

Patterson, upon seeing a possible respite arising in the travail of the settlers, promptly banned the use of nets to catch fish and ordered that all fencing demarcating property be removed. The garrison however, put up a fence around a wellsweep to prevent the settlers from obtaining water.

In April of 1784, a Yankee settler wrote to a friend in Connecticut relating to the state of affairs in Wyoming. The letter was published in *The Connecticut Journal* and *The Boston Gazette* and said in part referring to the soldiers, "And their daily insults are beyond anything that could be believed. The soldiers walk about with what they call shillalahs, and say they have orders that if an inhabitant gives them a wry word, to knock him down and beat him as they please. The insults and abuses are too numerous to repeat; and these abuses are all done by order and under the eyes of the military officers and some of the civil."

In a new petition to Congress for relief, Colonel Butler and several other prominent citizens wrote in part:

"And we are not only threatened of being beaten and abused with clubs, but are often threatened to be shot and put to immediate death. Many of our houses, lots, wells, and gardens lie near the garrison and under cover of their cannon: by which means we are continually receiving the greatest abuses and insults from some of the Justices as well as from the officers and soldiers. The said soldiers are continually walking the streets, and through every part of our settlement that is anywhere near the garrison, as well by night as by day—some armed with guns and bayonets, and others with clubs, insulting and assaulting whomsoever they please. Some of the inhabitants have been met in the street by this banditti, and have been beaten with clubs until their lives were despaired of. Others have been taken and carried into the fort, and there beaten with clubs by the officers and soldiers in a most cruel manner, and then dismissed."

Prophetically it was added:

"The merciless and mercenary land claimants have driven us almost to desperation, and unless we can have some speedy relief, we are inevitably ruined, and we must fly from this place with our distressed families, leaving our all behind us, our children crying for bread, and we shall have none to give them."

Ten days after the delivery of the new petition to Congress, sitting in Annapolis, Patterson made his move. On May 12th,1784, all the Yankee settlers were forced from their homes by detachments of soldiers and told to march back to Connecticut. Their homes and properties were immediately seized by Pennsylvania claimants. The expelled men, women, and children with just the clothes on their backs were forced to take the Lackawaxen Road northeast on foot. Thus exposed to the elements, a number of them died. One of the exiles, Elisha Harding stated:

"It was a solemn scene; parents, their children crying from hunger—aged men on crutches—all urged forward by an armed force at our heels. The first night we encamped at Capouse; the second at Cobbs; the third at Little Meadow, so called. Cold, hungry, and drenched with rain, the poor women and children suffering much. The fourth night at Lackawak; fifth, at Blooming Grove; sixth at Shohola; on the seventh, arrived at the Delaware, where the people dispersed some going up and some down the river. I kept on east, and when I got to the top of the Shongum Mountain, I looked back with the thought: shall I abandon Wyoming forever? The reply was, No, oh no! There lie your murdered brothers and friends. Dear to me art thou, though a land of affliction. Every way looked gloomy, except towards Wyoming. Poor, ragged, and distressed as I was, I had youth, health, and felt that my heart was whole. So I turned back to defend or die."

Meanwhile, Zebulon Butler and some Yankee settlers were able to escape to Sunbury where they told the sheriff there of the unlawful events that had transpired in Wyoming. President Dickinson and the Supreme Executive Council were notified and a runner sent to the Delaware telling the exiled settlers that they could safely and legally return to their homes in Wyoming. About thirty men immediately returned to Wyoming.

They found the Pennsylvania land claimants in complete possession of their homes and rather than enter into armed conflict, they took up residence in a mine cave in Wilkes-Barre Mountain to await the arrests of the claimants by Sheriff Antes of Sunbury.

Elisha Harding described life at this temporary strongpoint which the Yankees named Fort Lillopee:

"We went into the woods to a place called the coal-beds, back of Wilkes-Barre, where we continued about three weeks. Our living was not of the best. It consisted of chopped rye (about as fine as is ground for horse-feed), without salt. Our appetites were good, and when we drank the slop we did it in hopes of better fare. We were awaiting orders from the authorities to arrest those who had driven us off and taken possession of our houses and lands."

Sheriff Antes of Sunbury finally arrived in Wyoming to serve his warrants on the Pennemites but found them barricaded inside Fort Dickinson and was refused admittance. He returned a few days after and was this time accompanied by Benjamin Harvey. In the very presence of the Sheriff, Harvey was seized by Patterson's men, dragged off to the fort and beaten and abused in spite of the fact that he was sixty-two years old.

During this time, while the Pennemites were dividing up the land and property of the dispossessed Yankees, the Yankees made forays into the settlements and did some harassment of their own, beating a few Pennemites and driving off their livestock. In a few cases Pennemites were driven from their homes and threats were made against their lives with special treatment promised for Alexander Patterson. The Yankees were said to have threatened not only to murder Patterson, but to roast him as well!

Suddenly, Patterson proposed to allow the Yankees to return to their homes providing they returned unarmed. He sacredly pledged that he would not molest the settlers. Two Yankees, Captain Jabez Fish and John Gore, accepted the invitation and as soon as they entered the Valley they were immediately seized and severely beaten with ramrods before being banished from the town.

The Yankees now moved across the river to a group of unoccupied houses in Forty Fort. These they fortified and named their headquarters, Fort Defiance. When they received word that the Sheriff of Sunbury could not get armed men to serve warrants on the

Pennemites, the Yankees issued a call to arms under their new commander, Colonel John Franklin. It wasn't long before the first fatalities were suffered in this third civil war in the Wyoming Valley.

Sixty-two armed Yankees were proceeding from Kingston to Plymouth (then known as Shawnee) to work the fields when they were ambushed by forty of Patterson's Pennemites. Firing came from the bushes on the side of the road and two Yankees were killed. The fire was immediately returned as the Connecticut settlers fired into the bushes, wounding three Pennemites, the rest of whom fled to Fort Dickinson. Four days later, Captain Franklin at the head of another group of sixty-two Yankees, dispossessed every Pennemite family on the west side of the Susquehanna. Franklin also informed Patterson at Fort Dickinson that all Pennsylvania claimant families were free to leave the Valley without interference. Franklin and his men then crossed over to Nanticoke and, marching north, dispossessed every Pennemite family just short of Wilkes-Barre.

The next day, Franklin demanded the surrender of Fort Dickinson and gave the Pennemites two hours to do so. The Fort opened up with cannon fire against the Yankees, armed only with muskets. One Yankee was killed and the Fort remained in Pennemite hands under Patterson.

A relief column of Pennemites from Easton was intercepted by the Yankees—killing one and wounding three. This in turn brought the Pennsylvania Commissioners and four hundred militia under Colonel John Armstrong, former Secretary of War, to the Wyoming Valley.

The Commissioners demanded the surrender of arms on both sides. The Yankees immediately complied but not so the Pennemites. In their report to the Supreme Executive Council, the Commissioners admitted, "if ... as to the pretended titles of the Connecticut party, we have nothing to fear, and are convinced that had it not been through the cruel and irregular conduct of our people, the peace might have been established long since and the dignity of this government supported."

The doors of Fort Dickinson remained closed, causing the Commissioners to add, "We have dispersed the Connecticut party, *but our own people we cannot*."

The answer from Patterson, in the third person, to Commissioner Armstrong was, "Captain Patterson desires him to go home about his business if any he has—and bids him begone, begone immediately!"

With this defiant answer and challenge to his authority, Armstrong ordered the Yankees' arms returned for self defense. With this act, he received the trust of the Connecticut people.

The Commissioners again returned to Fort Dickinson and again demanded its surrender. This time their request was complied with and Patterson and his group were taken prisoner. Armstrong then met with Colonel Franklin and the Yankees, and promised them that if they gave up their arms they would not be made prisoners.

Colonel John Franklin describes what happened next: "I returned from my interview with Messrs. Armstrong and Boyd and informed our party as to what had taken place. They were fully satisfied. We met at the hour and place appointed. Armstrong and Boyd, accompanied by about 400 militia, appeared a short distance from us. We marched into an open field and grounded our arms, then marched from them a short distance, paraded in form, and halted. The Militia surrounded us, and Colonel Armstrong addressed himself to us in a sovereign manner, to the effect that we must consider ourselves his prisoners. Upon viewing the militia, I found that the party of Pennemites from the garrison and who had driven off our families and who we *thought were prisoners*, were paraded under arms to guard us. We were soon after marched to the vicinity of the garrison to the tune of 'Yankee Doodle,' played by drummers and fifers of the militia."

The Yankees were held prisoner in various homes for four days, during which time depositions from the various Pennsylvania land claimants were taken. With this done, thirty were handcuffed and formed in a column of twos and bound together by a long rope running from the head to the rear of the column. They were flanked on both sides by armed militia with fixed bayonets.

Colonel Armstrong gave orders to the guards that if any prisoner should try to escape, all the prisoners should be put to death immediately. With that warning, the first thirty Yankee prisoners marched off to Easton, sixty-five miles away along the Sullivan Trail. In spite of the highest security, three escaped and were never recaptured.

At the Easton jail the remaining twenty-seven prisoners were crowded into two small rooms. Their daily rations were limited to one pound of bread per man and water.

One of the prisoners, Elisha Harding related in 1838:

"I must record the generosity of a Jew, Michael Hart by name, who by Jewish custom, was taught to feed the poor. Every Friday he sent two young women with fresh beef soup and with beef and bread—a very comfortable meal. He has been long dead, but his memory will live with me while I have life."

The Start of the Yankee Prisoners to Easton (1784)

General Ethan Allen. Marble statue in the Washington D.C.

CHAPTER TWENTY-FIVE

Most of the able-bodied New England men were in jail, their penniless families evicted from their homes, their property seized, yet events swiftly took place to reverse their fortunes.

Forty-six other Yankees were sent off under guard to Sunbury, and Colonel Armstrong returned to Philadelphia to bask in the acclaim of the Pennemites for, at last, allowing them to occupy and control the Wyoming Valley.

To the unbelieving horror of the Pennsylvania land claimants and their supporters, the Sunbury prisoners were granted bail, and the bulk of the Easton prisoners escaped!

In Sunbury, Sheriff Antes had seen the injustices that the Yankees had suffered, and, in spite of the depositions submitted against them, he granted bail, and the Yankee prisoners were soon released.

More dramatic, however, were the events in the Easton jail—where twenty-seven Yankees were held in irons. One late afternoon, the assistant jailer unlocked the doors of the two rooms and unlocked the shackles of two of the prisoners, one from each room. Their job was to go down to the first floor to bring up bread and water. As soon as the irons on Edward Inman were released, he pounced on the jailer and choked him, took away his huge ring of keys, and with them, knocked the jailer unconscious. Inman was a very powerful man and after freeing his fellow prisoners, he ran downstairs, and shoving aside the chief jailer and his wife, he opened the outside gate for the escaping prisoners. They scattered out into the rainy night, and though eleven were recaptured, sixteen made their way back to Wyoming.

Colonel Armstrong rushed back to Wyoming with fifty militia, but not before the Yankees burned down Patterson's house through an innovative contraption. They built a platform mounted on wheels, one side of which had a high, hardwood wall with gun ports. While the Yankees sprayed their target with covering fire, the wagon was pushed alongside the house of their oppressor (Patterson) after they discovered it was where Patterson secretly lived. The Yankee fire was deadly and two of Patterson's aides were killed. Then, behind the cover of their moving wall, the Yankees threw fire brands into the house burning it down. Patterson escaped.

Shortly after this, Armstrong and his men arrived and attacked the Yankee fort in Kingston. The battle raged for an hour after which the militia retreated, losing one killed and three wounded. Two Yankees were wounded including Colonel Franklin who—with blood dripping from a wrist wound vowed he "... would never lay down his arms until death should arrest his hand, or Patterson and Armstrong be expelled from Wyoming and the people be restored to their rights of possession, and a legal trial guaranteed to every citizen by the Constitution, by justice, and by law!"

The next day, Armstrong, in revenge, dispossessed another thirty Yankee families who had recently returned to their homes. Armstrong then ordered his men into the fields to harvest a rich buckwheat crop planted earlier by the Yankees. A force of New Englanders under Major Joel Abbott silently surrounded the Pennemites at work. Unseen in the tall grass, the Yankees pounced on them before they could get to their weapons and took all their wagons, loaded with over a hundred bushels of grain. Across the river, the Pennemites at Fort Dickinson, seeing what had occurred, aimed their cannon at the field, but the Yankees used their prisoners as a shield and moved out of range back to Fort Defiance.

By now, Dickinson, the President of the Supreme Executive Council, used his influence on the Pennsylvania Assembly to right the wrongs done to the New Englanders. On September 15th, 1784, the Assembly ordered "the possession of the premises so forcibly entered and detained should be without delay restored to the persons who occupied them as aforesaid."

In addition, the Connecticut Assembly petitioned Congress to have Wyoming returned to the New Englanders. The resulting pressure culminated in the Pennemite evacuation of Fort Dickinson in November and its subsequent destruction by the Yankees. Patterson, Armstrong, and the Pennemites all left Wyoming for Philadelphia. Those who stubbornly refused to give up the homes they had taken were forcibly evicted by Colonel Franklin and his men.

The final determination of the property rights of the original Connecticut settlers, now in possession of the Wyoming Valley, was yet to be made by Congress. Toward this end, Colonel Franklin went to Connecticut to obtain the support of the son of an early Susquehanna Company shareholder. Because of his standing as one of the great patriots of the American Revolution, Franklin felt that his influence with Congress would help sway many uncommitted Congressmen to the Connecticut cause. This personage was none other than celebrated General Ethan Allen of Vermont!

On October 27, 1785 Ethan Allen wrote to "Colonel Butler and Mr. Franklin and such others as they see fit to communicate to, at Wyoming.":

> You have undoubtedly previous to this date, been informed that I have espoused your cause, against Pennsylvania. I proposed in August last to have made a visit to Wyoming, and to have consulted with your principle men, on the best measures of defense, but urgent business would not admit it. Extraordinaries excepted, I propose to make a tour of your hostile ground next spring.
>
> My father was an original proprietor in the Susquehanna purchase, and besides that I have since been considerably interested. Furthermore I am very sensible, that our cause is just and our title to the fee in the land indefeasible; add to this, you have been greatly oppressed by the land schemers of Pennsylvania, more so than any district in English America. In my opinion, that those schemers were *instrumental in bringing the common enemy against Wyoming* and consequently guilty of the destruction they caused....
>
> What a lawyer may suppose to be law, in this case I will not determine, but I think that as the Connecticut charter which expressly covers the disputed territory is eighteen years older than

that of Sir William Penn; and as we have a bona fide purchase from the Indian original proprietors, and been in the possession of it for the past twenty five years, and through the late Revolution has been an outpost and guard to Pennsylvania, the right of soil, by right belongs to the Susquehanna Company. If this is not a sufficiently authentic and legal title, it is in vain for mankind ever to acquire any lands whatever.

Probably the justice of our claim will have but little or no effect on our haughty antagonists, who seek our land and labors, it may nevertheless inspire to defend our rights with great zeal and fortitude to make us friends elsewhere particularly in Congress and justify our opposition, even to blood.

I hope that Congress will finally adjudge the right of soil to the Susquehanna Company, but whether they do or not, it is good policy to solicit for it, and in the meantime crowd settlements, add to your numbers and strength, procure firearms and ammunition, be united among yourselves. I hope to see you face to face next Spring, nor will I give up my interest to usurpers, without trying it out by force of arms; if we have not fortitude enough to face danger in a good cause, we are cowards indeed, and must in consequence of it be slaves, and our posterity, to Pennemite land thieves. Liberty and Property or Slavery and Poverty, are now before us, and our Wisdom and Fortitude, or Timidity and Folly, must terminate the matter.

I am, gentlemen, your friend and
humble servant,
Ethan Allen

A shareholder of the Susquehanna Company from New York wrote a letter to Colonel Butler, Colonel John Franklin, and Colonel Nathan Denison stating:

"... General Ethan Allen, having a large interest in Wyoming proposes to take up his future abode among you; and as he appears to be a great lover of peace and good neighborhood, I conclude you may like him as a neighbor...."

Ethan Allen made his visit to Wyoming in April 1786 and stayed at Colonel Butler's home in Wilkes-Barre. Colonel John Franklin commented:

"... General Ethan Allen paid us a visit at Wyoming, and proposed to settle amongst us, and to bring on with him a number of his 'Green Mountain Boys' and assist us in supporting and defending our rights against the Pennsylvania claimants. A large number of Proprietors' Rights were given to General Allen to induce him to espouse our cause."

Now, for the first time, a division arose between the settlers of the Susquehanna Company over the issue of allegiance to Pennsylvania law, jurisdiction, and sovereignty. Radical members of the Susquehanna Company such as John Franklin, John Jenkins, and Ethan Allen agreed to the need for a new state cut out of the Wyoming area and completely independent of Pennsylvania.

At the urging of more conservative Susquehanna Company shareholders, such as Zebulon Butler and Timothy Pickering, for compromise, the new President of the Supreme Executive Council, Benjamin Franklin, and the Pennsylvania Assembly gave the Wyoming area its own county, cut out of Northumberland County. The new county was named Luzerne in honor of the new minister to the United States, Chevalier de la Luzerne appointed by King Louis XVI of France.

Colonel Timothy Pickering was a New Englander from Massachusetts who had won the trust and confidence of General

Washington and the Congress for his excellent performance in the office of Quartermaster General and Secretary of War during the Revolution. He had become a citizen of Pennsylvania and because of his New England roots was assigned by Pennsylvania to go to Wyoming to organize the new county of Luzerne. This goal was a smooth transition of the county and its growing population.

Pickering announced the first election for county officers and approval of county laws and organization, approval of which implied an oath of allegiance to Pennsylvania.

John Franklin, John Jenkins, the Slocums, and upriver residents were committed to statehood, however, and were against any election which would imply submission to Pennsylvania!

Election day was tumultuous. As Miner stated, "It was a day of high excitement, even for Wyoming; indeed of riotous commotion."

Oration spiced with fist fights were the order of the day. People took to the streets to let everyone know their feelings for or against allegiance to Pennsylvania. Colonel Zebulon Butler in a familiar role rode his horse up and down through the crowd shouting, "I draw my sword in defense of the law, let every lover of peace and good order support me!"

The election was successful. Colonel Mathan Denison was elected to the Supreme Executive Council to serve under its president, Benjamin Franklin. John Franklin was elected to the Assembly, Lord Butler (Zebulon's son) was elected High Sheriff. Timothy Pickering was elected commissioner and termed himself a "fence viewer and overseer of the poor."

After the election, John Franklin went from town to town urging his followers to peacefully protest any allegiance to Pennsylvania or acknowledging its jurisdiction. Franklin continued his campaign of peaceful protest until both sides agreed to a "Town Meeting" type of forum. It was held in Forty Fort and the question discussed was whether the laws of Pennsylvania should be received and obeyed. Hundreds of people came to the meeting, most of the older people opting for allegiance and most of the younger people and new arrivals upriver demanding statehood.

Pickering made the first speech endorsing the Pennsylvania cause. This was answered by John Jenkins who asked:

"What security have we that if we comply, and put ourselves into your power, the State won't repeal the law and deal us treacherously as in the case of Armstrong!"

Next, Colonel Franklin called the compromise of a new county hollow and deceptive and denounced Pickering and all who supported him. With that, an enraged Colonel Hollenback threw the butt of his riding crop at Franklin's head. It was caught before it could do harm and this sparked a brawl with no holds barred. Scores of people exchanged blows. Finally, a vote was taken and it was moved to support the laws and adopt the compromise.

The Franklin forces had General Ethan Allen show up all around the Valley in his regimental uniform and cocked hat. It was to show that a true patriot chose the path of statehood and hinted that Allen could call down the "Green Mountain Boys" to insure the success of his choice. A few days later Ethan Allen quietly left Wyoming for home.

During this period the leaders of the opposing sides still maintained good relations, as seen by the following diary entry by Colonel Pickering.

"Colonel Zebulon Butler and Colonel John Franklin spent the evening with us very sociably. Mr. Franklin appears to be the leader of the warm supporters of the claim of The Susquehanna Company against Pennsylvania. Nothing was said on that subject. In the morning, having called to see Colonel Butler, he invited me to take breakfast during which time I made some inquiries relative to the dispute, and the proceedings of the meeting of the settlers the day before."

Before John Franklin and John Jenkins went to Philadelphia to take their places in the Executive Council and Assembly respectively, they had the following address distributed in both legislative bodies which said in part:

"The widows and orphans of those who fell in the common cause of America, *particularly in your defense*, have been plundered, despoiled of their goods, and driven from their habitations and legal possessions, with other inhabitants in general, and the whole treated nearly as inhumanely as by the common enemy; and many of our inhabitants have been killed, by the hostile attempts of Government to dispossess us of our lands and labors without the formality of a trial by law.

"Notwithstanding the great evils we have suffered from Your Government, yet in conformity to the Congressional decision of the jurisdiction of this territory (at Trenton), *we make the following proposition of amity, and submission to your jurisdiction and laws*—to prevent, if possible, any further effusion of blood, and to terminate all disputes to wit: Provided the Legislature of the State of Pennsylvania, will in the most explicit and unequivocal manner ratify, confirm, and secure to us the *right of soil* of the lands in the disputed territory, which we have purchased from the aboriginal proprietors and the State of Connecticut (part of which we have improved and are in possession of), that on this condition we the said inhabitants, will *submit to the jurisdiction and laws of the State of Pennsylvania.*

"Should this condition—which is the bone of contention—be complied with on the part of the Government, we indulge a hope and strong expection that harmony, justice, and peace will succeed the evils and hostilities which have heretofore taken place...."

When Franklin and Jenkins arrived in Philadelphia, they reiterated their offer to the Council and Assembly. They were then contacted by Benjamin Franklin who also requested that their petition be put before him and this too was done. The outcome however was inconclusive since John Franklin's petition was never acted upon.

The following year of 1787 saw increasing pressure by John Franklin, now referred to as the Hero of Wyoming by his followers, to include the Wyoming Valley in a new state including part of New York. As if to counter this movement, Colonel Butler was appointed Lieutenant of Luzerne County, thus putting him in command of the county militia. Benjamin Franklin began to suspect a conspiracy on the part of John Franklin to possibly engage the aid of Great Britain in setting up this newly proposed state and made known his fears to the Governor of New York, DeWitt Clinton. Benjamin Franklin was informed that a constitution for the proposed state had already been drawn up. Finally, on September 1, 1787, a warrant for the arrest of John Franklin was issued with a note to Zebulon Butler stating:

"John Franklin being a pernicious and seditious man and a person of disquiet mind, contriving, practicing and maliciously and turbulently intending our peace and common tranquility to molest and disturb, hath at several times and within the last six months in the County of Luzerne ... incited and encouraged several inhabitants to disobey our laws and resist our Government...."

Four strong, former army officers were secretly sent on a mission to capture John Franklin and return him to Philadelphia, and Pickering was informed of the mission. Franklin was returning from Wilkes-Barre from a political trip and was at River Street waiting for the ferry when he was seized from behind by the four men. He broke loose but was again seized and a noose was thrown over his head to pin his arms to his sides. Franklin called out for help, and his hands being free, he drew his pistols but was struck over the head and blood streamed over his face. It took four men to get Franklin on a horse several times but repeatedly Franklin threw himself off. Finally Timothy Pickering and his servant held a gun to Franklin's chest while they tied his legs to the horse around the horse's belly. The four men rode south, day and night to a jail in Philadelphia where Franklin was placed in irons and charged with treason.

An eyewitness report from Philadelphia was sent to Pickering stating: "...They say he fought the whole of them for several minutes before he surrendered. Five of them have receipts to prove the assertion—a black eye each. Franklin has a black eye and is otherwise bruised. How this will affect you, time will discover, but I hope his party is too contemptible to affect you or alarm anyone. It affords a great triumph here, and I sincerely hope that peace may follow violence.

"... Colonel Denison has this moment called on me. He has seen

Franklin. He informs me he seems disposed to be composed, though it is manifest, he is in the horrors. His plan of independency seems to lay heaviest against him."

In November, 1787, an election was held to select a representative to the Constitutional Convention from Wyoming, and by an overwhelming majority, Timothy Pickering was selected, and later ratified the new Consitution containing several safeguards which events at Wyoming helped to inspire. The new Constitution prohibited taking of homes and property without due process of law, the forced quartering of troops in private homes, the right of fair trial by jury, and the requirement that disputes between states be decided by the Supreme Court.

In the following June of 1788, the few remaining followers of John Franklin managed to kidnap Timothy Pickering in an attempt to exchange him for Franklin. Because of the national standing of Pickering as a Revolutionary hero, national attention became focused on his release and his abductors, in fear of the pursuing milita, turned him loose.

A few months later, John Franklin was released on condition he would not question the jurisdiction of Pennsylvania over Wyoming. By Christmas, 1788, there was peace in the Valley at last.

For the first time thereafter, in the whole bloody history of Wyoming, lasting peace came to the Valley. There is no place on the North American Continent that had been the scene of battles from the French and Indian Wars, three Pennemite-Yankee Civil Wars, constant Iroquois raids, and the Revolutionary War, all of which followed various intertribal Indian Wars. The Wyoming Valley, so steeped in blood, had at last found peace!

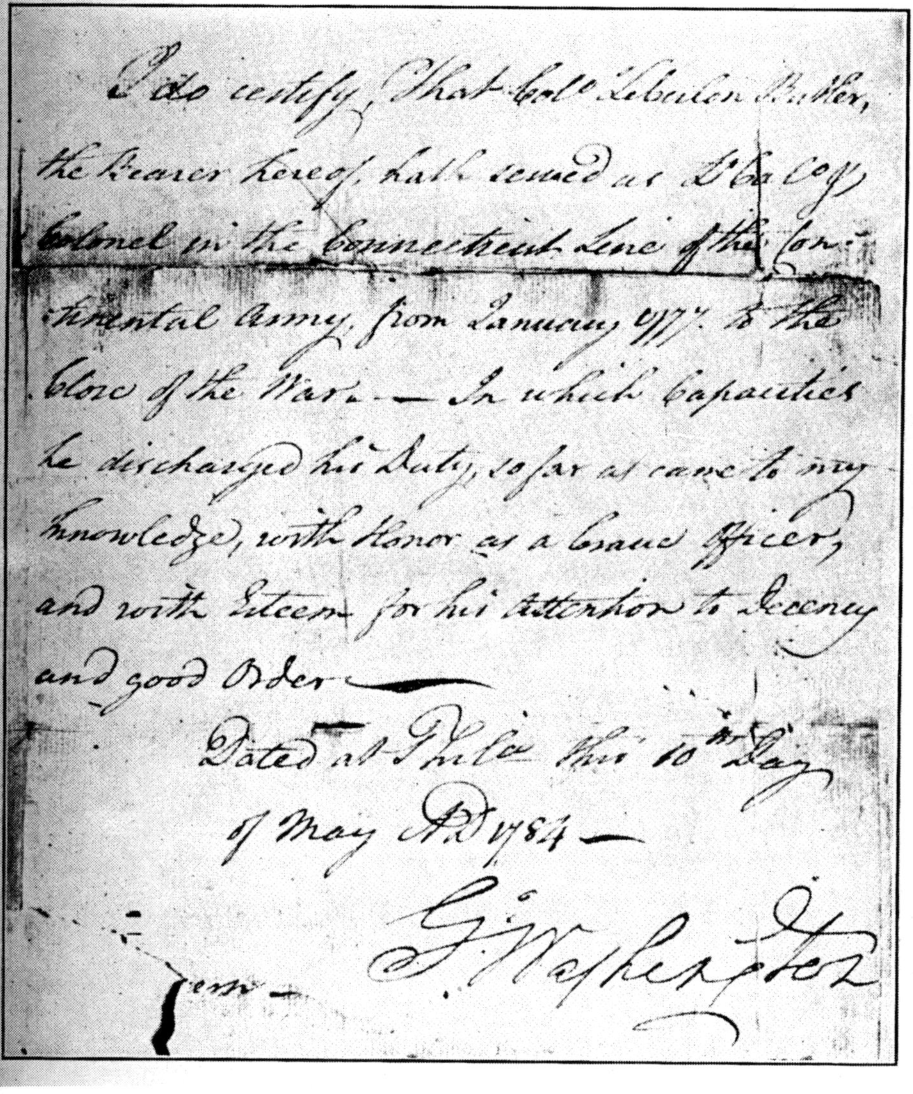

I do certify, That Coll° Zebulon Butler, the Bearer hereof, hath served as Lt Col of Colonel in the Connecticut Line of the Continental Army, from January 1777 to the Close of the War. — In which Capacities he discharged his Duty, so far as came to my knowledge, with Honor as a brave Officer, and with Esteem for his attention to Decency and good Order —

Dated at Phila this 10th Day of May AD 1784 —

G. Washington

Honorable Discharge of Colonel Zebulon Butler, 1784.

The Capture of John Franklin from an old wood cut (Courtesy of the Wyoming Valley Historical and Geological Society).

CHAPTER TWENTY-SIX

The years following the close of 1788 saw the frontier move on, and an influx of new arrivals from New England and other parts of Pennsylvania moved into Wyoming as the Valley flourished. However, the tapestry formed of previous events had left loose ends from the war-torn past that kept cropping up into the now-peaceful present.

In January, 1835, the owner of an Indian trading post at Logansport, Indiana, named Colonel George W. Ewing, went up the Mississineva River on a trading trip. It was getting dark as he reached an Indian settlement named Deaf Man's Village. He sought shelter for the night at the cabin of Maconaquah, a Miami Indian woman whom he had known for several years. She was sixty-two years old but looked much older due to a hard and rigorous life. Her name in the Miami Indian dialect means *Young Bear*.

"She provided me with a good supper and ordered wood to be piled on the big hearth, which surprised me as our supper was over and the Indian bedtime had arrived. After sitting a half hour or so and talking over ordinary matters about her crops and her cattle, I told her I would retire to my bed. She said, 'No, I have something on my mind, I am old and weak. I shan't live long and I must tell it. I can't die in peace if I don't.'"

She then proceeded to tell Ewing that when she was a little girl of five, living near the Susquehanna River, she was kidnapped by the Iroquois. She remembered that her father's name was Slocum and that he was a Quaker with a broad-brimmed hat. She also remembered there was a fort about a half mile from where she lived. She recalled too that she, young Nathan Kingsley, and her captors sought refuge that night in a cave (in what is now Francis Slocum State Park).

The next morning, Ewing left the home of Maconaquah to return to his trading post. There he reflected on the old Indian woman's story, and thinking that Lancaster was a town on the Susquehanna, he wrote the following letter to the postmaster of Lancaster, Pennsylvania:

"Dear Sir: In the hope that some good may result from it, I have taken this means of giving to your fellow citizens—say the descendants of the early settlers of the Susquehanna—the following information and if there be any now living whose name is Slocum; to them I hope the following may be communicated through the public prints of your place.

"There is now living near this place (Logansport) among the Miami tribe of Indians, an aged white woman who a few days ago told me that she was taken away from her father's house on, or near the Susquehanna River when she was very young. She says her father's name was Slocum; that he was a Quaker, and wore a large brimmed hat, that he lived about a half mile from a town where there is a Fort. She has two daughters living. Her husband is dead—she is old and feeble, and thinks she shall not live long. These considerations induced her to give the present history of herself—which she never would before, fearing her kindred would come and force her away. She has lived long and happy as an Indian—is very respectable, and wealthy, sober and honest—her name is without reproach."

The letter was received by Mrs. L. Mary Dickson, the postmistress who was also the owner of a newspaper in Lancaster, *The Intelligencer*. Mrs. Dickson didn't think the letter was important and put it aside with other, old letters where it remained for two years. The letter was discovered by a post office employee when the newspaper was sold by Mrs. Dickson to a newspaperman and politician named John W. Forney. Forney was given the letter by its finder and as a seasoned newsman, Forney saw a real story in the letter which he instantly published in *The Intelligencer* in July, 1837.

As luck would have it, the Episcopal Rector of St. James Church in Lancaster, Reverend Samuel Bowman, was a native of Wilkes-Barre and had lived there for twenty-two years. He read the letter and knew of the kidnapping of Frances Slocum in addition to knowing several members of the Slocum family. Bowman quickly mailed a copy of the letter to Joseph Slocum, brother of Frances.

The letter caused such a stir in the Wyoming Valley that the two Valley newspapers reprinted the letter on their front pages with banner headlines. Several members of the Slocum family immediately set out for Indiana to meet Maconaquah. Her brother Joseph, who went to see his sister, remembered that when the two were small children they had played at their father's blacksmith shop. On one occasion one of the children accidently hit Frances' left-hand, middle finger with a hammer on the anvil.

When the relatives came to greet Maconaquah for the first time, Joseph immediately noticed that the elderly woman extended a crushed left hand. They all embraced and cried with the sudden recognition that this was indeed the "Lost Sister of Wyoming," as the newspapers referred to her.

With the use of an interepreter, Frances told how the Iroquois took her and Nathan Kingsley to Fort Niagara where both children were adopted and kindly treated by separate Delaware families along the Genesee River.

Maconaquah informed her newfound family, "When the Indians lose a child, they often adopt someone in its place, and treat that one in all respects as their own. This is the reason why they so often carry off the children of white people."

Frances added that Nathan Kingsley died a few years after his adoption and that at the age of thirteen she moved west to Indiana with her adoptive family and later married a Delaware who moved further west. She decided to stay on and married a Miami chief by whom she had four children: two girls, and two boys. She was told that all the Indian farmland along the Genesee was destroyed and later occupied by Americans. Her two sons and her husband died, leaving her a rich widow with a large tract of land and livestock.

Frances' relatives urged her to move back to the Wyoming Valley. She refused, and in turn, offered half of her land to them if they would move to Indiana. The Wyoming Slocums politely refused.

Two years later, in 1839, Joseph Slocum returned to visit his sister in Indiana. He found her depressed over the prospect of being forced to leave her lands to move to Kansas. The American Government wanted all tribes moved out of Indiana to make room for land-hungry settlers.

On behalf of their sister, Joseph and Isaac Slocum appealed through their Congressman Benjamin Bidlack to the House of Representatives. A special bill was passed allowing Frances Slocum and her descendants to remain on their lands in Indiana. The rest of the Indian population, under armed guard, was moved overland through Illinois and Iowa to a new reservation in Kansas. Surrounded by new and unfriendly neighbors, Frances Slocum died a lonely, despondent figure in 1847 at the age of 74.

To the east, as mentioned, the Iroquois, too, had been moved into reservations with resulting moral breakdown, suicide, and drunkenness. It was then that a Seneca Indian, Handsome Lake, a veteran of the Battle of Wyoming, came forward to halt the disintegration of the Iroquois Nation—a legacy of Sullivan's Raid which grew out of the Battle of Wyoming.

Handsome Lake was no exception to the rule. He too had seen his life change drastically. Although he no longer had to go to war and be away from home, his freedom of movement and hunting were restricted to the relatively small reservation. Handsome Lake was not the first Seneca who questioned the reason for existence, but was content to turn to alcohol for solace. He began to drink heavily and in the Spring of 1799 he lay in his bunk in a feverishly sickened and drunken state. His breathing became imperceptible and the word went out that he had died. His relatives, Blacksnake and Cornplanter came to examine his body and finding it cold, went to get the neighbors to carry out the body and prepare it for burial rites. Blacksnake again touched the body to move it and found it had a "warm spot" and a half-hour later, breathing began.

Handsome Lake awoke to say that he felt well and that he had a vision. He stated that he saw four angels sent by the Creator to tell him that the Creator was sad and angry because of the current Seneca behavior. The Creator wanted an end to whiskey, witchcraft, love magic, and sterility medicine. Further visions revealed the need for peace and the preservation and revival of the traditional rituals and ceremonies. Handsome Lake came to believe that the Iroquois required civilization for a better life, but not the further restrictions of Christianity. Enthusiastic response to the new religion was dramatically received by the Council of the Iroquois.

To obtain material aid and to help advance his people, Handsome Lake wrote a letter to President Thomas Jefferson and was cordially invited to Washington, D.C.

Handsome Lake respectfully addressed Jefferson:

"Brother, I thank the Great Spirit above that I have a very bright day to talk with the Great Chief of our white Brothers. It is the Great Spirit's doing. The Great Spirit has appointed four Angels and appointed me the fifth to direct our people on Earth. I thank the Great Spirit that the Great Chief of my white Brothers is well and hearty. This is the first year since the Great Spirit appointed me to guide my people and give them knowledge, good from bad. He directed me to begin with my own people first and this is the reason why I have been so long in coming to my white brother.

"I am very much troubled, to find that my Brothers and my white Brothers have gone astray."

Handsome Lake went on to say that the guilt of the Iroquois was drunkenness and the guilt of the whites was seizure of Iroquois lands. Handsome Lake requested deeds to the lands the Iroquois retained and also tools and equipment to help the Iroquois help themselves. As a result of this meeting with Jefferson, plows, oxen, cows, sheep, wool-gathering equipment, and other farm equipment was sent to the various reservations. In addition, Congress passed a law prohibiting the sale of alcoholic beverages on all reservations.

Jefferson later sent a letter to Handsome Lake stating:

> ... Go on then brother, in the great reformation you have undertaken. Persuade our red men to be sober and to cultivate their lands and their women to spin and weave for their families. You will soon see your women and children well fed and clothed; your men living happily in peace and plenty, and your numbers increasing from year to year. It will be a great glory to you to have been the instrument of so happy a change, and your children's children, from generation to generation will repeat your name with love and gratitude forever. In all your enterprises for the good of your people you may count with confidence on the aid and protection of the United States and on the sincerity and zeal with which I am animated in the furthering of this humane work. You are our brethren of the same land; we wish you prosperity as brethren should.
>
> Farewell!
> Th. Jefferson

Handsome Lake's preaching stopped the downward cycle of the Iroquois after the Revolution and brought about a reformation under this new religion and moral code that survives to this day called Gaiwiio—The Old Way of Handsome Lake.

However, not all the unpleasant echoes of the past involving the Iroquois were abated into the present and future. Charles Miner, in a footnote made the following statement:

"Fifteen years after the battle, a number of Indians, among whom were several chiefs of distinction, passed through Wyoming, on their way to Philadelphia, on business with the Government. Apprehending danger, they sent word to Wilkes-Barre, and an escort of respectable citizens turned out to accompany them into town. In the evening, a council was held in the Court Room, where mutually pacific assurances were given. It is not suprising, considering their cruel conduct during the war, that the Indians entertained fears for their safety. On their return, passing on the opposite side of the river from the battleground, the old braves showed much excitement, talking and gesticulating, with great emphasis, and spirit, as they seemed to be pointing out to the younger savages the position, and incidents of the conflict. I met Red Jacket at Washington in 1827 or 8, and strove to lead him to talk of Wyoming, but on that subject his lips were hermetically sealed."

Mac-On-A-Qhuh (Frances Slocum). From an 1839 portrait by George Winter. She was the "Lost Sister of Wyoming."

CHAPTER TWENTY-SEVEN

The reverberations of the Wyoming Valley's past did not stop. Rather, they caused events to occur and discoveries to be made right into the Nineteenth Century.

As related earlier, Lieutenant John Jenkins had to work fast to gather up as many bones as he could find and bury them in a common grave in October, 1778. There was then the constant imminence of Iroquois raids and it is no wonder that the common grave site was lost.

As stated in a letter by one of Luke Pettebone's descendants, Payne Pettebone, "Considerable interest was awakened on the subject of suitably marking the place of burial of the slain in the Massacre of July 3rd, 1778 and some prospecting for the spot was had without success, because it was in the midst of a field which had been plowed over for many years, and the mound, if any had ever existed, was entirely obliterated."

The search for the site actually became a contest between two rival political clubs of Wilkes-Barre. A member of one of these clubs, William Swetland, a descendant of Luke Swetland, decided to search for the bones and he offered twenty dollars to a farm hand who had worked the land in which the bones were thought to be buried. The farmer made an iron rod six-feet long with a barbed point. After probing the land for about two hours, the bones were found and Swetland was informed of the location.

In July of 1832, a meeting of concerned citizens was held at the home of Fisher Gay, the owner of the land on which the bones were found. The group agreed to purchase the land but Gay would not hear of it, and donated the land. In the following Spring of 1833, the grave was opened and the bones packed into boxes, and, at the same time, stone blocks were quarried from the east side of the Valley to be made into a vault for the bones as well as the foundation for a monument to be erected. The vault was completed, and in December, the bones were respectfully interred in the vault which is in the exact spot where John Jenkins originally buried them.

According to Steuben Jenkins, in his speech at the 1878 Centennial, ninety-six skeletons were buried in the vault, sixty of which were found on or near the battle line, and the remainder, between the battle line and Forty Fort.

The monument was completed in 1846, in stages, due to uneven funding, and is sixty-two-and-a-half feet tall. The tablet on the monument lists the names of one hundred and seventy killed and forty-nine who escaped.

Meanwhile, the public began to see the need to protect Queen Esther's Rock, as pieces of the rock were being constantly chipped away by souvenir hunters. Finally, in 1895, the Wyoming Valley Chapter of the Daughters of the American Revolution had an iron grating built around it as well as an iron fence around its surrounding lot.

The site of both the Wyoming Monument and Queen Esther's Rock was known as New Troy. The name was supposedly supplied by a clerk interested in the classics in the land office when the first Pennsylvania patent for land in the area was granted to Jacob Bedford in July, 1807. The name New Troy continued to be used for more than twenty-five years and the New Troy post office was established in 1826 with Gilliam Swetland as postmaster. It wasn't until 1839 that the town's name was changed to Wyoming. It was commonly being referred to by that name, interchangeably with the Valley that it was part of, and the Battle which it was the site of.

Another relic had also survived Wyoming's bloody past. In March, 1837, a native of Wilkes-Barre, Frederick Hancock, was visiting the War Department in Washington. He asked to be shown a collection of enemy flags taken as war trophies in past battles. Hancock was led to the attic and shown several flags captured from enemy forces.

Hancock wrote:

"After some further examination, I was shown a very ancient looking British flag, and was informed that it had been carried in the 'Wyoming Massacre.' My attention was at once excited, and upon examination I found the following words written on the margin of the flag: 'The standard of the bloody, scalping Colonel Butler, carried in the Massacre of Wyoming.' The flag was much defaced and stained with blood and looked as though it might have been in the front of the battle on that memorable day."

The flag was eight-feet long by five-feet-four-inches in width with the Union Jack on a background of buff. In each of the four quarters of the flag, formed by the Red Cross of St. George, were two, blue, triangular designs. After the Revolution, and the disbanding of "Butler's Rangers," the flag was stored at Fort George. In the War of 1812, Fort George was captured by four thousand American troops and there the flag was found, and the comment on its white area added, before being shipped off to the War Department in Washington.

Frederick Hancock tried to get the flag presented to the citizens of Wyoming but the Adjutant General of the Army said that he had no authority to release the flag. Hancock then requested Congressman Joseph R. Underwood of Kentucky, who was present at the capture of Fort George, to help him put a petition before Congress to return the flag to Wyoming. It did not pass, however, because of opposing feelings that this was an *enemy* flag and as Congressman William Potter of Pennsylvania stated, would only "give a pang to the hearts of the few survivors of that fatal day and to the descendants of those who sleep the sleep of death."

Between 1837 and 1840 the flag was transferred to the United States Military Academy at West Point. There, in the Spring of 1840, a sketch in color was made of the flag on a scale 1/8th the size of the original by one Richard Smith, Assistant Instructor in drawing at the U.S. Military Acadamy on April 6, 1840. In 1903, historian Oscar J. Harvey, after much correspondence with the Adjutant of the U.S. Military Academy, was unable to locate the flag at West Point.

This author, however was far more fortunate. In the Fall of 1994, with just one letter and one phone call to the Curator of History, the lost Tory flag of the Battle of Wyoming was located in storage at West Point. The flag is registered as West Point Museum Accession #2430. It is hand sewn and made of silk. The following description appears in an article entitled "Notes on British Artillery Flags in the American Revolution," by Donald W. Holst in the Fall 1987 issue of *Military Collector and Historian*:

"There are two other British Union Flags in the collections of the West Point Museum; the first of which was at one time believed to have been carried by a Loyalist corps known as Butler's Rangers during the Susquehanna Campaign and which they were somehow supposed to have lost at the time of the Wyoming Massacre. This flag, the same as that illustrated in FIG 1, measured 69 by 105 3/4 inches and has a pear-shaped hole in the center of the St. George's Cross, indicating the probability that there had been a device (monogram or insignia), painted on the flag at that point."

Mr. Holst made a further comment on this pear-shaped hole:

"This could have been some sort of circular device surmounted by another object such as a crown. What little evidence that is available to us indicates the possibility that some flags may possibly have had a central device while others did not."

Figure 1. The Tory Battle Flag of Wyoming as it was sketched when it arrived at West Point in 1840. Note the writing on the white area on the right, identifying it as the Wyoming ensign and written by the soldier who captured it in Canada on May 27, 1813—the day that Fort George, Ontario was captured in the War of 1812 (Courtesy U.S. Army Photograph).

Figure 2. The Battle Flag of Wyoming as it appears today (Courtesy U.S. Army Photograph).

The Curator of History at West Point states that "the area where a royal cypher was 'removed' actually is not large enough to have ever supported one." This author is completely in agreement with this statement, the important factor is that this is a *battle flag* and those holes, in this author's opinion, came from musket balls piercing the flag in the heat of battle. This is borne out by Frederick Hancock's statement of 1837, when he first discovered the flag, that it "looked as though it might have been in the front of the battle on that memorable day."

The West Point Curator would not vouch for the flag other than to affirm that it had been at West Point since 1840. The overwhelming test of veracity, however, is the fact that the 1840 sketch of the flag, complete with the statement of authenticity in FIG 1, matches up tear-for-tear and hole-for-hole with the modern photograph of the reverse side flag of FIG 2 in storage today at West Point!

With regard to the written statement seen on the right side of FIG 1, relating to the flag's history and authenticity, this was written in ink on the white-silk area of the flag and may have faded with time. In any event, if it is still present, it would appear on the reverse of FIG 2. Proof of its presence must await further examination and testing, but the pattern of holes and tears leaves no doubt that FIGS 1 and 2 are of the same flag. It was FIG 1 that was shown to the octogenarian veterans of the Battle when it was proposed to return the flag to the people of the Valley. The sight of this flag sketch brought such a negative reaction from these eyewitnesses, that the flag was refused by them. Only the genuine flag that they saw on that July day in 1773 could have evinced such a reaction!

In March of 1995, this author wrote to President Bill Clinton informing him of the flag's discovery and its significance. The White House forwarded the letter to the Army's Chief Curator's Office, also in Washington. On April 25, 1995, Chief Curator Judson E. Bennett Jr. replied and confirmed that the flag at West Point was "of national significance" and was indeed the authentic Tory battle flag of the Battle of Wyoming.

Mathias Hollenback

CHAPTER TWENTY-EIGHT

More poignant than the fate and disposition of artifacts was the aging and passing of the great figures from the stage or the saga of the Wyoming Valley. The first to go was the proud and fearless Colonel Zebulon Butler who died at the age of 64 in 1795. The distinguishing traits of Colonel Butler's character, wrote Charles Miner, "were activity, energy, a high sense of honor, a courage moral and professional, that when duty called, knew no fear."

He rests beneath a flat marble slab in Hollenback Cemetery in Wilkes-Barre whose inscription has been almost obliterated by the elements:

Distinguished by his usefulness
At home and when abroad
In court, in camp, and in recess
Protected still by God.

The next great figure to pass on was the colorful and beloved Reverend Jacob Johnson. This was no "summer patriot," but rather one of the early "Sons Of Liberty," scornful of English rule and never hesitant to fight the enemies of his country with a unique mixture of fearless, political rhetoric, religion, and prophecy. His passing was as unique as his life.

At the age of eighty-four he had a dream, or as he put it, a vision, a forewarning of his death. The next day, Reverend Johnson went to the highest hill on his property (the current intersection of Franklin Street and North Street in Wilkes-Barre) and there dug his own grave, to his liking, but when finished, he returned home and calmly gave directions to his son regarding his funeral. He told his son to put his body in the grave facing east, so that he could see the coming of the Messiah over the edge of the Valley. Before the night was over, Johnson died peacefully. His remains were later removed to Hollenback Cemetery to make room for new streets. He was interred at the top of a hill in his new resting place, still facing east.

In 1809, Colonel Nathan Denison died at the age of sixty-eight. Although forced to surrender Forty Fort, he was able to bargain for the best possible terms of capitulation—resulting in no harm done to the women and children. In dealing with the Iroquois, he showed a perceptive degree of statesmanship in cordially receiving Iroquois peace overtures while keeping his powder dry and maintaining an efficient intelligence and early-warning system. His house still stands in Wyoming as a tourist attraction and memorial to this fine man.

Mathias Hollenback was a good-natured man who lived well into the Nineteenth Century. His early career as a merchant and his fondness for acquiring wealth played no small role in his efforts exerted in fleeing the Iroquois after the Battle of Wyoming with his gold pieces, resulting with the loss of his pants. This did not later stop him from selflessly helping and feeding the settlers fleeing Forty Fort or his elevation to near sainthood by the German press.

The most accurate testament to his fine character, however, can be found in an incident which occurred in Hollenback's later years. He had become a beloved and respected judge after the Revolution. Hollenback's reputation for integrity became an attraction for another protagonist of the Battle of Wyoming.

This other figure from the past was none other than Colonel John Butler. His reputation had suffered in England due to his published cruelties which took place in Wyoming. Butler's overriding desire in his later years was to be admitted to knighthood. With this goal in mind, he sent his agent to Wyoming to get a signature from an American participant at the Battle of Wyouing whose reputation for honesty was beyond reproach. The certificate on parchment swore that Butler's conduct at Wyoming was humane. Butler's agent chose Hollenback as the best candidate for a signature endorsing Butler for knighthood. The agent who called on the old judge was a bland and unemotional Englishman who stood by as Hollenback carefully read the certificate.

Hollenback looked the agent in the eye and asked, "Do you expect me to sign this?"

"Yes, sir, if you please," answered the agent.

"I shall not do it for it is not true," said Hollenback. The agent persisted that the statement was factual.

"It is not a word of it true, sir—I say sir it is a big lie," repeated Hollenback.

With that, Butler's agent put an open purse filled with British gold sovereigns on the table. The gold coins flickered invitingly in the firelight. However, it had the opposite effect on the old man.

"Gold! Gold!" he shouted, "Your king has not gold enough to buy me, sir."

Hollenback then hurled every possible epithet at the agent, and, pointing to the door, thundered, "There, sir, is the door; let me never see you again upon this business."

The agent was thankful he got out of the house alive and amazed that he actually found a man that gold couldn't buy.

Hollenback died in 1829 at the age of seventy-seven, leaving an estate estimated to be worth between three hundred and four hundred thousand dollars.

John Franklin was the last and possibly most powerful and energetic of the aging giants of Wyoming to pass on. In a speech he made on July 4th, 1828, three years before his death, he left his epithat for future generations:

"Friends and Fellow Citizens, you see before you a frail remnant of one of those who have faced the British cannon and heard the still more appalling yell of the painted savage at the horrible massacre of Wyoming. We gained for you the liberty you have enjoyed for more than half a century. In all human probability this is the last time our faltering tongue will ever tell to you on an anniversary of freedom, the story of our sufferings. May the Almighty strengthen you with virtue to defend your inheritance against foreign invasion as well as against domestic intrigue and military usurptions."

John Franklin died in 1831 at the age of eighty-three, and the last of the heroes of Wyoming had gone.

Life would go on for the Wyoming Valley. It would now have a peaceful present and future setting for a new prosperity. It's violent and bloody past was finally over. The name Wyoming, however, would live on in fame for a few decades more. In that time span, the name Wyoming became synonymous with bravery and tenacity.

Historian H. C. Bradsby wrote, as late as 1893: "In historical fame there is no spot on the continent so well known throughout the civilized world. Wyoming! The inspiring theme of historians and poets!"

The good name of Wyoming also had an inspiring meaning to Congressman James M. Ashley, of Ohio. He was a native of Pennsylvania and the Chairman of the Committee on Territories in the House of Representatives. In 1865, Ashley introduced a bill to provide a temporary government for a western territory which he wanted to name Wyoming. The bill was defeated, but three years later, the opponents of the name Wyoming agreed to create the territory, but only if it was named Lincoln, after the newly martyred president.

The name Lincoln, however, was discarded because, as its opponents pointed out, no territory or state (up to that time) had been named for an individual. The proponents of the name Wyoming stubbornly pointed out the American peoples' pride and familiarity with Wyoming's name, and that its meaning of "large plains" matched much of the topography of the new territory.

The bill passed in the House of Representatives, but in the Senate, proponents of Western Indian names held up passage of the bill. Finally, Senator James W. Nye, of Nevada, ended the debate with the statement, "Let's call it Wyoming." Thus evolved the ultimate honor for an eighteen-mile-long Valley in Northeastern Pennsylvania—a new territory, and ultimately, a new state was named after it!

Many other events and wars were to come and go, obscuring the luster and importance which American historians and scholars had formerly ascribed to Wyoming, for Wyoming Valley history is now all but forgotten in the new world of revised and politically correct American History. However, remembering Wyoming is crucial in learning from the past—how a small group of people under stress in an isolated area found the strength to overcome great odds and prevail. From this saga of the Wyoming Valley, our now great nation and people can only draw strength to face the future and once again, prevail.

COL. JOHN FRANKLIN.

Photo-reproduction of an engraved portrait in Craft's "History of Bradford County."

Colonel John Franklin from Craft's "History of Bradford County."

WYOMING.

IN MEMORIAM.

LIST OF OFFICERS AND PRIVATES KILLED AT THE BATTLE AND MASSACRE AT

WYOMING, JULY 3D, 1778.

LIEUT. COL. GEORGE DORRANCE.
MAJOR JOHN GARRET.
CAPTAINS.—JAMES BIDLACH, JR.,
AHOLIAB BUCK,
ROBERT DURKEE
REZIN GEER,
JOSEPH WHITTLESEY,
DETTRICH HEWITT,
WM. McKARAGAN,
SAMUEL RANSOM,
LAZARUS STEWART,
JAMES WIGTON.
LIEUTENANTS.—A. ATHERTON,
STODDARD BOWEN,
AARON GAYLORD,
TIMOTHY PIERCE,
PERRIN ROSS,
ELIJAH SHOEMAKER,
LAZARUS STEWART, JR.
ASA STEVENS,
FLAVIUS WATERMAN,
JAS. WELLS.
ENSIGNS.—JEREMIAH BIGFORD,
ASA GORE,
SILAS GORE,
TITUS HINMAN,
JOHN OTIS,
WILLIAM WHITE.

PRIVATES.

JABES ATHERTON,
CHRISTOPHER AVERY,
—— ACKE,
A. BENEDICK,
JABES BEERS,
SAMUEL BIGFORD,
ELIAS BIXBY,
DAVID BIXBY,
JOHN BOYD,
JOHN BROWN,
THOMAS BROWN,
WILLIAM BUCK,
JAMES BUDD,
AMOS BULLOCH,
HENRY BUCK,
JOHN CALDWELL,
ISAAC CAMPBELL,
JOSIAH CAMERON,
JOSEPH CAREY
[illegible]
COLE,
ROBERT COMSTOCK,
(THREE BROTHERS) COOK,
CHRIS. CARTRIGHT,
JOHN COURTRIGHT,
ANSON CORAY,
RUFUS CORAY,
JENKS CORAY,
SAMUEL CROCKER,
JOSEPH CROCKER,
JABES DARLING,
D. DENTON,
CONRAD DAVENPORT,
ANDERSON DANA,
JAMES DIVINE,
GEORGE DOWNING,
LEVI DUNN,
WILLIAM DUNN,
—— DUCHER,
BENJ. FINCH,
JOHN FINCH,
DANIEL FINCH,
ELISHA FITCH,
CORNELIUS FITCHETT.
ELIPHALET FOLLETT,
THOMAS FAXEN,
JOHN FRANKLIN,
THOMAS FULLER,
STEPHEN FULLER,
—— GARDNER,
GEORGE GORE,
—— GREEN,
SAM'L HUTCHINSON,
WILLIAM HAMMOND,
SILAS HARVEY,
BENJ. HATCH,
CYPRIAN HEBARD.
LEVI HICKS,
JAMES HOPKINS,
NATHANIEL HOWARD,
JOHN HUTCHINS,

PRIVATES.—ISRAEL INMAN,
ELIJAH INMAN,
JOSEPH JENNINGS,
SAMUEL JACKSON,
ROBERT JAMESON,
HENRY JOHNSON,
—— LESTER,
JOSHUA LANDON,
DANIEL LAWRENCE,
WM. LAWRENCE,
FRANCIS LEDYARD.
JAMES LOCK,
CONRAD LOWE,
JACOB LOWE,
NICHOLAS MANVILL,
JOB MARSHALL,
NEW. MATHEWSON,
C. McCARTEE,
A. MULEMAN,
ROB'T McINTIRE,
AND. MILLARD,
JOHN MURPHEY,
JOSEPH OGDEN,
JOHN PIERCE,
ABEL PALMER,
SILAS PARKE.
WM. PACKER,
HENRY PENCIL,
NOAH PETTIBONE, JR.
JEREMIAH ROSS,
—— REYNOLDS,
ELISHA RICHARDS,
ELIAS ROBERTS,
ENOS ROCKWAY,
TIMOTHY ROSS,
JAMES SHAW,
DARIUS SPAFFORD.
LEVI SPENCER,
JOSIAH SPENCER,
CONSTANT SEARLE,
ABEL SEELEY,
JOSEPH SHAW,
ABRAHAM SHAW,
ELEAZOR SPRAGUE
AARON STARK,
DANIEL STARK,
JOSEPH STAPLES,
RUFUS STEVENS,
JAMES STEVENSON,
NALOR SWEAD,
ICHABOB TUTTLE,
JOHN VAN WEE,
[illegible]
BARTHOL'W WEEKS,
JONATHAN WEEKS,
PHILIP WEEKS.
PETER WHEELER,
STEPHEN WHITON,
ESEN WILCOX,
JOHN WILLIAMS,
ELIHU WILLIAMS, JR.,
RUFUS WILLIAMS,
AZIBAH WILLIAMS,
JOHN WARD,
JOHN WILSON
PARKER WILS
—— WADE,
WM. WOODRINGER,
OZIAS YALE,
GERSHOM PRINCE (Col'd).

MONUMENT AT WYOMING, PA.

Of 25 or 30 Officers and Privates of independent companies (attached to one of the Conn. Reg'ts and encamped at Morristown, N. J.) who left the regiment without leave, and hastened to Wyoming to participate in the battle of July 3d, the following were killed: Capt. Rob't Durkee, Capt. Sam'l Ransom Lieut. Timothy Pierce, Lieut. James Wells; Privates, Sam'l Cole, Daniel Denton, Wm. Dunn, Daniel Lawrence, and Constant Searle.

MARTYRS WHOSE MURDER AROUSED THE CIVILIZED WORLD

The front page of the program of the celebration in 1878 of the Centennial of the Battle of Wyoming. The names listed above are inscribed on tablets on the Wyoming Monument. The news of the inhuman death of these men aroused the sympathy of the nations of Europe and as a result, in the belief of some historians, played a large part in inducing them to proffer the military aid which ultimately proved so effective in bringing victory to the American cause. The Centennial was elaborately celebrated here. On July third exercises were held at Wyoming Monument from 9 a. m. till late in the afternoon, with an intermission for dinner. A parade of the Grand Army of the Republic, municipal bodies and civic and benevolent societies was held on July fourth; it was reviewed by President Hayes. On the following day a Grand Regatta on the Susquehanna attracted crews from clubs of New York City, Philadelphia and various towns in New York and Pennsylvania.

Reprints from the Wyoming Centennial Program appearing in the *New York Daily Graphic*, July 1, 1878 (This and next two pages).

161

THE DAILY GRAPHIC: NEW YORK. MONDAY. JULY 1. 1878.

NUMENT, NEAR THE SPOT WHERE THE BATTLE OF WYOMING WAS FOUGHT, JULY 3, 1778. 2—FORTY FORT IN 1778. 3—FORTY FORT IN 187

THE CENTENNIAL OF THE MASSACRE OF WYOMING.

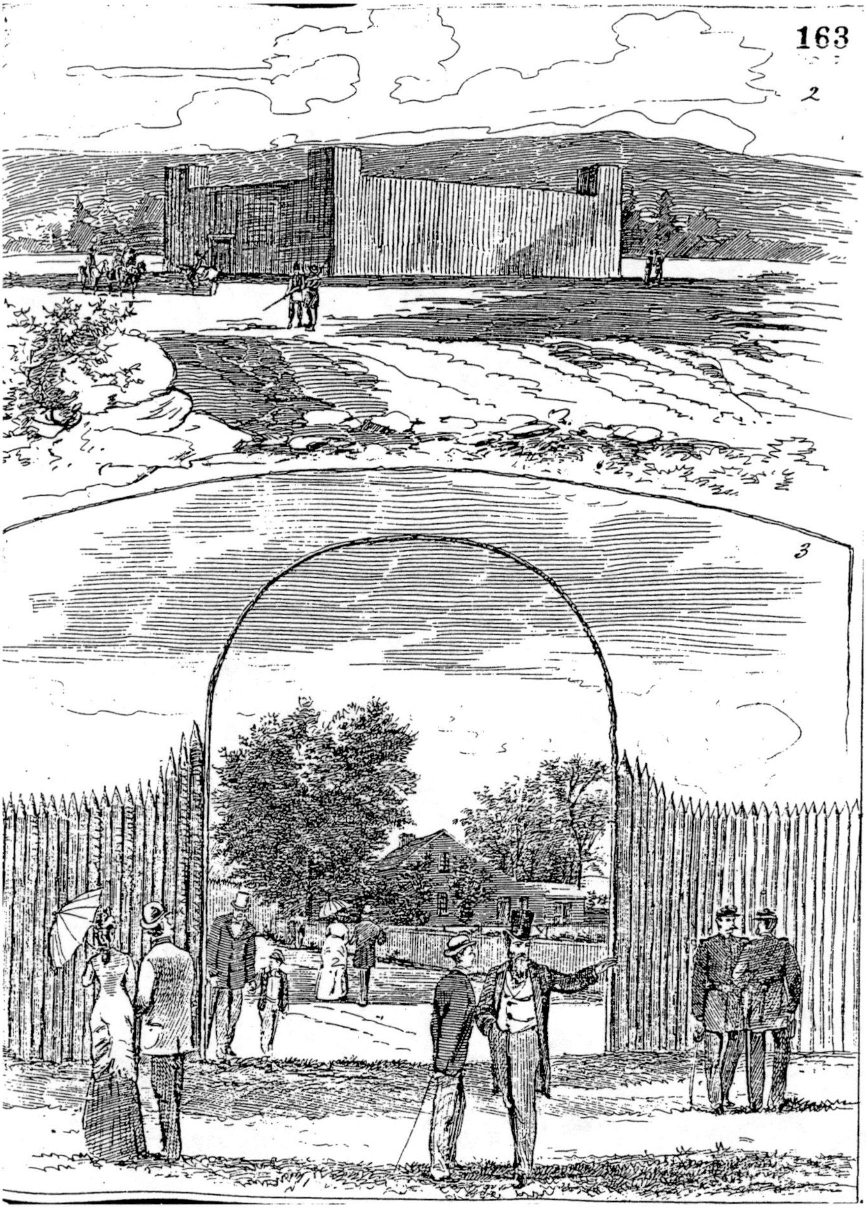

Number 2 is Forty Fort in 1778 and Number 3 is Forty Fort in 1878

Grave marker at Hollenback Cemetery in Wilkes-Barre, located at its highest point and facing east, as requested by Jacob Johnson just before his death at the age of eighty-four (Courtesy Ken Newman).

Remember Wyoming. Enhanced by Diane Belusko from a small, early 19th Century woodcut.

EPILOGUE

The River apparently flows as two. One is the River which we see in the reality of the present, the River which has seen its once-pristine status polluted by coal mining, industry and untreated sewage—and then, later, returned to a cleaner state. The River which now affords us beauty, recreation and solace.

But, in the heavy mists and quiet of the dawn, there is another River. Stand by its shore and, through the gray fog, the outlines of reality and time become blurred.

Here and there, through small breaks in the mist, your eye catches movement and your ears pick up faint sounds. The glide-by of ghostly birch canoes paddled by sullen men with painted faces. The muffled splashing and screaming of terrorized men, dashing headlong into the water on the opposite bank, now lost in fog. The intermingled high-pitched war whoops. Indistinct outgoing barges, crammed with blue uniformed men, to the faint strains of "Yankee Doodle" on fife and drum, barely reaching your ears.

The visions and sounds carry the message—do not forget things as they were in the Wyoming Valley. Do not change the past to suit the present, for the River of the Past is the same River of the Present. And there remains one River—the River that says, "Remember—Remember Wyoming, for this is a Special Place."

Plaque from the Governor of the State of Wyoming to the people of Wyoming, Pennsylvania, dated 1976 in recognition of the State-Valley connection forged by history (Courtesy John & Janice Shaver and Ken Newman).

BIBLIOGRAPHY

Amory, Thomas C., *The Military Services and Public Life of Major General John Sullivan*, Keanikat Press Inc. Port Washington, New York, 1868, Repub. 1968.

Boyd, Julian G., *The Susquehanna Company, Connecticut's Experiment in Expansion,* Yale University Press, New Haven, Connecticut, 1935.

Bradsby, H.C., *History of Luzerne County,* S. B. Nelson and Co. Chicago, IL 1893.

Brewster, William, *History of the Certified Township of Kingston, Pennsylvania 1769-1929*, Smith Bennet Corp., Wilkes-Barre, Pennsylvania, 1930.

Bruchac, Joseph, "A Mohawk Village in 1491—Otsungo, America Before Columbus," *National Geographic Magazine*, Volume 180, 04, October 1991.

Cadzow, D.A., *Archeological Studies of Susquehanna Indians*, Pennsylvania Historical Commission, Harrisburg, Pennsylvania 1931.

Carmer, Carl, *The Susquehanna River*, Rinehart & Co., New York 1955.

Cook, Frederic, *Journal of the Military Expedition of Major General John Sullivan Against the Six Nations of Indians in 1779,* Document, Wyoming Valley Community Association, Wyoming, Pennsylvania.

Erwin, Marie H., *Wyoming Historical Blue Book,* Bradford Robinson Printing, Denver 1943.

Evans, Annette, *Frontier Women of Wyoming Valley,* Wyoming Valley Community Association, Address, July 14, 1767.

Flick, Alexander, *New Sources of The Sullivan-Clinton Campaign in 1779,* New York Historical Association, (reprint) New York 1921.

Godcharlies, Frederick A., *Second Pennemite War*, Proceedings of 145th Anniversary, Wyoming Community Association, Wilkes-Barre, Pennsylvania 1923.

Griffis, W.E., *Wyoming, The Pivot of the Revolution*, (reprint) Proceedings of Wyoming Community Association, 132nd Anniversary, Wilkes-Barre, Pennsylvania, July 6, 1910.

Griffis, W.E., *The Rise, Glory, and Fall of the Iroquois Confederacy*, Proceedings of the Wyoming Community Association, 136th Anniversary, Wilkes-Barre, July 8, 1914.

Griffis, W.E., *History and Mythology of the Sullivan Expedition*, Report of the Proceedings of July 3, 1903, Wyoming Community Association, Wilkes-Barre, Pennsylvania.

Hall, Charles Herbert, *History of Wyoming Borough 1935*

Hanlon, Edward F., *The Wyoming Valley, An American Portrait*, Windsor Publications, Woodland Hills, California, 1938.

Harvey, Oscar J. *A History of Wilkes-Barre*, Volume I, II, III, Wilkes-Barre 1909 (Locally published—no publisher named).

Jenkins, Steuben, "A Paper on the Names of Those Connected with the Massacre of Wyoming," Wyoming Community Association, Wilkes-Barre, Pennsylvania, July 3, 1885.

Johnson, Frederic C. M.D., *Pioneer Women of Wyoming*, Wyoming Valley Historical Society, Wilkes-Barre, Pennsylvania 1901.

Joyce, Mary H., *Pioneer Days in the Wyoming Valley*, Wilkes-Barre, Pennsylvania 1927.

Lottick, Sally Teller, *Bridging Change,* Wyoming Historical Society 1992.

Miner, Charles, *History of Wyoming*, J. Crissy, Philadelphia, 1843.

Moquin, Wayne, and Van Doren, Charles, *Great Documents in American Indian History*. Praeger Publishers, New York, 1973.

Murray, Elsie, *Teoga*, Athens, Pennsylvania 1939.

Murray, L.W., *Notes on the Sullivan Expedition of 1779*, Athens, Pennsylvania 1929.

Parker, R., *Parker on the Iroquois*, Syracuse University Press, Syracuse 1968.

Peck, George, *Wyoming*, Harper Brothers, New York 1858.

Petrillo, F. Charles, *Harvey's Lake*, The Bookmakers, Wilkes-Barre, PA, 1983.

Savelle, Max, *Seeds of Liberty*, New York 1948.

Smith, Charles Emory, *Commencement Address*, Union College, Philadelphia Press, June 26, 1889.

Stone, William L., *The Poetry and History of Wyoming*, 1873.

Urbanek, Mae Bobb, *Wyoming Place Names*, Mountain Press Publishing Company, Missoula, Montana 1988.

Wallace, Anthony F. C., *Death and Rebirth of the Seneca,* Knopf, New York, 1973.

Wallace, Paul A. W., "Address July 4, 1966," Wyoming Community Association, Wilkes-Barre, Pennsylvania.

Whittemore, Charles P., *A General of the Revolution—John Sullivan of New Hampshire*, Columbia University Press 1961.

Wilcox, William A., *The Flight From Wyoming—3rd Person Eyewitness Account by Mercy Ross*, Wyoming Community Association, Wilkes-Barre, Pennsylvania, July 2, 1887.

Wise, Sidney F., *The Other Side of the Battle of Wyoming*, Directorate of History, Department of National Defense, Canadian Forces H.Q., Ottawa 1971

ADDITIONAL SOURCES

Debates and Proceedings of the 2nd Session of the 38th Congress and Special Session of the Senate. The Congressional Globe 1865.

Military Collector & Historian Vol. XXXIX, No. 3, Fall 1987 Washington, D.C., Holst, Donald W., "Notes on British Artillery Flags in the American Revolution."

A Picture Tour of Wilkes-Barre and the Historic Wyoming Valley, Herbert E. Atkins Publishing, Wilkes-Barre, PA, 1932.

Program for the 1878 Centennial of the Battle of Wyoming, Reprint-Illustrations, *New York Daily Graphic*, July 1, 1878.